I'M FREE

AWARENESS OF WHO YOU *Are* BY DISCOVERING WHO YOU ARE *Not!*

ERIKA KIND

BALBOA.
PRESS
A DIVISION OF HAY HOUSE

Translation from German:
Anja CR Schaefer www.DISCUSPublishingServices.com
and Chris Gaydon www.gaydon.de

Balboa Press books may be ordered through booksellers or by contacting:

Balboa Press
A Division of Hay House
1663 Liberty Drive
Bloomington, IN 47403
www.balboapress.com
1 (877) 407-4847

Because of the dynamic nature of the Internet, any web addresses or links contained in this book may have changed since publication and may no longer be valid. The views expressed in this work are solely those of the author and do not necessarily reflect the views of the publisher, and the publisher hereby disclaims any responsibility for them.

The author of this book does not dispense medical advice or prescribe the use of any technique as a form of treatment for physical, emotional, or medical problems without the advice of a physician, either directly or indirectly. The intent of the author is only to offer information of a general nature to help you in your quest for emotional and spiritual well-being. In the event you use any of the information in this book for yourself, which is your constitutional right, the author and the publisher assume no responsibility for your actions.

Any people depicted in stock imagery provided by Thinkstock are models, and such images are being used for illustrative purposes only.
Certain stock imagery © Thinkstock.

Printed in the United States of America.

ISBN: 978-1-4525-9370-8 (sc)
ISBN: 978-1-4525-9372-2 (hc)
ISBN: 978-1-4525-9371-5 (e)

Library of Congress Control Number: 2014903754

Balboa Press rev. date: 2/26/2014

CONTENTS

PART 3: JOURNEY TO FREEDOM

PART 4: REALIGNMENT

PREFACE

A life in happiness and well-being begins with a decision.

For a long time I was dominated and controlled by fears and outside influences—probably like everyone who had taken this book into their hands and began to turn the pages over. From infancy to adulthood my life was overshadowed by destructive thought patterns. I was afraid of almost everything—scared of strangers, of being on my own, of sicknesses, of failure, of flying, of being laughed at, of not being accepted, of the unknown, of having to stand up alone, of not meeting others' expectations, of losing control, of examinations, of heights, and much more. Fear was my daily companion. Additionally I was shy, full of complexes. I had no mind of my own. I could easily be influenced, and I did not have a spark of self-consciousness. I believed in everything you can think of except in me. At least I thought that I believed in something. I never got the idea that I should change this condition or that I was even able to have an influence on it. I was convinced of being a victim of circumstances, and because I believed this so thoroughly, I created my life accordingly. That's how it simply was. I had accepted all chains as real parts of myself. Yes, I thought, *That's how I am and how I will always be. That's life. Bad luck!*

But one day when I already had kids of my own, something started to change. More and more frequently I had the feeling that something inside of me that I could not even identify was taking over the control in certain situations. It was as if a new course had been set for me. One time I was put on the give-up track and then on the outburst-of-rage track, and another time I was put on the must-keep-things-under-control track. Slowly I noticed that I was controlled by something that felt strange to me and that I did not really want. I perceived it as a foreign element, as something that in reality was not a part of me. When a certain point was passed, I just let it happen. The more often I experienced and noticed this, the more I started to search for the reasons that made me react reflexively and usually succeeded in gaining mastery over me. I had become curious and began to research first within myself, then in my surroundings, and there starting with my past. I began to put the puzzle pieces together and was interested in finding out what was really going on inside and outside of me. Books about different subjects—mostly spiritual literature—found their ways into my life. I had training, and I attended seminars and workshops. In the course of time I encountered more and more people who were in similar situations. They were constructive aids for me or gave me valuable hints. At that time I had already read numerous books about the power of thoughts and the law of attraction, and I had also watched many documentaries about these subjects. I trained myself diligently in the application of this law. When I talked with friends or family members, I was able to more and more observe what effects thoughts could make on our lives, respectively what we ourselves make of our lives because of our self-made thoughts. It was amazingly interesting. More and more signposts came to me very naturally.

One day when I had reached a specific point on my path, somebody was placed at my side, someone who showed me a way to find the way back to myself. He had to deal with similar problems like I did, and we noticed many parallels in our thinking, our perception, viewpoints, hopes, and dreams but also in our experiences and patterns from our pasts. A very close fraternal relationship developed. As we were able to connect with each other because of our similarities, we mutually began to show each other our strengths. We exchanged experiences and knowledge, and while we were dealing with the other's difficulties, which were reflected in us, we worked on ourselves at the same time. Because I was hoping that he saw the same in me as I saw in him, I made great efforts to gain strength in order to be strong for him. In doing so, I learned to look at things from a higher perspective and to see them in a different light. Our mutual encouragement and examination of things from different perspectives on behalf of the other continually opened new horizons in us. It was a constant give-and-take at an enormous speed. As he believed in me and encouraged me to follow my feelings and to have confidence, I regained faith in myself.

One day I stood up and started to face my fears one by one. I began to question one viewpoint after the next and to bring light into the new perspectives. I had enough of continually being prevented from what I really wanted to do and realized how little truth was included in most of my adapted belief patterns. For example, I sometimes said to myself, "I cannot do this. I cannot make it. I have not been trained enough. I am not good enough." As time went by, I enjoyed saying good-bye to these distortions of my mind. I even made a list of fears and worked my way through them and stopped giving in to minor and bigger fears that spontaneously arose all day long. I really searched for them so that I could consciously eliminate them. Every time I faced a fear, something peculiar happened. Instead of a fight and new fears resulting from it, I experienced *inner silence and peace.* There were no more fears. I recognized fear as nothing more than an illusion that I myself had invented and that had been caused by adapted belief patterns. The more often I had these kinds of experiences, the easier I noticed that I had taken steps in the right direction, steps that I would not have dared to make a couple of weeks before. Some hurdles I did not even notice anymore. My self-consciousness grew enormously because I recognized what I was able to do and the fact that I could accomplish all I wanted to accomplish. All these realizations were initialized by this wonderful connection to my soul partner. Without him, this book would not exist because I had never thought that I was not capable of writing a book but mostly because I would not have the knowledge and experience that, thanks to our special connection, led to these contents.

Of course, there are still fears and insecurities arising in me, but today I encounter them in a completely different way. As I had already realized how illusionary some fears were, I am not afraid of encountering them anymore. To me, fears are nothing more than unsettled issues on a checklist that I need to work through. The more problems I have dealt with, the clearer my views get and the more veils are lifted. I don't postpone difficulties anymore. Whenever a fear or insecurity arises, it's the right moment to face it.

What could be more beautiful than regaining faith in one's own existence? There is an enormous power within each of us. Every one of us came into this world with a special task—an individual fate—and this fate can only be fulfilled by the individual. We can only fulfill our fate when we unfold our whole potential and faithfully listen to our inner voice—no matter what our environment tries to talk us into. We are only able to trust our inner voice when we are consciously perceiving what happens in our lives and when we are asking critical questions like, "Is this or that opinion about myself really true?" When we are totally honest with ourselves and don't hide behind reliable but wrong securities proclaimed by public opinions, we will be able to let go of what we are not. We must be aware that common opinions can only lead to limitations but never the freedom of being ourselves.

With this book I would like to show that nobody is alone with his or her fears and the resulting symptoms and consequences. This book shall encourage you to look underneath your bed and to find out that there is no monster hidden there. It will show you ways to get rid of bondages of fear and self-imposed prohibitions. The main effect of this book is *to show the reader a way to recognize who he or she truly is*. The only thing you need is openness and the will to change your current situation. You have already made the first step by dealing with this subject, not turning your head away anymore, and taking this book into your hands. No matter how deep your True Self might be buried, it was always there. It is there, and it will always be there. It is the wisdom within you that has elevated itself above the ego. When you become aware of your True Self and are able to feel yourself again, you clearly see that all fears and obstacles only existed in your head. Finally you are able to unfold your whole potential and to bring your uniqueness into this world. This is the one and only reason for being here.

With gratitude I would like to pass on all experiences, encounters, and occurrences that I have faced to reach the point where I am standing now. All that I transmit on the following pages are my own profound experiences and observations, knowledge from books, from innumerable conversations with my mentor and humans of all ages and origins, and from my own therapeutic activities. My main concern is to share these realizations with as many people as possible. They shall be shown the possibilities of helping themselves in order to follow their own paths and to fulfill their dreams and wishes, which might have been suppressed through fear. Naturally this individual path has to be taken by everyone for themselves. We never walk alone, but we must walk this path by ourselves. One thing I can promise is this: It's possible! From the bottom of my heart I wish you much joy and God's blessing on this fascinating journey called life.

Acknowledgments

To my husband, Bruno, thank you for walking a certain path with me, a path sometimes made of soft grass and moss and sometimes made of stones and rocks. There was a time when we didn't know if we could make it. I am so happy that we did. When our journey went through the darkest jungle, inside of me the brightest light of awareness was turned on, which I needed to experience in order to show it to the world. Thank you for laying a seed into our crisis, which let our relationship grow up to a higher level.

To my friend and companion Patrick, your belief in me has given me the courage to dig deeper into my heart to find my True Self again. Only because of this I was able to discover numerous miracles of our being and of life itself, which I can place in this book today. Without you the person who wrote this book wouldn't have even been born (yet). Therefore, this book wouldn't exist. Thank you for being the brother I had always wished for and for offering the security that I can always count on you.

To my best friend Irene, thank you for all the feedback, criticisms, and confirmations. Thank you for our talks and for letting me be part of your happiest hours and of your most challenging worries. You are the most wonderful friend someone could wish for. Thank you for your uncomplicated and open mind, the fact that you are there for me, and the fact that you let me be there for you.

To my translating angels, Anja and Chris, my dear friend and mentor, thank you for all of your efforts to help me bring this book into the English world.

Thank you to everyone who ever crossed my path, touched my life, or walked by my side for a while, to everyone who challenged me in a way that forced me to look inside. All of you have helped me to become who I am today. And I love who I am.

I thank myself that I started to get up, to listen and follow my inner voice rather than outer opinions or the approval of others, that I started to follow the path of my conviction and of this burning flame that lights my way of intention. The greatest love of all is to love oneself. The greatest happiness lies within this self. This insight changes the way you look at things … and then the things you look at change.

INTRODUCTION

Every person already has felt the desire to be free. But what is freedom? It seems to have different meanings for everyone. For one person it means to possess a specific car. For another person it means to be self-employed or to leap into the blue on his Harley or maybe to be single. Sometimes the moment comes when the motorbike trip is finished or when one feels lonely because he or she is single. Is freedom something that we once have and then lose again? Is freedom something what we only experience from time to time? Does freedom exist at all? The bad news is this: No, freedom does not exist as long as we are looking for it in the outer circumstances of our lives. The good news, however, is this: Yes, real freedom does exist but only when it emerges from within. Even the most suppressed slave can be free at any time. Basically we are all free at any moment in time. Yet in those moments when we feel that we are oppressed by circumstances, we can be free at the same time.

We experience freedom when we realize who we really are. This is where the problem actually lies. Through all the attachments and accepted belief and thought patterns from our environment, over the years we have successfully controlled and suppressed our True Selves, and now we are virtually not aware of them anymore. What we can see are the moral and social structures that we have incorporated throughout our lives without knowing if they really correspond to our nature. Nobody fits into a set scheme. Through the social universal thinking, we are often convinced that these upbringings are a part of us, although it's obvious that they hinder us in living the kind of lives we are truly meant to live. When we feel uncomfortable and unhappy, it's a good sign that a lot of conditioning doesn't correspond to our real essences. If we were in tune with ourselves, we would feel peaceful, content, and joyful. Human beings are not mass products, and what's right for one person might be unacceptable for another. We are all unique individuals with the most differing preferences, aversions, and abilities. Everyone has the right to live out his uniqueness and to share it with his environment. We are not competitors but cocreators, and achieving an awareness of this difference allows us to become creators in this world and make it a better place for ourselves and everyone.

To reach freedom and to realize what our true nature is, we must at first be aware of what it is not. By understanding where we come from and by consciously dealing with our thoughts and emotions, we can remove the veils that cover our True Selves step by step. With the knowledge of every part that does not correspond to the nature of our True Selves, we unveil the view of our core and therefore regain our inner freedom continually. The recognition alone that we make our own lives difficult simply by not living them leads us to the most important and decisive breakthrough to regain self-awareness. Eventually a being appears who is free of fears, self-doubts, and destructive thinking and one that is now able to fulfill its fate with strength, self-responsibility, and enthusiasm. When you realize what you are not, you begin to see who you really are. When you see who you are, you also see your own path. When you have recognized it, you feel spontaneously the deep connection between yourself and your path. It feels familiar and safe. It simply feels *right*. Even if the rest of the world cannot agree with your new course in life, nothing and nobody will be able to prevent you from following this route. This is because you are now in harmony with yourself, with your inner wisdom, and with your fate.

This book is meant to demonstrate in a practical and easily understandable way what moves us to suppress our wonderful, true existence. I explain how simple it is to live a life in joy, harmony, and contentment instead of a life in fear, insecurities, and deficiencies. We achieve this by straightening up and renaming things. Through reorienting our perspectives and shifting our thoughts and emotions from destructibility to constructiveness, a new life begins. In this life we are able to implement our longings and dreams. It's a new life in which we can free ourselves from shadows of the past and from unclear phantoms of the future. It's a life where we can simply live without the feeling of having to prove something to somebody or to justify ourselves. It's a life in freedom!

I have experienced myself all the knowledge, insights, and proposals for solutions that I mention in this book, and I successfully apply them in my own life. The more puzzle pieces I was able to put together throughout the last years, the clearer my notion of the unbelievable size of the complete picture that still needs to be assembled became. Already this small insight is so mind-blowing that I wouldn't want to withhold it from anyone. As the universe wanted to make sure that I really feel what I am writing about, it sent me all kinds of tests. During the work on this book, I went through every single chapter again and readjusted it according to my newly won recognitions. I went through intensive times and was pushed to the limits of my physical capacities. With my deepest conviction I can guarantee that every sentence contains its deepest truth and that I now have a much deeper relationship with the creative energy called God than ever before. Through the writing of this book it was possible to make the biggest evolutionary step in my life.

It is not possible to handle these chapters separately. Every chapter's final result contains many aspects that are interconnected. For this reason, recurrences and repetitions within the single chapters are inevitable. Everything is connected and cannot be looked at separately. I regard many statements and cross connections as very important and have woven them into the chapters repeatedly with full intention. I feel that hence many connections can be comprehended better. The more fundamental certain details and recognitions are, the more often they automatically occur and the more weight they therefore gain in their message. This has the additional advantage that the individual subjects are illuminated from different viewpoints in different contexts and thus make their interconnectivity more obvious. The result is a well-rounded image. We humans are no machines with identical attitudes. What one person can better accept from this side, the other might better perceive from a different perspective.

In the first part of this book, I will introduce you to your True Self. It is to give a rough idea and an overview. Many questions might arise from this. Parts 2 to 4 of this book contain detailed information and explanations about part 1.

The content of this book is not a call to rebel against the outside world, the past, something we have experienced, or somebody who influenced us at some point in our lives. Everything we dealt with up until the current moment has shaped us into who we are today. We developed new qualities out of the hardest moments, the biggest challenges, and the deepest crises. This book is a tool with which the reader can find a way to reach within him or herself, a way to let go of destructive ideas about the self and his or her life. It is about not denying yourself, about being authentic and living your life in tune with your True Self in regards to yourself and the outside world. Whatever happens out of love can never be anything else but a blessing!

Enough of introductory words! Now dive into a world that not only consists of problems and sorrows and see what the dark veil of fears was able to successfully hide from your eyes. Discover an unknown energy that leads you toward fulfillment of your dreams. Experience the moment when you can finally say, "I'm free!"

RENDEZVOUS WITH GOD
A SPIRITUAL FAIRY TALE

I sat beside a lonely mountain lake in a North American Indian reservation. From a distance I heard the drums and flutes of the Indian tribe close by. After I had sat meditating beside the lake for a while, I stood up and bent down over the water. I wanted answers. I looked into the water and asked myself if it would reveal to me who I really was. I looked at the mirror image, but instead of receiving clarity, the water got murky and darker. The longer I stared into it, the more I was drawn closer until, without having noticed it, I was immersed. To my amazement, I had no fear and was even able to breathe normally.

Although the lake seemed to be incredibly deep and I could not perceive anything but darkness, I continually reached toward the ground of the lake. After a short time I was able to see a light below me. Driven by curiosity, I moved faster to come closer to this warm and bright radiant light. Arriving at the bottom of the lake, I saw that this light came from the inside of a cave. Standing in front of the entry, I noticed that for some reason no water could enter the cave. It was located in the middle of the lake and seemed to be surrounded by an air bubble. I entered the cave, and the water swiftly dripped from my body. I was totally dry in an instant. Now I stood in a hallway that was illuminated by the bright light from somewhere farther back. After I walked toward the light, I arrived in a kind of hall where a big fire burned.

Three figures sat around it. My gaze—yes, my whole

attention—was attracted by this fire in a weird, almost magical way. From a glaring white to a dark red, the fire consisted of all of the colors from the color palette. The single nuances continually changed. Still it seemed as if the balance of colors remained perfect inside of it. When it became darker in some areas, other parts became brighter. Sometimes it even seemed to be so balanced that the whole fire seemed like just one single color that consisted of a mixture of all the colors.

Now I looked at the three persons sitting around this fire. They sat in the shape of a triangle. One person sat directly behind the fire. One sat on the left side, and one sat on the right. The place in front of the fire was still empty. Every person sat on a stone, and there was also a stone on the free place. They wore long, light gray robes, and their heads were hidden underneath hoods. While I examined the whole picture, I noticed that the three seemed to be connected with the fire in a special way. The light of the fire seemed to completely surround them, but it could also have been possible that the figures supplied the fire with their light.

I was impressed by the whole scene. Instead of being frightened, I perceived the atmosphere as a very peaceful and harmonious energy. A warm, pleasant feeling arose within me. It was as if I was in a deeply familiar and trusted environment. Now the person behind the fire lifted his right arm and pointed to the stone in front of the fire in order to encourage me to sit down. Overwhelmed by what I saw and felt, I took a seat.

The figure who had offered me the seat lifted his hood and let it fall backward. An elderly, very strong-looking man appeared. His eyes looked at me not only with attention and wisdom but also with an unbelievable kindness and understanding. His hair was long, snow white, dense, and slightly curled. With a loving sparkle in his eyes, he said, "Why did you come?"

Although I was still so amazed by all these impressions, I answered as if I was sitting next to a very close friend, "I want to know who I am."

Now the figure on my left side moved and likewise lifted his hood. I looked into the knowing and equally loving eyes of a younger man with longer brown hair. He asked me the same question, "Why did you come here?"

I almost had the feeling as if the three had been waiting for me. My joy about so much goodwill as well as the love that started to burn within me almost made my cry with inner movement and the feeling of shelter. "I am here because I want to know who I am," I answered.

Then the figure to my right lifted its hood, but I could only vaguely perceive an almost waterlike, continually changing face. It did not frighten me. It was just interesting to study this face. This being also asked a question, but I could not hear it with my ears. Instead, I somehow perceived it in my thoughts, "Tell me why you came here."

After this figure had asked me the same question, I felt the flame increasing within me. It was as if each one of these three nourished me with warmth and love through their attention. "I have come to find out who I am."

Now something fascinating happened. The three figures slowly stood up, and the old man opposite me slowly drew the other two into him until they were entirely absorbed. When I looked into his eyes, I could also see the other two within him. Pure love, wisdom, and power were revealed to me. In a flash I realized who I just faced in person, and I fell on my knees. I had just spoken with God! Filled with unspeakable gratitude and the feeling of the greatest honor that a simple human being like myself could ever receive, I said in tears, "God, is this you? Did you call me, an insignificant little human being? How did I deserve so much grace?"

God answered, "My beloved child, it's not me who called you. You called me. To enable you to understand that I am always with you and there for you, I guided you here. The grace that God is always there for you is your right. My permanent presence is not only everybody's fundamental right. It's a simple fact with eternal validity. Even when you often complain that I had left you, in these moments I am closer to you than you can imagine. You approached me with a question, and I will try to explain to you a few things so that you find the answer to your questions yourself. Look into the fire. What do you see?"

God's love, His smooth voice and calming energy had centered me again, and so I was able to experience this conversation with a previously unknown inner calmness and thankful happiness. Wow, I had really spoken with God and He with me! The only really odd thing about this was that it was not odd at all. Everything seemed to be totally normal and natural.

"I see a fire. Oh, it strikes me that there is no wood or other burning material. I can't see anything that's burned in this fire or by what it can nourish itself."

"This is because it does not need nourishment. It nourishes everything that exists. I am this fire. This fire is the all-encompassing energy. It's the Source of life. This universal energy carries everything that is within it and can therefore never decrease. Everything that was created out of this energy will always remain a part of it. It might alter its shape. You can see the fire moving. But it never gets less. It stays the same. What else do you see?"

"I see that this fire consists of an unbelievable number of colors that continually change or even wander around. Why is that so?"

"I am glad that you asked this question. Every single flame is a being like yourself—even when it only flickers shortly. The different colors, the changing colorizations and sizes of the flames represent the current state of consciousness and the mood of the individual beings. The higher a flame flickers, the more unconscious it is because it tries hard to remove itself from its Source of creation. But it doesn't work. Every flame remains connected. If it was separated, it would die, but as it is impossible for a flame to be separated from the fire, it can never die. Remember what you perceived when you entered this room. You saw a luminous connection between God the Father, God the Son, and God the Holy Spirit with the fire of eternity. This is because I am this energy and therefore inseparably connected with it.

The different colorizations equally represent the state of consciousness. The lighter a flame is, the more it is aware of its belonging to the mother flame, and the darker it is, the less it is in tune with itself and its origin. So that the equilibrium is preserved, a law exists. It is the universal law of duality. When single parts of the fire are getting too dark, the brighter others become. The more conscious the whole mass is, the more similar the colorization gets. The farther from the core some flames flicker, the closer to the core another part stays. Thus, everything remains in its harmonious order."

"Does this mean that in reality I am a part of the universal fire?"

"You are already on the right track to see the truth clearer, but you must let your flame burn brighter to dissolve the veil of distortion and to see really clearly. A flame of the fire you see here burns inside of you. Such a flame burns in every being—always. The less you are aware of this flame and the less you consciously turn to this flame, the smaller it becomes in you. Nevertheless, it's always there and can never fade. As soon as you turn your attention to it, it is fed and immediately starts to expand. Thus, you sense the connection with your True Self dwelling in your human body. You just have made the experience yourself how the flickering of the eternal flame within you feels through giving attention to your question and therefore to your inmost self. Every time when I encouraged you to concentrate on the essence of your existence by asking questions from God the Father, God the Son, and God the Holy Spirit, your light increased. This flame is nothing less than your True Self. With every question and every answer, you connected more and more with it. This special feeling of the all-encompassing God's love inherent in you really blossomed. It fulfills you and gives you the feeling that what lives within you is bigger than the body hosting it. You sense the power and energy corresponding to your true nature and origin. In this moment you know that this power enables you to accomplish all and to put everything into action that you can imagine.

"I created you out of the same substance as me. It is pure energy and the only thing that in reality exists and out of which all life consists. All life that I created has this energy at its disposal to create the contents of its life. You all are creators. You have the means to create. The key to your power lies within your heart. You have access to it at any time. You just have to reconnect yourself and let your light shine, and you will see.

"Your immortal, omniscient light is a part of this big divine fire; however, it's pure divine energy. Now you know that you are—because of what you truly are—at any time connected with me and therefore with your origin. When you feel yourself, you feel me. When you believe in yourself, you believe in me. I am always with you, and nothing can ever separate you from me. The only things that can provoke separation are your unconscious thoughts, but even they cannot cause real separations. They are simply illusions or distortions of your mind. They might decrease the flame because you are getting more unconscious, but they never have the power to extinguish it. This light dwelling in your body illuminates your path. Feel it, feel yourself, and let it shine. The brighter it gets, the clearer you can see. Feel yourself and shine so that you can better see your way. It's the road of your personal fate and therefore leads directly to me.

"My dear child, do you now understand that you are not here because I called you but because you called me? You are not dependent on my attention toward you because it is—as I explained—always there through your origin. However, it's of no use to you as long as you are not open for me.

"You are here because of the attention you give to yourself and therefore to me. This attention nourishes your own light and restores the balance again. You have made a trip into your own heart. Before the water seemed to be dark, but now you see that it shines brighter the deeper you dive into the lake and therefore into your own heart. You went through the dark curtain of illusions, false perceptions, and distortions and found your beautiful, brightly shining light.

"To get to the heart of the issue, you looked inside of you and found me. Do you know now who you are?"

I awoke in this moment. Although I knew that it was just a dream, I still had the feeling that it had really happened. Even though I could not see the dreamed images anymore, something remained that has not changed until today. My light shines brighter than ever before, and my belief in myself is getting stronger every day. I searched for myself and found God. Or was it just the other way around?

Erika Kind, 11/15/2010

And the soul, afraid of dying
never learns to live.

—Excerpt from the song "The Rose"

REALIZE WHO YOU ARE...

PART 1
OUR TRUE SELF

I am the abundance that created me.
—Source unknown

WHY DO WE EXPERIENCE
WHAT WE EXPERIENCE?

hat we encounter in our lives as circumstances, events, incidents, or persons many people call fate. With the term *fate*, most people associate an unpredictable force that shapes our lives according to its inclination and mood and to what we seem to be abandoned to. That's utterly not true! Everything we encounter is simply a reaction to our actions—actions in terms of thoughts, feelings, and the resultant activities, habits, and targets we have set for this lifetime. Two things cause something to happen in our lives. In the course of this book, I will give an overview of these two causes and will automatically go step-by-step deeper into the details.

1. OUR PROGRAM OF LIFE

The one and only reason for our earth life is to acquire knowledge— in fact, to acquire as much knowledge as possible. I am not talking about knowledge from school but about spiritual knowledge. We all come here in order to grow and to mature, to increase our frequencies, and to eventually integrate *all* knowledge within us and thus become consciously one with our Source of creation. But this does not end with reading a few spiritual books or faithfully going to church each Sunday. It's about knowledge that we absorb by making experiences during our journey through life so that they become parts of us. Thus, we have integrated this knowledge without having to even think about it any further. But of course, we have set not only one target to accomplish in our lives but many! However, we really want to have achieved some of these goals by the end of our earthly lives. And to achieve them, we are confronted with all we need to do so. All this is never to be understood as punishment!

We will encounter aids on our way so that we get the full benefits from them. This can be pleasant; however, more often than not, it is very unpleasant, which has proved to be the most effective way to learn the lessons set.

2. WE ATTRACT WHAT WE THINK AND BELIEVE

Faith starts with a single thought. It can be a thought arising in us, but we can also absorb it from outside. No matter what kind of thought it is, when we think it often enough, it will ripen until it becomes the truth. It may be thoughts that we like to think but also thoughts that cause us to feel uncomfortable. When we often enough hear that we are dumb and then when something stupid happens, we automatically think, *Oh, man, am I stupid!* Then this idea is strengthened over time.

From an early age we are exposed to many sources of information, which we use to guide ourselves and our beliefs. Through education, school, friends, media, relatives, and much more, we are confronted with different rules and opinions. Some of them have been absorbed consciously; others have crept in almost imperceptibly. All of this information that you have stored inside of you as true from outside sources corresponds to a large extent to the belief of others who have completely different programs in life from you. The beliefs of these people have most likely been formed in the same way by unconsciously absorbing and accepting information for decades. Now it has become apparent that many of our thought patterns have not emerged from our own inner convictions but are mixtures of trained and often subconsciously accepted thoughts.

But why do our thoughts and beliefs influence the events in our lives? Whatever we focus on, whatever we act out with conviction, with what kind of attitude do we encounter the happenings in our lives? All this is essential for what life gives back to us! I am talking about the law of attraction. Like attracts like.

We will always find or become in our lives what we put our attention to and what corresponds to the vibrations we emit. When we focus our thoughts on fears, faults, and shortages, we will always be faced with situations that confirm these convictions. Whatever we feel inside of us as a conviction connects us to the same energy frequency on the outside. So what we get is mostly the result of the kind of energy we radiated in the first place, according to our perspectives of our lives and ourselves.

We have come here to create our own realities, and we see the world the way we want to see it. And the way we want to see it is manifested for us. Returning to the previous example, if we are of the opinion that we are stupid, then the universe will confirm our point of view and provide us with everything that makes us look stupid. It will provide us with misfortunes but also with persons who confirm our point of view repeatedly. It doesn't matter if these ideas really correspond to our true being or if they are absorbed suggestions from outside. Whatever we expect from life, wherever we put our attention on—*wanted or unwanted*—will manifest. This is the second reason why things happen in our lives the way they happen.

When we come into this life, we have *our program of life*. But the realization of our program of life is strongly influenced by the second statement, which is that *we attract what we think and believe*. The real problem now arises in the second statement. As long as we block our own true beliefs and viewpoints by set ways of thought structures, negate our feelings, and deny our true needs and wishes, we are not able to know why we have incarnated and what our life program really is! To recognize our own truth and to be able to see the paths that we have to travel in order to fulfill our deepest purpose, it is essential that we first work on the second statement. We have to clear up all the debris that we have dumped for decades in front of our True Selves.

The following example explains this thought. Everyone carries bags around with them. Let's say we carry backpacks—backpacks for the equipment needed to walk from point A to point B in our lives. This backpack contains the spiritual provisions for our journeys of development. From an early stage we start filling this backpack. We pack everything into it that we consider necessary and useful. We pack many small food parcels that we receive from others—with the best of intentions or as intentional stumbling blocks. Every experience, every belief pattern, and every incident is placed in this backpack. It is necessary to pack everything because every single parcel has the function to show us something, and it did the trick!

But we reach stages in our lives when we use the parcels in our backpack because we need them; however, we sometimes forget to throw away the packaging. Now it is time to throw away the empty packaging. Herein lies the problem. We kept on placing things in our backpack but never removed any of the used stuff. Instead, we kept filling the backpack, and it was constantly getting heavier and heavier. What seem to be burdens now are not the things we pack and could be things we really need but rather the empty packaging and all the spoiled food that has accumulated and started to stink. Since we have been carrying it around with us for so long, we have long since forgotten about it. We just feel this heaviness, but we cannot define where it comes from. In addition, we are often no longer able to absorb new information because the backpack is full of old stuff and there is no room for anything new.

Once we become aware that we carry a lot that's not relevant at all anymore, the process of introspection begins. We take the bags from our backs and consciously open them—maybe for the first time in years. Now the time has come to clean the bags out! At first we will find the newest packaging that we have put into the bags and take that out. The oldest packages are at the bottom and will be taken out last. It is not recommended to just dig down blindly into the backpack, as this could prove to be very unpleasant and painful. We might not be prepared to look at what we then take out. Removing the upper parts helps us and prepares us to go deeper gradually. It is the same as when you start to look deeply into your heart. We are first confronted with those feelings and situations that were added last. These are easier to understand. Each level prepares us for the next lower level and so on. Once we have eliminated all unnecessary garbage or at least taken a look at it, we have created space (room) to welcome new things with a newfound ease in our lives. This process of clearing out belongs to the first statement, the process of self-discovery!

For both the first and the second statement, we are equipped with a navigation system that informs us constantly whether we are on our correct path or not. We always feel if something is good or bad.

If we, for instance, feel a resistance within us when we hear, "Remain modest! You don't have the right to have a bigger car. You don't deserve it!" then it's an obvious signal that this way of thinking does not correspond to our inner truth. It might correspond to the truth of Mr. Smith on Smith Street but not to our own. Everybody has their own truth, which is composed of all the previously mentioned aspects. Therefore, there can be no single truth in many issues. By the way, it's *never* true that we don't deserve something! We are all precious beings who only deserve the best!

Distinguishing between what belongs to our True Selves and what is foreign storage might be the hardest part to work on as one of our spiritual tasks. When we have accomplished this and understood how the universal laws operate, we have absolved a significant learning step to win the battle against our own ego thinking.

The realization of who we really are and why we have come into this world is the best basis to successfully go through our earthly existence.

Once we have uncovered the view of ourselves, our navigation system can unaffectedly specify the course to the real reason of our existence without losing the satellite reception. Then we can see our own truth.

This book shall be a torch to light the path from your false self to your True Self.

You alone know your own truth, because you're the only one who sees through your eyes.

THE STORY ABOUT THE EGO AND THE UNCONSCIOUS SELF

*J*o help understand more thoroughly how we have reached the situation of having to increase our state of awareness by repeated incarnations, I am paraphrasing a wonderful story of the regression therapist Jan Erik Sigdell. This story depicts why we believe that we are separated from our Source and why we consequently created the ego. It also illustrates that this seeming separation is not real at all and that we are not only connected with our Source but also with one another.

God viewed His creation and called it good. There was a large number of beings, and all of them carried inside of them a seed to allow growth to complete goodness, a seed of perfection. Joyfully and playfully they grew up in their paradise. They had a free will and were able to make decisions. Thus, every being could go its own way, which was in accordance with its nature.

Now because of this free will, it happened that one of God's creatures had a new idea. It thought, *What if we emancipate ourselves from creation? Can't we also be without God?* And it further thought, *Let's live to the fullest and become independent. We want to go our own way and choose for ourselves.* The being presented his idea to the others, and many of them were interested. And they went to see God.

God argued, "That's not possible, because we are all one. We cannot separate from one another, as then the stream of life's energy in the universe would be interrupted, and you would not be able to exist."

But the being who had the idea did not really want to believe this. He wanted to try something to put it into action. Some of the beings who were first interested in his idea turned back to God, but others completely committed themselves to this new idea. The being who initially had the idea became their leader. "If it's true that we have a free will," it said, "then it must be possible!"

And God let it happen. *The renegades will eventually learn from their experiences,* He thought. *But with those ideas they will be able to cause a great deal of harm in creation and disturb the holy order.* That's why God created a special space for them where they could live out their concepts. In this space they were shielded from the rest of creation, for its and their own protection. Now they could live their illusion of emancipation from creation.

But it would be impossible for them to exist this way without continuously being connected with the divine life's energy. If the connection was interrupted for only one moment, they would immediately cease to exist. It would be as if they never had existed at all. Therefore, God needed to supply them with His own life's energy across the borders of their separated space.

However, so that they could indulge in their illusion completely undisturbed, God arranged it so that they were unable to see the light of that energy. He took their awareness of being connected with His energy away from them. This way, and for the first time, the unconscious self-emerged through the separation of the conscious part of their personalities, which has been called ego since then. From that day on, the ego has existed as that part of being believed to be independent and living out the illusion of separation.

The leader of the beings realized that some kind of life force was necessary within this space of seeming separation from God. He felt fulfilled with that divine energy, whose cause was now unconscious to him as well. As he was not able to see that it was God who still let His energy flow through him, he believed that he radiated his own energy to these beings. In particular, he feared that they would cease to exist without this energy and that they would be lost for him. Eventually he needed them to live out his idea. What benefit would he gain from being alone after all?

So it was something radiating that emanated from him. These beings experienced it as light, and therefore, they called him Lucifer, the bringer of light. As they now dwelt in a world of illusion, they could not see that this was not the real light anymore but a modified form of the divine light radiating throughout the world and being transmitted by their leader.

In former times they all ate the fruits from God's tree. Now they could not remember this tree and ate the fruits from the tree of illusion instead. They were not aware of the truth anymore and therefore thought that this was the Tree of Knowledge.

Now our ego still picks the fruits from the supposed Tree of Knowledge and does not realize that in reality it's the Tree of Illusion. Only our unconscious self continuously lives on the Tree of Life, as otherwise we could not exist one more second.

The world of illusion consolidated, and its beings received physical bodies. So that they could continue to exist, the beings were separated into male and female parts—two different aspects of God, after whose image they were created in the first place. As everything else was invisible to them, they did not see that all this was God's creation. He wanted to secure the existence of their playground so that they could continue to live their illusion. And it was good because with their very limited consciousness they could not cause so much damage anymore. Although they were endowed by their Creator with much power and enormous abilities, this was now slumbering deep within them without even being noticed. The physical bodies had properties so that they could not exist by themselves. Everything in the physical world undergoes a process of natural decay. This world was not originally planned in creation.

It was supposed to only exist until the beings found their way out of the illusion. The leader of these beings was highly developed when he had his unfortunate idea. He knew more than the others. Within himself he found the ability to create, and he added his own creations to the material world. He had the idea of a self-sustaining circulation of life's energy. An embodied being should eat the bodies of other beings in order to be eaten by others again. This was a method to retain the available energy despite the natural decay of the physical structures. The one who is eaten passes on life's energy to others. And the person who eats other bodies can incorporate life's energy at the expense of other beings.

So the principle of killing came into being, and with it came the eating of meat. In the beginning it mainly happened among beings of different kind and less within the same species. This led to greed. "I want more of life's energy. Where can I get it?" From now on, this was the main ambition of most of the beings trapped on this plain. In the world of illusion the so-called right of the strong arose.

Besides their physical bodies, all embodied beings possess a sense of self, a soul core. (It is different though in animals and plants than it is in humans, for which the world of illusion was created as a self-contained playground.) Whoever ate another being could only absorb the life energy of its body but not its self. When a body was eaten or when it died through natural collapse, its sense of self had to move away from it and proceed to a new body so that it could remain in the world of illusion until it would eventually find its way out of it.

Reincarnation therefore belonged to the world of illusion, as many lives in many bodies can be necessary until a soul (through development and maturity) is able to fulfill the conditions, allowing it to leave this world of illusion. Even if a man reached the required insight, he still carried burdens from previous lifetimes with him so that a few more embodied lives were necessary in order to be free. He had to make up for many things and to reconcile with those beings he had caused suffering to. He also had to give back everything he had taken and to forgive those who had caused him pain.

By and by these beings became even more unconscious in their world of illusion and completely controlled by their egos. They were unable to understand that in reality they were inseparably interconnected with one another and that nothing could ever function differently. Already evidenced by the fact that we eat, we are connected with other beings and with the whole of nature, which offers material food for all and connects them with one another. Nature's divine light lies hidden everywhere. If we were consequent in our efforts for emancipation, we would have to stop eating. This would mean a slow death for the physical body. Yes, we would also have to stop breathing, as the breath connects us with everything that breathes. A fast death!

The bringer of light, who brought us the apparent light, was way ahead of us in his development when he fell away from God and took us with him as he fell. He sees more than we do. He also understands that he cannot exist without us, and therefore, he does not want to lose any of us. Thus, he even enhanced the illusion and made it as difficult as possible for us to leave this world. He increased our greed for possessions and power in order to attach ourselves to the world of illusion even more. Therefore, we have to make amends and pay our debts before we are able to get out of here. But to settle our old bills, we need more time, and during this time we run into the danger of relapsing.

Lucifer even succeeded in connecting our subconscious idea of life's force or our "ability to live" so deeply with the material world that the ego believes matter is the most important thing in life. He let us go on believing that the life force especially had to do with those kinds of things that are more permanent than our bodies. We discovered that gold and precious stones are much more unchanging than everything else in the material world. Gold does not get rusty. Jewels don't weather. They even remain beautiful when everything else perishes. Since then our greed has been especially focused on these materials. We wanted to possess as much as possible from them, believing that we would be stronger and more viable or at least have more convenient lives as a result.

We are not aware anymore of the fact that someday we have to give everything back—if not in this lifetime, then in another lifetime. We did not even shrink from taking other people's lives or from stealing their material possessions. Many of us have to pay debts back in order to correct our mistakes. We even have to give back the lives that we once took away from others. (Often we have to have these souls as children and raise them.) No man gets out of here before he has not paid his debts back in full.

The longer this process takes, the better for the bringer of light. He knows that he must eventually give back everything that he has taken from creation, and this is what he dreads.

At first there was only one way to get out of this world again—the individual, personal way of insight, development of awareness, and settlement of the "open invoices." But time after time the number of individuals who found their way out of here diminished, as the bringer of light kept inventing more means to bind us to the world of illusion.

God saw that the circumstances for the souls got worse and sent ambassadors to draw their attention to what they had forgotten. In the course of time, around these divine messengers belief systems and religions emerged by which the bringer of light felt threatened. For that reason, he caused strife and misunderstandings. By human weaknesses the teachings were distorted, and finally every group considered the beliefs of the others to be heresy, although originally they had all taught the same thing but only in a different form.

One of the divine messengers was called Buddha, the enlightened. He taught forgotten knowledge about the way out of the illusion. He did not directly speak of God. This was not necessary. He knew that everybody who entered this way back to their origin would sooner or later realize that it was God Himself. (Self-developed God-consciousness is worth far more than every learned theory about Him!) He would rather speak of the most important conditions to walk along this path, which are love and compassion. These are the true keys to liberation. Without them, no one ever finds their way out.

Buddha's teachings gradually fell into oblivion.

Less and less people were really able to follow the path he had shown us, even when they externally declared their faith in him. And God saw that a newer and stronger message was needed—a message that would address more directly against the influence of the bringer of light, as in time he had succeeded in twisting all previous messages. So He sent Christ in this world—Christ, the spirit and the power of love, which is the basis of creation. A being representing the most important of all principles of creation is of such a high nature that it cannot be embodied in only one single human being. Therefore, the power of Christ incarnated in the whole of mankind, but an already redeemed person took up the task to serve its mouthpiece, and so He incarnated as Jesus.

This fairy tale illustrates where we come from and the fact that we still carry the divine spark within us all because physical life would be impossible without it.

There is this divine spark within each of us. It is a part of the former whole. It is a part of the universal energy. Through this spark, we are and remain forever connected with one another. Simultaneously this connection means that through our own development we have an influence on the development of other souls. Sometimes we receive, and sometimes we give. Sometimes we see the signposts that are transmitted by others. Other times we are the transmitters. Sometimes we even help others by allowing them to help us because they have to deal with something they would not have dealt with without us. Whatever we have to learn in order to work our way out of the illusion mentioned by Jan Erik Sigdell happens in accordance with the divine order, an order that we often cannot understand with our minds but can with the wisdom of our souls. Now if we try to determine this order ourselves with our minds (because we know it so much better), we might even block the way to a problem's solution or ultimately even hinder our life plan—or at least we may delay its fulfillment. For this reason, it is necessary to also accept experiences and situations whose purpose we at first cannot see.

Yes, all of us, every living being, every plant, and every stone are connected with one another through the divine spark. It awakens the bodies we inhabit. Let's have a look at the night sky now. How humble and small we might feel when we are looking at it! Nevertheless, we are important enough to play a significant role in this huge whole, and everybody has a plan customized for his or her individual needs. All plans are closely interrelated in a perfect way. People enter our lives and leave them again in order to give us something or to receive something from us. We are all here to help one another, and we are also responsible for one another.

The divine spark radiates within all of us, and we must become aware of this. *It is nothing else than our immortal soul.*

THE SOUL

To put it concisely, we are soul, individual souls, individualized expressions of the divine.

Soul is what we truly are. In principle, the aim of our existence here is the recognition of who we are. With this realization we are able to follow that inner call, which shows us the way to our destination. That's what life is all about. Often we instinctively go our own way anyhow. But when we understand that this impulse is triggered by an inner knowledge—a knowledge that permanently resides inside of us and that can be called up any time—then we realize the real strength and power that we carry within us. Then we can consciously put our visions into action with more success. Our souls—the True Selves—is provided with this power at all times. Moreover, all wisdom that is needed to recognize what our tasks here on earth are—and to live up to them—is all anchored in the soul.

We all derive from the same Source. We can call it what we like—the universe, God, energy. In the end it's all the same. We all carry that spark of our origin within us. Without this divine spark we are unable to survive. What would a body be without a soul? The soul can live without a body but not vice versa. This means that beings with identical origins are spread over the whole earth. Everything that exists has the same Creator. And we all have a part of the Creator within ourselves because we *are* where we come from. Exactly this part is our soul.

So we all come from the same Source and return to it after the death of our bodies. Think of it like this: All souls live in an immense field of energy, and they are all connected with this field and one another. To put it another way, we ourselves and all creation together *are* this energy. The energy that we carry within us is the same energy as our place of origin. We are not only all connected with the Source but also with one another. This is why we continually influence one another with everything we do, no matter which nation, race, or age we might belong to in our earth lives. Like the description in the fairy tale, we are in the process of self-realization. We can experience this self-realization in the hereafter, which is actually our home, here on earth or on other planets. An incarnation on earth brings by far the most realizations and quicker ripening of the fruits of our harvest. So if we have decided to gather our experiences here on earth, our souls send parts of themselves into human bodies. This emitted aspect of our souls—also called the *Higher Self*—is the spark that fills our bodies with life. It is always energetically connected with its big brother during the whole incarnation period. There is no separation. The concept of separation is an illusion of the mind. One may imagine this like sun rays breaking through the cloud covers. The rays reach the earth but remain inseparably connected to their Source. Without their connection to the sun, the rays could not even exist just like the soul could not exist without its connection to its Source. Everything that the incarnated part experiences is saved in the soul. When the mission is fulfilled (when we die), the incarnated soul part gets rid of its physical body and floats back to its Source.

Soul mates, for example, are aspects of the same soul. Thus, they feel very familiar to each other. During their first meeting they often have the feeling that they have known each other for an eternity. This means that they are pieces of the same cake.

There is so much more that can be said about the soul. This issue itself could fill innumerable volumes. But what I would especially like to emphasize is the interaction of vibrations. As our souls commonly come from a huge field of energy, we are directly connected with one another through it. We are one! Thereby, we automatically influence one another in our ripening processes. When we develop, we increase our own vibration and transmit it to the energy field. Through this field the other souls receive these vibrations. However, it is the same case with negative vibrations, and this means that the vibrations we send out are also our responsibility. We not only go through our development processes for ourselves individually but for every other being as well. The higher the vibrational rate of the individual, the more the whole level of awareness rises. One could also imagine this like the class average in an examination. The better your own grade, the more the average rises, and the lower your own grade, the lower the average. So if we have reached a higher level of development through all the insights and experiences that we have made in our lifetimes, we emit higher vibrations and thus have a positive influence on the vibrational rate of the matter around us.

And so this means that with every development, with each bit of work on ourselves, and with all obtained knowledge, we not only do a service to ourselves but to the whole of mankind. This is how we support the increase of vibrations, and sometime we will together reach that vibrational rate through which we will finally be liberated from the world of illusion.

IDENTIFICATION WITH THE EXTERNAL

Erroneously we tend to identify with what surrounds us. We usually identify ourselves with our bodies. For example, we say, "I am slim," or, "I am ill." But that is actually not true. It might be true that one's body is ill or slim. But that's not true of the "I." The body can be compared with a car. We get into it because it takes us from A to B. Then we get off again. It is the same with the body. It is at our disposal so that we can experience this physical existence. And we must care for it so that it is maintained for us as long as possible and so that we can have as many experiences as possible. Would we ever think of saying, "I'm starting to rust," just because the car is getting rusty? That's not very likely as we are not the car, although we can get into it. We are not the body either! We just have bodies that give our souls homes for the duration of our incarnation, but we are not this body.

As many people identify with their bodies, it is a tragedy for them when their bodies, for example, starts to age or when health issues arise. Our bodies are perishable. When we identify with something that is perishable, we sink into depression when it starts to decay. It is the same with everything we might own. When we identify with our possession, we will suffer great agonies when we are losing it—money, houses, cars. We own money, houses, and cars because these things can be enjoyed and because they bring significant benefits that embellish or facilitate our lives. We are not our professions either. We practice these because they are (hopefully) fun, fulfill us, and provide pay. With the earned money, we can buy ourselves many things that make our lives pleasant. We can afford houses, cars, good food, nice trips, and much more. We can have it all because we like it, but we are not these things. If we make our whole purpose in life and what we believe that we are dependent on our professions, what happens when we for some reason cannot practice them anymore? We would cease to function. We would have lost ourselves. But this cannot be because we are still here. Therefore, we are not what we have.

We can never be something that is perishable. We can only own impermanent things for a certain period of time. And even that sentence is too specific. In principle one must say that perishable things can only be used for a certain period of time. Eventually we have to give back all that is impermanent. But the time when we have to give back the alleged possessions does not always lie in our own hands. It is the same with relationships. We cannot own a relationship, a person, or even love. Love is something that we are given freely. A relationship with a partner is a gift one has to take care of. It is a gift that first of all serves as a great teaching aid. Within relationships—whether it's a friendship, a partnership, or a connections among family members or relatives—we learn much about ourselves. But if we are of the opinion that we own our relationships, we make ourselves dependent on them. As we are only connected to people as long as we can learn something from these relationships, we will feel lost when they come to an end. Everything around us is impermanent. What never perishes is what we are—our True Selves currently inhabiting bodies. Love never ceases to exist. It is love that enables us to live. Love created us. It is love that keeps us alive and that binds us together (whether we are aware of these connections or not). This love is inside of us, within our bodies. It exists in our True Selves. It is love that we feel when we feel ourselves. It is love when we realize inner peace, gratefulness, compassion, and joy. Love is the basis for our existence. It is the cover of our souls, which they permeate at the same time. We are this love, and love is us. All that exists in this physical world is subjected to futility. But what remains forever are our True Selves, which consist of pure love only. It is all we really have, what we are, and what we can never lose. Everything else will disappear sometime. The identification with something external only brings suffering, as one day we must let go of it. The only thing that brings real satisfaction are our True Selves because we never have to separate from them. Indeed, we cannot even separate from our souls.

"Happiness, fulfillment and purpose in life are all inner concepts. If you don't have inner peace and serenity, then you have nothing," says Dr. Wayne W. Dyer.

This short phrase suffices: I am. Therein lies all that's necessary. You are soul, this immortal core within you. Soul is really the only imperishable thing. Soul is our existence. It is the life within us. Without it, we were not viable. It is so much bigger and more powerful than the body surrounding us. However, the outer circumstances might change, whatever might have been given into your hands or has been taken away again. Nothing can really happen to us because what we truly are is indestructible. All knowledge, all experiences, and all realizations from previous lifetimes are stored in our souls. It is our inner voice, our essence, and therefore, our True Selves remain intact after physical death.

> You are eternal consciousness currently residing in
> this wonderful physical body, because it is exciting and
> joyful to be creative in this space-time-reality.
> —Abraham – Esther and Jerry Hicks

I Love, Therefore I Am!

Pretty much everyone knows Descartes's quotation, "I think, therefore I am." This would mean that as long as we are able to think, we exist. The reverse would say, "When I don't think, I am not." Or it might suggest that as soon as our brains do not function anymore and our bodies die, we cease to exist. Can this really be true?

Our ability to think is a proof for our physical existence. But our true existence is imperishable and independent from the physical body. We are eternal life. And during this eternal life we occasionally dive into bodies through which we can experience things we could not experience without it. It is not the brain that gives life to this body. The brain is just a control center and also part of the body. What awakens the body to life is the "I am." It is our soul—the divine spark, the energy where we come from and which enables us to live physical lives.

The True Self is only enabling us to give a body the possibility to think. Actually the phrase should be the other way around. "I am, therefore I think." But there is still a small inconsistency. Our True Selves feel, emit energy, and radiate vibrations. But the thinking belongs to our brain and to the physical part of the body. The "I am" within us is wisdom and love. And we feel this love with our hearts, not with our minds. It is this area where the spark that keeps us alive—God's light, our soul—is situated. The "I am" was created out of love, and therefore, we are love to the very core. God is love, and love is God. God is immortal. When we feel this love, we feel God, the root of our existence. When we feel love, we feel the immortal within us. And the immortal is our soul, our "I am." When we feel ourselves, we feel love, and we feel God.

Even when our bodies die, we still exist. Then we recognize our true existence again. We are always, with or without bodies, with or without thinking.

The sentence should be read as follows: "I love, therefore I am."

THE MEANING OF LIFE/OUR MISSION

Every one of us said: "I will enter this space-time-reality together with other beings and assume a clear and specific identity". You also said: "I will love it and allow it to completely fill this physical body—this space-time-reality. This environment will inspire me to let the powerful energy, which I am, to flow into the manifestation of targeted, specific wishes. By this, I powerfully drive the development—and it will be my great pleasure."
—Abraham – Esther and Jerry Hicks

Our souls—that means every part of us because we *are* soul—is a part of God. God is everything—every being, every stone, every tree, and every planet. We can imagine God as a chocolate cake. In this cake all ingredients are spread out evenly—the flour, the eggs, the sugar, the chocolate, the butter, the baking powder, etc. If we cut out a piece of the cake, it contains the same mixture of components as in the whole cake. Even a crumb consists of the same ingredients. So God is the cake, and we are a crumb of this cake. Being soul, we are made from the same substance as God himself. We are all a small piece of God. God experiences himself through us. We are ambassadors of God, and everything we realize and experience God himself experiences through us. Therefore, it is an act of gratitude to give the best we can in order to fulfill our tasks here. Being divine means that your counterpart is divine too. This concept helps us understand the following phrase from Jesus: "Inasmuch as you have done it unto one of the least of these my brethren, you have done it unto *me.*" - Matthew 25:40 KJV. Whenever we do something good for another person, we also do it for God. In other words, we do it for God *and* for other people, and through the interconnection we also do it for mankind and for ourselves. This is a very figurative explanation why all actions, thoughts, and words eventually return to us. We receive what we are. When we make sure that we are satisfied within ourselves, we radiate our satisfaction to the universe. It has nothing to do with egoism when we have a good time as long as our well-being is not consciously uplifted at the expense of others. We feel good when we are truly happy. To be happy means to realize God within us. To realize God within us means to see God in everything. This implies that we know deep inside us that God is omnipresent.

Whatever we have to do on this planet, we don't do it just for ourselves. We are all a part of the whole and therefore closely interconnected. Everybody collects information for the benefit of all. Hence, we do everything we do for every one of us. It should be our purpose in life to support others to likewise give their very best, to experience their own beauty, and to share their happiness with others. We are all doing this without being aware of it anyway. In fact, through the different tasks that we need to fulfill while we are here, we add a special individual touch of perfection to the whole.

DESTINY AND FATE

We all come from the same place and have the same light within us. However, each of us comes here with his or her own program individually tailored for the person. Before we incarnated, we ourselves determined what we wanted to accomplish and to experience in this lifetime. For this reason, every one of us has different goals and dreams. This leads to the fact that some issues can be huge problems for some people, whereas other people do not even notice them.

We chose certain targets for every incarnation. These targets are insights we definitely want to achieve or feelings we want to experience. We can call these targets our fate or the central theme in our lives. We ourselves chose the targets we want to reach. In order to really get to them, we must follow a specific path. This path contains our preferences and aversions. It also contains the perspective with which we look at all things. Our point of view causes thoughts and actions that bring us into situations. We also come into contact with the people who aid us and through whom we are able to receive our required realizations. Sometimes we must get a complete contrasting view in order to experience a moment or receive the aha effect. By this aha moment, we perform a perfect U-turn with the effect that the realization is irrevocably anchored in us now.

This individual way to our realization includes the body the way it is. Perhaps we have not chosen our bodies in detail. But we agreed that the body should be exactly in such a way so that it could serve us best to reach our targets. This agreement also includes all limitations our bodies might bring along with them. By setting us certain limits, the body automatically prevents us from deviating from our original plan. This means that if we are not meant to be runners, we will not have the required body structures, and we will not be able to develop the necessary stamina. If we are not meant to be supermodels, we will likewise not fulfill the necessary conditions. But if we are meant to live our fate as singers or artists, then we will bring a special talent with us, and if we are supposed to work as craftsmen, our hands will be very skillful. We are automatically prevented from doing certain activities by allergies or health issues that make it impossible for us to carry out these activities. Our genetic and intellectual dispositions correspond exactly to the needs we have in order to achieve the objectives pursued. Unfortunately far too often we spend much time with finding out why we don't meet certain beauty standards, why we have cellulite, or why we have one or two kilos in the wrong place. Why don't I have the super mane my neighbor has? Why do I need glasses? Why do I have a birth mark? Health issues also belong to these limitations, especially disabilities that direct us into specific directions and prevent us from going the wrong way. All these things are aids that help us to adhere to our original purpose. When we understand that we have set our targets ourselves and that we have agreed to use the necessary tools, we will cease to struggle against unchangeable circumstances. If we stop dealing with them and accept them through recognition, we automatically turn ourselves to those subjects that we set when we came here. If we cease to ask, "Why?" we save much time and energy, much of which we can invest in our true path more constructively. I want to point out that in some cases a limitation of the body, a missing arm or leg, or another disability can show us that everything is possible in this world and that there are always ways to fulfill our inner calling. If it is meant for that person to find ways to overcome his or her physical or mentally boundaries, he or she will definitely know it through this burning fire in his or her heart.

Think of the story of the brave and admirable Temple Grandin. She was diagnosed with autism and labeled as having brain damage at the age of three in 1950. Since the child wasn't talking, Grandin's mother spoke to a doctor who suggested speech therapy. She hired a nanny who spent hours playing turn-taking games with Grandin and her sister. This way she started speaking at the age of four. Her mother supported her in a way that gave her everything she needed so she could live a normal life. In spite of her disability, Grandin graduated middle and high school, although she was always ridiculed by her schoolmates. Grandin went on to earn her bachelor's degree psychology from Franklin Pierce College in 1970, a master's degree in animal science from Arizona State University in 1975, and a doctoral degree in animal science from the University of Illinois at Urbana-Champaign in 1989. Grandin is a philosophical leader of both the animal welfare and autism advocacy movements. Both movements commonly cite her work regarding animal welfare neurology and philosophy. She knows the anxiety of feeling threatened by everything in her surroundings and of being dismissed and feared, which motivates her work in humane livestock-handling processes. Grandin's interest in animal welfare began with designs for sweeping, curved corrals intended to reduce stress in animals being led to slaughter. Grandin also started to talk about her life with the diagnosis autism to help aggrieved parties. She first spoke in public about autism in the mid-1980s. Based on personal experience, Grandin advocates early intervention to address autism and supportive teachers who can direct fixations of the child with autism in fruitful directions. She has described her hypersensitivity to noise and other sensory stimuli. She claims she is a primarily visual thinker and has said that words are her second language. Grandin attributes her success as a humane livestock facility designer to her ability to recall detail, which is a characteristic of her photographic memory. Grandin compares her memory to full-length movies in her head that can be replayed at will, allowing her to notice small details. She is also able to view her memories using slightly different contexts by changing the positions of the lighting and shadows. Her insight into the minds of cattle has taught her to value the changes in details to which animals are particularly sensitive and to use her visualization skills to design thoughtful and humane animal-handling equipment. Temple Grandin is an example of how to live your own purpose rightly because of a disability. She took the advantages she got from her disease and turned them into a powerful tool to live her fate and equally bring hope and constructive help into the lives of others. As she lives her life according to her fate with all the necessary boundaries, she allows the God inside of her to flow into the world for the benefit of the whole.

In connection with our goals, we have not only chosen our bodies and our personalities but also all the people with whom we are in contact throughout our lifetimes, starting with our parents, brothers and sisters, friends, and partners. With all of them we have made arrangements. They all help us make the experiences that we came here to make. Every one of us was given a role that he or she plays in order to promote the development of ourselves and the people close to us. For this reason, we should not judge anyone who plays the role of the "bad guy" in our lives. It is a wonderful soul that agreed to become unpopular in order to help us develop. Let's take the example of a soul that wants to learn assertiveness and self-esteem. If this person never came under pressure and never experienced humiliation, if the individual instead continually received support and confirmation of his or her subservience, this person would never feel the urge to break out of his or her submissiveness, stand up, and appreciate his or her own existence. All people we meet teach us something, whether we experience them as friendly or unfriendly. Every being we encounter is a teacher for us, even if we don't consciously recognize it. Before their and our births they decided to play roles in our lives, and they will play exactly the role that is necessary for our development. It was our decision. We ourselves compiled the program for our incarnation, and it is our decision to alter these roles while we make progress.

The arrangements we made with other Souls also affect our assistance in their lives. These Souls are not only a part of our life, at the same time we are a part of their life, so also because of this we have taken over a responsibility toward mankind as a whole: By following our path, we comply with our plan, and by doing so, we enable others to remain on their paths too. The program of our incarnation is saved in our souls. Our minds do not know it. It is part of the transient body. Therefore, we easily diverge from the ideal path as soon as we bring the mind and thus the ego into play. As each has his or her own personal program, everybody can only know for him or herself what is right for each respectively, even if the rest of the world has a different opinion. If we follow the call of our souls, we will always be correct. Always! This does not mean that life is a walk in the park. It means that we pursue the fate we have chosen and that everything is at our disposal for its fulfillment. Only when we have gone through and experienced everything we had on our checklist will we successfully return to our Source. When we understand the meaning behind our incarnation and all occurrences in our lives, it is much easier to follow the route chosen by us before our birth and to accept all its consequences. Then we are also able to accept everything we encounter and to be thankful for it with the deepest conviction, that it helps us for our development and further progress.

Although we have this program, which leads us to our predetermined objectives, nevertheless we have free will. We can follow our plan or turn it down. Equally we ourselves decide in what kind of way we want to proceed. This means that we can chicken out, postpone, or move forward. The full program will be pulled through anyway, as it was our free will to start it in the first place. What an intelligent arrangement! We would never make decisions for certain challenging experiences while already being in this physical body. But setting it up from our wise selves with a higher perspective before we incarnated doesn't let us out. It was our free will anyway! We cannot negate its main topics. It will accompany us uncompromisingly until we look it in the eye, as it is the real reason why we are in this current incarnation. We will therefore be confronted with the same things over and over again until we have accepted them. God's love is unconditional. God takes our requests seriously and continually supplies us with everything we need so that our wish to learn what we came here for is fulfilled. And when we are in danger of losing our way, he will send us means and helpers that unmistakably draw our attention to this condition. But don't worry! We will always be confronted with just the right circumstances that we are able to deal with. All challenges are always tailored to our current state of consciousness. Even within our main topic we reach different levels of development. We work on them in stages. It would be impossible to handle such a task at once. It is like learning a language. We have to go through one lesson after the other until we are more or less able to speak the language. Although we understand more after every comprehended lesson, there is always more to learn.

So there is this thing called fate forcing us to learn certain things, but at all times we have our free will. Neither God nor guardian spirits will ever interfere with our free will. We have our free will to decide in what kind of way we want to learn our lessons. It determines our destiny. Destiny is not something that simply happens to us. Destiny is the way we move forward to reach our targets. There will be consequences depending on how we face things and on how we deal with circumstances and occurrences. We cause these consequences with our thoughts, words, and eventually our actions. We therefore have an influence on our destiny. Even if unpleasant things happen, we have the chance to deal with them positively by understanding that they are simply teaching aids guiding us to our next realization. On the other hand, we can be against them, negate them, express displeasure, fall into self-pity, and talk ourselves deeper and deeper into something. By doing so, not only do we attract all of the negatives we don't really want, but through our permanent resistance against a perhaps simple experience, we even cause an inner tension against our self-determined path. On the other hand, if we trust that with negative situations there are special tools sent to us that bring us back to our senses and help us to remember which direction we should take and what it's really all about, everything runs smoothly. We can compare this with a house. We are the architects, and the house is our earthly life. After our decision to incarnate, we design the blueprints for our lives. When our plans are finished, everything can begin. We begin to construct our lives in the moment when we as souls enter bodies.

The shell construction is definite, but of course we may continually make changes. Some things transpire easily, and other things are more difficult. We can always make adjustments to the interior. We can design it luxuriously or simple. However, there are cornerstones that cannot be altered, as they belong to our true fate and therefore will keep us within our life program. Trying to move a key wall, for example, can result in part of our house falling down. And it is very hard to restore it to the previous state. On the other side we now know for sure that this point cannot be changed and that we have to find a compromise by accepting it and by harmoniously integrating this key wall into the remaining construction. It is also up to us how we look after our house. Do we keep it clean, always ready to welcome guests? Or do we have hundreds of locks attached to the doors and windows? The main plan is definite, but it is our free will as to how we organize it. This metaphor could be spun out endlessly.

Even if we are sure that we are on the right track—yes, even when we are really sure that we are following our life's path—it does not mean that we can escape from all stumbling blocks. As I said, we are here to learn. We gained admission to one of the rare places on this planet. It is no all-inclusive holiday (it's more like an on-the-farm holiday).

We can feel absolutely in tune with what we do. We can be fully involved in an activity and have a sense of fulfillment for it, but nevertheless, obstacles may be put in our way. Often this might make us wonder if we are really on the right track or if it would be better to give up everything. Hence, it is important to understand the following: If we feel that we are on the right path, if we pursue our activities with passion, then it is very likely that we are really on the right track. But let's compare this with the construction of a house again. A room is not finished just because the windows are installed. It still has to be painted. The floor covering has to be chosen and laid. Lamps need to be mounted and furniture placed. Perhaps the furniture even needs to be assembled beforehand. What I want to say is this: To pursue our fate does not mean that we automatically obtain a license for lifelong freedom from any kind of setbacks or obstacles. On the contrary, in order to successfully reach a target within our fate, we must retain the necessary skills. A true healer or spiritual teacher has to get over very painful experiences so that he or she is able to understand this life and to feel with other people so that people take him or her seriously.

How many people want to be rich? There is hardly anyone who would oppose this. How many people play the lottery, and how many of them really win high amounts? A win on the lottery only makes sense when the time and the appropriate maturity level is in alignment with the individual's fate. Naturally I already hear objections. But there are so many lottery winners who spent their whole wealth within a few months and now even have a mountain of debt. A lottery win does not necessarily have to be a target. For some people the meaning of such a win is not the receipt but indeed the loss of the money in order to learn the lesson about why they are here. When we lose everything—with everything, I mean outer circumstances, material possessions, and relationships—all that remains is what we really are, and this is what we can never lose. Hence, sometimes the total ruin is the only possible way to find our way back to our true essence and to become aware of it. Moreover, we recognize that everything external is only borrowed and subject to decay. We should enjoy it and use it, but we should not fall into the illusion that we are these trivialities.

Whatever happens to us is part of our learning process. There are no injustices because we learn something from everything. We even learn the most from those circumstances we consider to be unfair.

It is very important to learn that we were not presented with a preprinted life path but that we also have possibilities to change it. We ourselves were the wire-pullers of the plan for our incarnation. Nothing happens against our will. What annoys us in our daily lives and all the obstacles we encounter serve as challenges to reach the next stage of knowledge. We cannot blame anyone for any circumstances or incidents except ourselves. Our request to design this incarnation the way we wanted to experience it in order to reach our desired level of maturity was fulfilled. It's anything but punishment. It is an honor to be here. This will become increasingly clear in the course of this book.

What Do Our Dreams Show Us?

Dreams, wishes, and longings lie dormant in each of us. Each of us has already felt the need to realize this or that. There are dreams like being on the stage, traveling around the world, following a special profession, visiting a particular place, learning an instrument or a language, giving up smoking, etc. Some people simply get going, and others dodge their longings. They use excuses like these: "I am not capable of doing this." "I have never done something like this before." "It takes too much time." "I am too old enough." But why do we use these and similar excuses? Because fear is in between, and we don't want to admit that. We rather search for explanations for why we think that we cannot reach certain things. Nevertheless, our dreams and wishes stay, and in the end we live unhappy lives— unhappy with ourselves and with our environments, which we wrongly blame for not being able to reach our goals. Or we put the blame on the circumstances for not being able to live our dreams. Probably everybody has once reached this point in his or her life.

Our dreams don't spring from our minds. They are an inner call reminding us over and over again of the direction of our path and of what we want to experience here. When we give positive attention to our dreams, we automatically follow our fate and encounter exactly those occurrences and persons who are necessary for its realization. But the more we leave our path, the louder the inner voices get and the faster we are confronted with situations that cause us to think and to get back to our original route.

Let's imagine our life path like a dead straight street. Naturally there are always ups and downs, but as long as we stay on the street, it carries straight on fluently. It starts getting difficult though when, by making way for difficulties, we go farther and farther astray or when we even become entangled in undergrowth at the side of the street. We realize it pretty quickly when we have lost our way. We can see it in our minds by experiencing unpleasant feelings, physical reactions, or certain occurrences or persons. These are the moments when we have pain, suffering, or fears, times when we feel that nothing moves any further. Or we may have moved into directions we absolutely do not want to pursue. Those moments are necessary so that we reflect on our lives, notice the deviations, and begin to listen to our inner voice again. As soon as we have gone through such crises, we are stronger than before and rise like phoenixes from the ashes with new realizations. We have learned a lesson and thus pushed ourselves back on our own path. And at the same time we have come further. We have taken a big step. Hence, it is very important not to condemn unpleasant situations, as we learn a lot from them. Many aha moments in our lives are connected with prior pains. Only when it starts getting unbearable, we feel forced to think everything over and to find out if it would be better to change something. Why should we ever change something as long as everything is running like clockwork? We must feel it in order to absorb it. Only then have we really learned something.

Every life path is as unique as each of us. Hence, there is no universal solution for the challenges appearing on our path. There is a particular solution for each particular person in his or her particular situation, but this solution needs to be found by the individual. Often we need to be completely down to be able to find the solutions that lie in the depths. We ourselves have to discover it. As long as we only follow the advice of others without feeling the right decisions inside of us, we might be able to find a way out of the current situation, but we will not learn the essence of the lesson and therefore not be able to absorb anything. Another consequence is that we will be confronted with the same or similar circumstances at the next opportunity. Every path that we have to walk has never been taken by anyone else before, and it never will be. Every path is new territory, and it is perfectly designed for the needs of the individual. Thus, we might be able to accompany others on their paths for this life, but we are not able to walk these for them.

Our dreams show us the direction we need to take. By realizing our dreams, we deal with everything that we have planned to experience. For this reason, it is so important to carefully give attention to our inner voice. If we don't follow the hints of our True Selves, we might not be able to experience some things that originally were on our agenda. Some of the things we have not dealt with yet are thrown in our faces over and over again until they have become so unpleasant so that we finally have to look at them. So it is not necessarily all about reaching a particular target but about pursuing it with seriousness, conviction, and passion—no matter what the result eventually looks like. We must know that on the way to our target we discover all those important realizations.

GIVING AND TAKING

We should be grateful to every person, every situation, and every single occurrence in our lives. Our life paths often intersect. Sometimes we share the same path with another person until this person or we ourselves get to a fork in the path and the ways separate again. We have many tasks to fulfill on our way, and these are also linked to the tasks of others. At the right moment we are there for other people and them for us. Some encounters are only like a gentle touch, and through others a new task begins—perhaps even *the* task. It is a continual giving and taking. We always give and take in tune with our true being, with our fate, and with the divine order. It is important to equally balance out what others gave to us. True gratefulness is important in the first place. Take it and be grateful. If someone needs your help, be at his or her disposal. It is a harmonious circle. Give to those who need something and receive when you need it. Sometimes we are givers, and sometimes we are takers. We learn the most for ourselves when we help others.

Putting us aside and adjusting to the needs of the other person enables us to have insights and realizations that are not obvious as long as we remain buried within ourselves. By doing so, we help the other person while at the same time we receive enormous knowledge for ourselves. This is because we are now able to see our own situation with distance. Of course we can be sure that something can be found in every encounter that is supposed to cause insights. By giving, we immediately receive—and not only in one kind of way but at least in three.

- the lesson that can be learned from the situation of the other person
- the good feeling of having done something good
- the good feeling of gratefulness radiated by the other person

Through the energy that has emerged from our insights, more positive things are drawn into our lives that are accompanied by further realizations.

Even if the other people do not express thankfulness, we can be sure that they were helped anyway. Simply the good feeling of this certainty reconnects us with our inner light and with our Source. Now we can better understand the saying, "Giving is more blissful than taking." Give ... and you are given. The more you give, the more you receive. This is the law of attraction.

COMING TO THE RIGHT DECISIONS

Decisions always have to be made. Sometimes they are crystal clear for us, and sometimes we rack our brains and weigh all the things involved without really knowing for sure what we shall do eventually. But there is also some good news. Every decision we make is exactly the right one! Even if we change our minds after we already made a decision, it is exactly how it should be. It is senseless anyway to be at odds with decisions that have already been made because we will never know through a realistic comparison how it would have been if we had chosen differently.

Let's take a simple example. You want to rent a house. After you have already made selections, there are still two houses on the shortlist. Both are basically what you have in mind. House A is more expensive, but it is situated more centrally. House B is cheaper but lies more out of town. In the end, the advantages and disadvantages cancel one another out. So what do you do now? Let's imagine that you decide in favor of house A. What sense does it make to permanently wonder if house B would have been more sensible because of the cheaper rent? If you decide in favor of house B, you will never know how things would have turned out with house A. Perhaps the central location would soon have become a nuisance to you because of the high volume of traffic, or you would have had loud neighbors. From whatever side you look at it, you will never come to a conclusion because you are not able to live both decisions. No matter which house you take, it will be perfect for you. You will experience exactly what you are supposed to experience.

Simplified, it is our task to follow our own path and to deal with all challenges we encounter. They are there to allow us to reach the end of this stage. With every step we come closer to it. Through our dreams, we visualize these destinations. We experience a lot of ways to their realization, and we meet very different people.

Everything we have experienced has made us what we are today. Our whole life is a unique and exciting journey. Enjoy it and anticipate what adventures wait ahead of you! As we all have our own travel route with perfectly matching tasks, only we ourselves individually can decide where our journeys lead us. Nobody else can know it, and therefore, no one should want to make the decisions for others.

I wrote a little poem about longings. Our dreams and longings are reminders of our soul that there is something waiting for us.

When you give yourself the permission to follow this inner call and bring your soul's voice in alignment with your mind you have the most powerful team in your back to make your dreams come true.

Longings

You're longing for wisdom.
You're longing for love.
You're longing for freedom
and help from above.

Your longings are signposts
full of passion and strong.
They are the drive
to hang in and move on.

To feel a deep longing
is your wake-up call
to follow your purpose,
to conquer it all!

—Erika Kind

THE TARGET

We have demanded independence, and because of His love, God gave it to us. Now we have to learn to deal with the consequences of this independence. We received our free will, and therefore, we have the possibility to determine how fast and in what kind of way we want to develop. Incarnation after incarnation we work our way up to the light. This does not mean that we move from independence to dependence, it means that we are on the way to our oneness with God, our Source. It means that eventually all crumbs will be united with their original cake again. Among others, we have to recognize this difference through the veil of distortion, which the ego throws over us.

Although every one of us is born into this world with his or her own program, we all have the same target—to eventually realize that we are eternal beings of God. When we realize this, we are above all material things. We do not judge anymore. We don't identify ourselves with appearances and superficialities, and we appreciate every being the way it is because we know that it is like us and that it has incarnated for the same reason as we are. Through this realization we have automatically resolved our life's theme. But we only reach our target by realizing our core and by understanding that this physical life is not our true existence but a role in this theater. I don't mean the intellectual understanding, as this often comes pretty easy but is stuck to the surface. I mean the absolute consciousness about who we truly are and why we came here. As long as we still have the slightest doubt that in reality we are eternal, almighty, loving energy, we will orient ourselves over and over again toward physical circumstances, identify with them, and experience suffering, even though less often and less intensive with advancing consciousness. On the other hand, this means that whenever we perceive negative, emotionally straining feelings caused by outer circumstances, we are shown that our consciousness is dimmed. Otherwise we would not allow ourselves to get involved in these kinds of complications any further. All this might appear to be so distant that it's beyond reach. It is unnecessary to fall into desperation again for this reason because that's exactly what we shall learn incarnation for incarnation. It is a process of development. Hardly anyone of us has already reached full consciousness. If that is the case, he or she would probably not be here anymore. What every individual is able to do at this moment are exercises *making us aware of the unconscious.*

There is nothing you cannot be, do, or have. Whatever your wish might be: We want to help you to receive it. But we also

love your momentary status—even if you don't like it—as we know how wonderful every step on your journey is and will be.
—Abraham – Esther and Jerry Hicks

You will make an incredible discovery. Given the distance you have to cover in order to reach your goals, you encounter the most unbelievable challenges. Some are pleasant, and some are not. Through your clear aim, you will not be able to draw back because you know what you are doing all this for. Perhaps you will detect, time after time, that it is not absolutely necessary to reach your aim but to go your own way toward it—a way supplying you with everything you want to experience and to learn here. You will recognize the meaning of this sentence: "The path is the goal." The more attention you give to your path and the more joyful you accept every challenge, the faster your visions will become true.

There is no way to Happiness; Happiness is the way!
—Dr. Wayne W. Dyer, *Living the Wisdom of the Tao*

Simplified we can say as follows: "We live in order to learn and to apply in our lives what we have learned." This way we grow and put the puzzle pieces together until the whole picture is complete again.

OUTER INFLUENCES

In the course of time—beginning with our birth—we are characterized by our environment. We are trained to obey the rules and regulations, to behave morally, to have good manners, to be adaptable, or even to accept a subordinated role. A little boy who is just about to learn how to speak does not know much about this world, about hierarchies, and moral or social rules. He learns from the persons in his surroundings. These are his parents, brothers and sisters, friends of the family, relatives, teachers, etc. He discovers how he is perceived by the people close to him. The boy receives information about his behavior and his appearance from all these people. He is told what's wrong and what's right, what is pretty or ugly, smart or stupid, skillful or clumsy, etc. Little by little, the child is given social and religious regulations and belief systems to take with him. The child collects all this information and saves it like a computer on his hard drive. He accepts all these statements as facts because he does not know any better. All the statements about the environment, his surroundings, or even about the boy himself are absorbed into his belief system. The more often he absorbs the same statements, the deeper they are anchored within him. They are taken as facts. The little child cannot differentiate yet between different points of views and does not understand that people can have different opinions on the same subject. He cannot understand yet that every person perceives him differently. Nevertheless, he stores within him everything that he thinks to be most useful. Throughout our childhood these belief systems and thought patterns that are taken from outside sources become anchored within us and become stronger. We learn that we are rewarded when we meet the expectations of others and that we are punished when we don't behave properly. Time after time this child, which might already be a teenager or a young adult by now, does not perceive at all anymore that he does not live his life according to his own standards, but he lives and expresses the opinions of others. That's why later in our lives it's so hard to differ between the permitted characteristics from others and our own convictions and tendencies. We were trained to be good girls or boys by following the sociably accepted rules. As it was important for our survival to be loved and accepted, we obeyed these rules.

It is true though that throughout puberty and at the latest during adulthood, our true nature breaks through again and again. Hence, tensions arise within us because our true nature does not correspond to many of the influences we took from outside. But because we have submitted ourselves to a long-term training program to obey social rules, we don't understand the source of our inner tensions. Now a small or big battle starts inside of us. What are we fighting against? Against what society considers to be right or wrong or what we have practiced our whole lives? Or against what we had suppressed for many years and what actually is unknown to us, although in reality our True Selves are calling? Of course, we will fight against the unknown, the unwanted, uncomfortable individual being that supposedly insists on its right for realization with thoughtlessness and egoism. The voice of our True Selves starts to defend itself because it cannot identify with all those belief patterns that were—certainly with the best of intentions—stamped on everyone so that we are able to live decent lives. Our True Selves call us to wake up so that we can begin to go our own individual way. We are now asked to find our own opinions and convictions and to differentiate them from those of others so that we can live in harmony with our true nature and successfully follow our own task and destination.

The reason why we don't trust our own inner voice can be found in those imprints that have been trying to convince us that we have to follow the voice of the masses, not our own. Our inner voice is viewed to be uncomfortable because it tries to make us do things we shouldn't do in the eyes of the general public. As the years go by, we therefore refrain from doing many things that we feel that we must do, not because we don't want to do them but because we think that we have to meet the expectations of our surroundings. Thus, we believe more and more that we have to continually prove something to others and that we are only worth something when we receive the approval of our surroundings. By becoming like this, we risk that we live the dreams of others, not our own. We often go against the destiny we feel inside of us, and we bury our longings deep within us. As our minds do not know our true path, our minds then go with our imprints and habits and not with our inner voice—this silent voice that is continually trying to bring our true longings back to our minds. Being reasonable, adjusted persons, naturally we follow the voice of our minds and not the voice of our souls. What happens next? We realize that we don't feel good. In reality, we don't want to do what we have decided to do. We feel misunderstood, and often we feel isolated. So we feel separated, although—like I already said—we are always connected with our Source and with one another. What mainly happened through the wrong perception of separation is the loss of trust in us and in our guidance and our origin. We feel lost, and we still don't realize that we just have to get back inside of ourselves. The loss of trust points to the lack of love—and where no love is—fear arises. Our minds interfere and think that they can decide what's right and what's wrong. In fact, the mind is part of the brain and therefore part of the mortal body. It is only a part of the physical life. It's the mind that stored doctrines and belief patterns within it, and therefore, it can only go with what it knows. Our minds do not have the knowledge about our life path. In other words, the wisdom of our souls shows us the way, and the mind has to solve the arithmetic problems of life. It has to organize everything and to recognize difficult situations in our daily lives as well as handle them. The soul decides, whereas the mind is in charge of carrying out the decisions.

At this point I would like to emphasize that I am not telling anybody to drop everything and to evade his or her responsibilities just because something goes against the grain for the person. Duties and responsibilities don't necessarily have to be heavy burdens. If, for example, two people decided to start a family, they made this decision out of love. They wanted to give birth to children and give them their love and attention. Being a mother of three children, I know it only too well how demanding and challenging this task can often be. Having accepted that kind of responsibility, it will always remain for all time. It is the consequence of a previous decision and an action. For many years we were limited in our mobility. We experienced many short nights and were unable to make plans for one single day. Nevertheless, we cannot simply turn around and leave just because we—understandably sometimes—feel that it's all getting too much for us. With this example I want to show that we simply have to come to terms with some circumstances in our lives and that we—if necessary—must make changes in our way of thinking or behaving in order to bring back an ease to life. Even the most wonderful occurrences bring their challenges with them, whether it's parenthood, relationships, or work.

It can also be totally different as we can see in the following example: Suppose that a man has been a carpenter for twenty years and that he has been putting his whole heart into his job. Now in the past five years his work has become more and more unsatisfactory. Instead of compelling himself to carry out the same profession for the next twenty years just because he had made this choice sometime in the past, it would make more sense for him to become aware of the interests now prevailing. We change and develop continually, and whatever was right for us twenty years ago does not necessarily have to be right for us today. If we feel that this is true, then a new training or the combination of our old profession with an additional training might be variants. We never do anything for nothing, and in the course of our lives we are able to combine many abilities we have once acquired with others. If we finally merge them with the talents we were born with and those abilities we might already have developed, then we are following our inner voice and are going with the flow of our own individual growth. We should never shirk our responsibilities. This would be nothing but running away, and we would sooner or later be caught anyway. We must learn to deal with the facts of life and change whatever we are able to change instead of being petrified out of habit or because of our obsolete wish to meet the expectations of others.

The Permitting of Influences

Wayne Dyer puts it like this: "What other people think of me, is none of my business." We have no influence on the behavior of others. We can only influence our own thoughts and the emotions associated with them. If somebody has a problem with our behavior, with our characteristics, or with our personality, it is at person's problem, not ours! This person lives in his or her own reality just as you and I live in ours. Just like you act the way you feel is right according to your current level of information, your counterpart does the same. This person acts out of his or her conviction and according to his or her subjective point of view just like you do. When we become aware of that, it's easier for us not to take everything personally. Everyone has to go his own way, and everyone does it the way he or she feels is best. Of course, we should listen to the views of others. As they view the situation with detachment and therefore illuminate it with a different light, their perspectives might be very helpful and could lead us to a broader viewpoint. Everyone eventually has to decide for him or herself. Even helping somebody can have a big influence on you if you think that you must take responsibility and regulate the problem for that person. This will not work anyway. You can be there for the other person in order to accompany him or her, but you cannot solve the individual's problem because if the person does not go through his or her own experience, he or she cannot learn anything. Be helpful, have an open ear and an open heart, but avoid solving his or her problem by making it your own. If you do that, you burden yourself with things that are not your business. To recognize this might even be one of your learning lessons!

Objectively speaking, we should not make mistakes that hurt other people or expose them to additional burdens. Sometimes the chemistry's just not right. This has nothing to do with seemingly inappropriate actions or statements. It's simply the case that the other person basically feels disturbed by something we did or said. It is like two magnets facing each other with the same poles, thus repelling each other. Maybe we reflect something in the other person that he or she does not like in him or herself, or we accomplish something that our counterpart would like to accomplish but is not succeeding.

There are many reasons why some people react to us with negativity. As long as we don't do anything on purpose to fuel this negativity like provoking or hurting, their reactions should not irritate you. Of course, it might make sense to find out if there were unconscious actions or statements that hurt or upset the other person. We reflect something to others, and they reflect something to us as well. When we act according to our best knowledge and conscience, everything is all right. We are the way we are. Everyone follows his or her own program, and every program is justified. It's our decision not to dictate to others what they have to do or talk them into something that might only be good for us. Everybody who is asked to do so can and should share his personal view on a certain issue. Equally everyone should be aware that there is never only one solution for a problem. What seems to be perfect for one person would be a catastrophe for the other. It's okay to offer help and to give advice but please accept it if the other person decides to go into a completely different direction.

We are all individual beings with the right to express our individuality. Even if some people don't understand this, it does not mean that we are on the wrong track. As long as we listen to and go with the wisdom of our soul, we act out of love—out of love for ourselves and for everything surrounding us. Acting out of a place of love is always a gift and a blessing. What happens out of love can never be wrong because then we act holistically with the voice of our Source, and at the same time we give others the opportunity to grow with our actions. When we have anchored this knowledge within us, we can no longer be influenced from outside sources in negative ways.

Nobody can ever hurt you. Nobody can ever frighten you unless you allow it. "The less I care about the approval of others, the more approval I receive," Dr. Wayne W. Dyer says in *Living the Wisdom of the Tao*.

Insecurities, self-criticism, and fears can arise when we make ourselves dependent on the approval of others. Once we feel that we don't receive their approval, we think that we did something wrong. As we were actually convinced that we handled the situation correctly, rejections disappoint and irritate us even more. That's the main reason why we doubt ourselves. Among others, the cause for making ourselves dependent on the approval of others is the belief in being separated from one another. As every single person here on earth has to follow his or her own path, which differs from every other path, it is absolutely impossible to always receive the consent of the environment. But if we know that it is important to pursue our own path—because eventually only our own path can lead us to happiness—sometimes steps must be taken that perhaps no one understands. How far would we have come if we always only had gone along with the opinion of others? Electric lights, cars, airplanes, or any other technical achievement once were completely new ground and required the courage of the individual to override society's critical and uncomprehending voices and to take an uncertain step into the unknown. We have to have pioneers for new ideas and developments—people who rise above the mass and who point out grievances. There is a first time for everything. For example, many laughed at Galileo and even denounced him just because he got the idea that the Earth was a sphere!

Please be aware that you have to fulfill your individual task here. Therefore, your existence here is so important as only you can fulfill your purpose the way it has to be fulfilled. Of course, it gives us a boost and extra power to receive a certain confirmation from outside, but we should not make ourselves dependent on external reactions and not allow anyone to discourage us. Instead, we should always follow our inner call and convictions. Deep inside of yourself you know exactly what you have to do, what you want to do, and wherein your happiness and satisfaction lies.

By following your intuition and believing in yourself and your ideas, you will make an amazing observation that the situation changes. Right in the moment when you make yourself independent from the approval of others, when you believe in yourself and follow your path, people will begin to treat you with respect. If someone is so convinced of something and does not allow him or herself to get distracted, there must be some truth in it! This supports the statement that we cannot directly influence the behavior of others, but by changing our own patterns of thinking and behavior, we can have altered auras that can influence others.

As long as we believe in finding happiness and satisfaction in outer circumstances or persons, we have to deal with one disappointment after another. We cannot expect others to change to make us happy. It's not about being made happy by external sources. It's solely about realizing that true happiness comes from inside and that it starts within ourselves. The point is that we do not have to change at all. We just have to let go of all that doesn't belong to us and therefore find the way back to our true identity.

Töricht haschen wir auf Erden
nach des Glückes Irrlichtschein:
Wer sich quält, beglückt zu werden,
hat die Zeit nicht, es zu sein.
—Nikolaus Lenau

Since I cannot simply translate a poem, I put the meaning of the German words into an English poem here:

Happiness is not a gift,
but we unfortunately do not see.
Instead of yearning for its light,
we could live happily.
—*Erika Kind*

Dr. Wayne W. Dyer says, "My destiny is mine to control: *When you acquire enough inner peace and feel really positive about yourself, it's almost impossible for you to be controlled and manipulated by anybody else.*"

Whenever we appreciate and enjoy what we have and what we are, we dissolve bonds of expectation for the future at the same time. It's the only way to dissolve entanglements with circumstances and persons and to step forward with our new independence toward everything we want to experience. This is real freedom!

The Ego

*I*n the fairy tale outlined in "The Story about the Ego and the Unconscious Self," we already got to know a pretty pictorial image of the ego. The ego is a false idea of our True Selves invented by our minds. It's a wrong self. It's the idea of identification with what we have, what we do, the way we look, our bodily features, our professions, our material possessions, etc. In other words, this wrong self is identified with externals. It is identified with everything that surrounds our True Selves.

Broadly speaking, the ego is—when misapplied—nothing else but a troublemaker arising from our unconsciousness. It tries to convince us that we must live in a state of constant competition with our environment. It's typical for our ego to make us believe that we are separated from God, from every other being, and from our own souls. According to our ego, we must therefore be better or worse, prettier or uglier, richer or poorer, smarter or sillier than our environment. The ego is concerned with being better, getting more accomplished, and possessing more. It can also try to talk us into the contrary, saying that we are weak, that we have no right of care, or that we are not able to do this or that. Above all, it wants to be right and to defend and enforce our viewpoints. Whatever it tries to convince us of, it will continually make us believe that we are lone fighters that are separated from everything and from everybody. If we noticed that we are all equal, that we all rise from the same Source, and that we are all here for the same reasons, then we would realize that we are *not* separated but that we are one and interconnected. The ego would then have no power over us anymore because we would not need its support any further. With the illusion of separation, we are bound to the ego. It tells us that it carries great wisdom inside of it and that we need this wisdom to be protected.

The ego sees itself as the opponent of our True Selves. However, there is quite an imbalance between them, as the overinflated ego only prances around and has no real power—except for the power to wrap us in illusions. Our True Selves are pure love, wisdom, peace, calmness, and inner harmony. The ego, on the other hand, is loud and continually filling our minds with chatter. It is loud so that we don't hear the calm and peaceful voice of our souls, and in time we even forget the existence of this other voice. It wants to convince us that our right to exist is primarily to put ourselves above others. It pretends to be our only true ally and tries to blackmail us, to keep us small, and to put us under pressure. The ego tries to make us believe that we depend on it, and that's what we do as soon as we identify ourselves with it. The identification with the ego results in permanent pressure to perform.

The ego wants to hold you back. It lives from your identification with it because in reality it is dependent on you and your illusion of being dependent on it. The ego needs to maintain this illusion. It sends you feelings of fear as soon as you start questioning its rules. But in reality it has no power over you whatsoever, and it is only an invention of your mind. As soon as you connect with your True Self and feel the bond with your Source, it inevitably disintegrates. In this moment you recognize that you were really mistaken. Naturally the ego wants to prevent you from this recognition. It talks you into the belief that nothing besides the material world exists, that you are your body, and that you are only worth something and allowed to feel good if you are better than others when you adorn yourself with possessions and when you are in the right.

You created the ego out of the belief that you are separated from your Source. You needed somebody who agreed to everything that you did and who supported your perceptions. Therefore, you had the feeling of not being alone. But the ego is not a person. It's an illusion, and you gave it a real character and made it a part of yourself. Only that could keep it alive, and when you asked it for advice and sought protection in it, you nourished and strengthened it.

The ego will undertake everything in order to maintain the illusion of separation from your Source. It will even go so far as to make you believe that something like a divine Source does not exist at all. Dr. Wayne W. Dyer explains this in a very impressive way. I am rendering it here in its spirit, not word for word. "We are where we come from. All that exists derives from the same Source. So if we all originate from the same Source and if everything that exists, every human being, every animal, and every plant carries the essence of this Source—because we are what created us—then how can we ever be separated from one another and especially from our Source?" This is one of the great errors and lies that have been built up by our ego.

Dyer also found a very matching definition for the ego in the following acronym: Edge God Out (EGO).

That's exactly the purpose the ego pursues. It can only stay alive when we exclude God from our lives. As soon as we realize that we are all connected with this incredible energy and with one another and that consequently we are never alone, the lies of the ego are instantaneously revealed.

Because of this connection, we are always presented with the right persons at the right time. They might be aids to help us move forward easier, or maybe we are tested to see if we are ready for the next step. We ourselves also touch other people's lives in order to give them what they might need at that very moment. Think of a difficult situation in your life, and you will remember that somebody showed up to hold your hand, someone who gave you valuable tips and clues for the solution and who comforted you. Because we are not separated but interconnected, an enormous network was able to develop. Through this network we all are continually supporting one another's life plans. One can compare this with electricity. We are all interconnected via cables, but because of our unconsciousness, we don't know anything about this energetic connection with one another and with our Source. When we become aware of this reality and flip the switch to turn on the electricity, the energy can flow freely from one to the other, and hence, we can interact constructively. So when we activate the connection with our Source by flipping the switch, we have exactly the amount of energy at our disposal that is needed to shape our lives to our greater good!

The Ego Is Transient, and the Soul Is Eternal

The ego derives from our thoughts. The thoughts derive from our brain, and our brain belongs to our transient selves. Therefore, the ego is transient too. The ego knows that it is mortal and that it automatically ceases to exist when our bodies die. Therefore, so that the ego lives as long as possible, it wants to keep a tight hold on us throughout our lives. But there is a catch. In the moment we leave our bodies, the ego must reveal itself. All of a sudden we come to the clear conclusion that in our whole earthly lives we allowed ourselves to be deceived by the illusion of the ego. It was like having a blindfold placed over your eyes, preventing you from realizing the real intent and purpose of your incarnation. At the same time we have intuitively always been aware of this purpose through a dream, our dearest wish, or some kind of special ability or talent. The ingenious ego has always succeeded in making us believe that we *must not* give in to our longings and ideas. If we had done so, we would have unmasked it. We would have dived into a world of abundance, fulfillment, joy, creativity, and freedom and would not have been able to identify with the statements of the ego any further. The horizon of the ego is very limited. It only knows our physical existence. It does not know anything about our life plan.

An excerpt from "A Course in Miracles" says that making the ego our journey's leader will cause chaos and fear, since the selfish and limited ego never knows the path of the unlimited and wise soul.

"When you make the mistake of only searching for the HOLY SPIRIT inside of you, scary thoughts will arise. This is because you – by adopting the position of the ego – accept the ego as the leader of your journey. This inevitably causes fear" – Dr. Helen Schucman - *A Course in Miracles*

The horizon of our True Selves—our immortal souls in which all knowledge is stored because it is part of what created us—is unlimited. Our soul is a part of the universe. It knows the divine plan and reminds us of it through our inner voice. As soon as we let go of all the fears that are created by our ego, we are able to perceive this voice again. It is totally in tune with our life path. In the moment when we are aware of our inner voice, we are in peace and harmony. We also notice how smoothly we move forward now. Many of our blockages and lifelong fears can be taken off like a coat. Naturally we will encounter new obstacles. By overcoming them, we are lifted up to the next level. We will accept new hurdles with thankfulness because we have understood that through them we are given a new chance to grow and develop. We will welcome them with open arms and not shrink back with fear like we did before because we put the idea into our heads that we were incapable, were not courageous enough, or could even expect punishment. We understand now that we only encounter hurdles because they are a part of our life plan and that they will keep showing up on our path until we have learned the lesson. When we consciously accept these tasks, we will additionally receive all kinds of support.

Other than our True Selves, the ego is mortal. Our True Selves emerge from the divine Source. Thus, they live forever. Listening to which voice makes more sense? To the loud chattering illusionary ego that's always trying to make you believe that there is only this one physical life and that you must strive to over trump others and convince them of your uniqueness? Or does it make more sense to listen to our inner voice—the voice emerging from our True Selves, the all-knowing part of our Source, giving us love and bonding, knowing our life plan in detail and at the same time guiding us with compassion so that we can pursue our fate?

HOW DO I DISTINGUISH BETWEEN THE VOICE OF THE EGO AND THE ONE OF MY TRUE SELF?

When the ego is talking to us, some kind of pressure can be felt. The ego is egoistical. It only sees itself, its own survival, and its own advantages. With all its might, it is always desperate to deceive you and to convince you of its own power. It will tell you lies, and in the belief that they are the truth, you pass them on to others. On this foundation of lies you establish a self-image that further and further deviates from your true nature. The ego makes you believe that the world is a dark and cruel place and that life is a struggle. Furthermore, it will convince you that you have no right to be happy, although in reality this is your fundamental right. On the other hand, it can also lead you to bring things of joy into your life at any price, no matter if it is at the expense of others. Whenever it can, it will talk you into having a bad conscience when you take the liberty to pamper yourself or even to love yourself. It might also guide you so that you place yourself above everything and everybody because you are allegedly worth more than your counterpart. On the one hand, it will convince you that you must stand above others. On the other hand, it has to keep you small so that you will not have the idea of running away from it. According to the ego, your life is about suffering and struggle, a struggle that must be won without the chance to be won. The ego will drive you to become better, faster, and greater. Or it will make you become resigned so that you give up and see yourself as a loser. When you believe that you are a loser, the ego will confirm it for you. It will set itself up as a friend who not only understands you but also strengthens your destructive self-perception. All in all, we don't really feel good. We feel stressed because despite all wrong identifications and thoughts, we perceive our True Selves again and again and our real inner voice trying to make us follow our true targets.

The voice of the soul is the voice of God. It's calm and patient. Despite all attempts of the ego to keep it quiet, it is always there. It sends you your longings and your dreams so that you remember your real purpose. Your True Self is light, love, and happiness. It always feels good, as it is *you*. This identity, this absolute familiarity, is radically opposed to the artificial ego, which blackens the view. Our True Selves are based on all-encompassing love. If you ever allow yourself to open up for this love, you will never forget this feeling. From this moment on you will exactly know how your True Self feels and how it sounds. It's not like the state of being in love with another person. It's the divine love from where we originate. It's that kind of love that gives us new chances every day. This love knows no jealousy and no ambitions to acquire possessions. It is absolute harmony. You feel it right in the moment when you sink into yourself, find the divine spark inside of you, and consciously connect to it. Go deep inside yourself. Feel the light that you are and the spreading sensation of warmth in the area around your heart. Connect yourself with this light. This is what you are. When this feeling of comfort spreads inside of you, it can happen that your eyes fill with tears. This is an unmistakable sign of being connected with yourself and at the same time with your Creator. Now you feel God. You feel him inside of you, and you know that he has always been there. Look around you, and you will realize that God is everywhere. He is in everything, every human being, every animal, plant, and mineral—yes, even in the wind that blows around you. You will be aware of the permanent presence of God, and you will be grateful and look at everything around you as a gift that was given to you so that you could fulfill your purpose on earth.

A simple exercise to steal the ego's thunder and to turn to your True Self is contained in the following sentence by Dr. Wayne W. Dyer: "When you have the choice between being right and being kind, just choose kind."

If we don't give in to the pressure of the dogmatic ego but follow the smooth and compassionate voice of our souls, the ego immediately falls silent. Making this experiment is really worthwhile. Watch your feelings! On the face of it, you might see yourself as a winner when you feel in the right. In fact, this feeling is not fulfilling for a longer period of time because it is not a real part of our heritage. It dissolves because it is like an artificial outwardness. It even causes us to wrongly believe that we don't feel better because we have not been fighting long or hard enough yet, so it tries to make us do more things to justify ourselves. Eventually our dissatisfaction grows because it's simply a bottomless pit. But if we—after we have *consciously* chosen kindness—look inside of ourselves, we will notice that a warm feeling of contentment and harmony is beginning to spread. This feeling fills us with love.

Our biggest fears don't grow because we are afraid of the darkness but because we are afraid of the light. The ego can only survive as long as it can make us believe that dark abysses dwell in us and not bliss or happiness. As we have allowed the ego to become so powerful, we trust it. But if we ever realize the power and energy that we are in reality, the ego would cease to exist. So it persuades us not to look too deep inside of us or listen to our inner voice because we put ourselves in the danger of encountering our deepest abysses. The ego knows that there is no darkness but light inside of us. The deeper we go, the lighter it gets. When we have finally discovered our light, the ego is seriously worried about its survival. With all its might it will try to convince us that we are not worth perceiving this glory and that we are only imagining it. It will make us believe that we don't deserve being healthy, powerful, and marvelous and that we are not worth fulfilling all our talents and abilities. The ego even wants us to label this light as darkness.

I truly hope that you see your bright shining light while you are reading this book and take away the ego's elixir of life.

MY EGO—MY ALLY

Nothing we encounter and experience throughout our lives is meaningless or happens without a reason. This includes the ego. When we understand the nature of the ego, we are also aware of the benefit it can have for us. Everything around and within us act as tools to proceed, to learn, to grow, and to mature. We should try to look at the ego from this perspective. All these tools are given to us with love so that we—according to our own initial wish— are able to learn our lessons. Everything happens out of love. Our true nature is love. When we love ourselves, our love includes the ego. The ego is our own creation, and through our love it's becoming soft. Opposing it just nourishes it again, but when we have love and respect for ourselves, little by little all hardening will dissolve. We don't have to fight against anything. Fights never lead to victory. Fights cause resistance and new resistance. Love is soft. Love allows everything to flow. Love spreads tranquility. Love dissolves resistance, and shared love causes more love.

We are living in a world of opposites. Exactly these opposites are the source of our realizations. For this reason we are keen on incarnating on earth because the world of opposites leads us to clear and intensive knowledge and understanding. The ego belongs to the world of opposites as well. By the pressure that had built up inside of us because of the influence of the ego, we are literally pushed into searching for ways out of the self-made prison so that we can come to a deep knowledge of ourselves, others, and the fundamental idea of creation. He who once was imprisoned experiences newly won freedom with much intensity and thankfulness. The one who once felt small really appreciates the realization of his or her individual greatness. He who once felt isolated now understands that loneliness is homemade and that it never existed in reality. When he unveils the ego and experiences the dissolving of illusions, this then comes along with the feeling of real freedom.

So this is pretty much the essence of what this whole book is about. The insight actually lies in unmasking the ego and recognizing your True Self. Following the ego blindly throws you into a homemade prison of pressure, fear, and endless competition, a prison constantly seeking the approval of others. When you are aware of what part of you is ego and what part is your True Self, you have the opportunity to differ and then step into a world of joy, happiness, peacefulness, and real freedom.

It is certainly not about annihilating or excluding the ego from our lives. On the contrary, that would only cause more tension and fights, which again feeds the ego. We only have to learn how to properly deal with it. If we make use of the characteristics of the ego accordingly, we can transform it to an ally of our True Selves. The ego is ambitious and has a strong will. It encourages us to turn our words and intentions into actions. So when we harmonize the ego and the soul with each other, we are in charge of the best team, combining inner wisdom with the ability to practically implement our ideas into matter. With the soul as the legislative power and the ego as the motor and advisor for the physical world, we have an unbeatable team with which we can conquer the world.

Part 2
Origin of Fears and Blockages

I free myself from the prison of my imagination.
—Source unknown

Why Do We Have Fears?

*I*t is not always the big fears that make our lives hard. It's mostly the many little ones that we face throughout the day. Even if there is a big fear taking over from time to time, it mostly consists of an accumulation of little fears and unpleasant and formative experiences. This is what makes it so difficult to give a general heading to this big fear. It is triggered by one of the small fears. It comes from nothing and appears suddenly. It catches us with an iron fist, blocks our minds, and prevents us from thinking clearly. Often these kinds of fears have complete control over us, and what frightens us most is that we usually don't really know where these fears come from at all. If we knew this, we would have access to them and could do something about them. Therefore, a new fear can develop—the fear of the fear.

Short Definition of Fear

Fear does not exist. It's an illusion that has settled in our heads through thoughts. These thoughts have come from outside and are not in resonance with our true nature. Everything that corresponds to our true nature emerges from inside of us. What comes from the inside is peaceful. If we absorb outer disharmonious influences that are long and intensive enough, we identify with them one day. As soon as we identify with them, we assume that they are a part of us and believe that they arose from inside of us. Out of unconsciousness, we cannot distinguish anymore if these emotions are our gut feelings or caused by adapted belief structures. Hence, the illusion has passed over to a self-created but distorted reality. As soon as we have manifested this fear inside of us, we are blocked, and it starts getting more and more difficult to tear down this wall again.

Fearful thoughts arise from the absence of love (and consequently of faith)—the absence of pure, true love that created us and that lives within us. Fear is not a personal attribute or characteristic but an emotion emerging from our thoughts because of a false image of ourselves and what surrounds us. To put it briefly, fear emerges from the illusion of being separated from our Source—an illusion that the ego tries to make us believe.

Fear knocked at the door, faith opened it and no one was outside.
- Source unknown

The foundation stone for all fears lies in a loss of faith. I don't mean the belief that everything is going to be the way we want it to be. I mean the kind of faith that everything is going to be the way it is supposed to be and that all is good no matter how it is. If we don't feel this kind of faith in us, the thought prevails that we must be in control of every situation, over all circumstances, and even over other people. The mother of all fears is the loss of control.

It does not matter what kind of control we consider. What frightens us so much is mainly what comes after the loss of control, and this is not knowing what the future might bring. The fears of an incurable disease and also the fear of flying are based on this uncertainty. I myself was a total control freak. Everything had to be clearly structured in detail, and there was hardly any room for unforeseeable occurrences. As long as everything went as planned, my life was in order. But as soon as something deviated from this plan, everything in me worked against the acceptance of the new situation. The most dramatic events happened when one of my children fell ill. When this happened, I literally panicked. The panic did not arise out of fear for the child but because I did not know how the illness would develop. I had no control over what was happening. Of course, I made my children nervous when I took their temperature every thirty minutes. I thought, *How will the night be? Do I act correctly? Shall I take the child to the doctor as fast as possible? Will I be able to adhere to my deadlines? Or do I have to throw all my plans out the window?* Just by the fact that one child was sick, I felt completely overwhelmed. And I have three children. Of course, shortly after the recovery of one child, one of the other two or both fell ill. At least I was afraid this would happen.

The problem of not being in control over what happened caused feelings of powerlessness and helplessness in me. Although today I can only shake my head about my former self, it's easy for me to feel again these feelings while I write these words. I could even sense it physically. My stomach was tied in knots. I got diarrhea, and out of nervousness I could hardly eat anything. My thoughts all circled around this issue. I could not concentrate on anything else and was not resilient at all anymore. How much easier everything would have been if I had made myself aware of the fact that everything only took place in my head. I could have saved so much energy and nerves with the right thoughts, faith, and acceptance.

Besides love and hate, fear is one of the strongest emotions. Fear mostly arises out of the blue. We hear something, see something, or smell something, and all of a sudden we get scared. Hence, it's often a feeling that's stored somewhere within us and that's activated by the corresponding key words. But why do we feel fears at all? What gives us the reason to have fears? Mostly we are afraid of things that we don't know. But something being unfamiliar to us does not necessarily have to mean something bad. We could equally burst out in joy and laughter. But no, just to be safe we are struck by fear. Why are we afraid of the unknown? Because the mind is unable to draw on experience. For this reason, we lack imaginary safety and therefore faith.

To sum up, it can be said that fear arises from a lack of faith. When we have little self-confidence, we don't believe in ourselves. Instead, we get insecure. We don't dare trying out new things because we are worried about things going wrong. Or we fear that others might laugh at us and make us feel humiliated. The fear of failure emerges. Then comes the fear of not meeting expectations— our own expectations but mostly the ones of our environment. Therefore, there are many things that we don't even try.

We also fear losing control that arises from a lack of faith. It gives us a feeling of security when we seem to have the rudder in the hand and when we feel certain about upcoming events in the near or distant future. When we manage everything ourselves, we believe that we know what we can expect and that nothing can go wrong. For a while this is likely to go well, and we might even feel that our belief has proved us right—that is, until we encounter situations that show us it is impossible to control everything (e.g., the loss of a job, the death of a person close to us, or individual actions and the free will of others). Then we feel helpless and at the mercy of our circumstances. We then fall into a feeling of desperation. Our world, which was built on control, collapses like a house of cards.

When we have a lack of faith, we are also afraid of sharing our thoughts and feelings with others. Out of the deep emotional fear of being hurt, we bury our true emotions and thoughts in us. Perhaps we have already made the experience that our openness was shamelessly exploited. Who wants to get hurt or humiliated? This leads to closure, isolation, and possibly depression.

Fear can spread in waves. Often it does not only encompass a moment but moves our lives in a wrong direction. Therefore, it can have a sustaining and burdening influence on our life situation. We might close our eyes to the outside world, pretend to be someone else for camouflage reasons, hide our sorrows and fears within us, get a gastric ulcer, and develop eating disorders, depression or even panic attacks because the built-up energy must unload somewhere.

We might start to possibly misuse drugs or alcohol. In the worst case, it might result in suicide.

I am consciously repeating this statement again: Fear results from a lack of faith, and a lack of faith results from a lack of love, namely self-love. To develop a satisfactory solution, the most important and effective way starts within us. There is no use at all in blaming our outside world for what happens to us. Achieving our goals lies in our own hands. There is one thing we should realize. Fear—and I am talking about the restrictive, blocking fear that holds our unique being and abilities imprisoned in a dungeon— is not a part of our True Selves. The essence of every individual being's True Self is love and light. Every human on this earth is so unique. Every single human has the right to express his or her uniqueness and to share it with his or her environment.

If one feels no love, one has no faith either. If one has no faith, one feels lost. One tries to please everybody and is afraid of not meeting their requirements and expectations. One feels like a lone fighter. But if we discover that we are always connected to the Source that created us, whether we notice it or not, we can realize it consists of pure love and helps us to achieve everything. Then we would never feel the slightest breath of fear. Then we have real unconditional faith that everything happens for our own good, that everything is a part of our life plan and has been sent to us with love—no matter what it is. Now we know that nothing can ever happen to what we truly are. We are immortal, and we are here to fulfill our purpose with all our heart!

Fear is like a mirage. As soon as one gets closer and faces it, it disappears because it is just a deception of the mind.

Is Fear a Protection Mechanism?

It is said that fear can be something good. It supposedly prevents us from getting into dangerous situations. However, fear must not be confused with intuition. Fear is a negative energy. Fear means restriction and imprisonment. It is like a chain restricting our zest for action and preventing us from pursuing our inwardly felt tasks because they don't fit into our thought patterns.

If fear was a protection mechanism, one could argue that it's good to have a fear of heights because it prevents us from approaching the edge of an abyss so closely that we put ourselves in jeopardy of falling into the depths. I don't necessarily feel that this is correct. Of course, with a fear of heights, one will never intentionally approach the edge of an abyss, and this will keep that person away from many dangers. On the other hand, despite a fear of heights, one might get into a situation where one must surmount an enormously steep and long flight of stairs. Precisely because of this phobia, one might panic and fall. Why are so many people afraid of riding in cable cars? Because they think of a possible failure where the cable breaks and the cable car falls. Here we got it again! Such fears develop because we start making up all kinds of horror scenarios. There is no reason why we should not look very carefully at the system and avoid using it when it makes an obvious bad impression on us. But considering something as principally terrifying has nothing to do with an inner alarm system that solely with self-made thoughts cause fear. Hence, fear is directed by our brain and has nothing to do with intuition. It is not a protection mechanism but a homemade blockage.

Certainly the mind can protect us from certain dangers. For example, we have learned from past experience that touching a hot plate causes great pain, or the mind informs us that it's not a good idea to look for protection underneath a tree in a thunderstorm. In these cases, the influence of the mind is fully justified. In this book, however, I am referring not to these practical fears but to fears that are more like bad excuses preventing us from the manifestation of visions or the expression of talents and abilities. We like using excuses so that we can pull ourselves out of certain situations—excuses like these: "I have never done this before." "I am not capable." "I don't dare it." "I am too clumsy." And then the topic is finished! This has nothing to do with a bad feeling. It is a spontaneous reaction to fear of a certain activity so that we don't have to deal with it.

The real protection mechanism is not called fear but inner voice. There's a significant difference between the two. Meanwhile, I like being guided by my inner voice but in no case by fear. When we have to make decisions, we immediately notice our inner voice. It either feels good or bad. We get a queasy feeling, or joy and enthusiasm arise. Our bodies begin to react negatively, or we get a boost of energy. That's our inner voice, and we should learn to listen to it again. But it has nothing to do with the fears controlling us. Our inner voice might cause a feeling of fear, but in this case, the fear is not the root but a means of our intuition. This kind of fear only lasts for a short time. It does not accompany or burden us for months or years. Permanent fears have no protective function. They are walls blocking our view so that we don't see that there is nothing behind them or that we might see something beautiful on the other side. Probably every one of us has already got over one or another hurdle and noticed, "Well, actually it was not all that difficult." Did we not gain strength afterward? Fear keeps us small. It's not a part of our real personality but buzzes around and lulls it.

Of course, in the beginning it's not easy to know if we feel fear acquired for years or decades or if it's our inner voice telling us that we had better let it be. In this case, we can ask ourselves, "Is this really true? Is it really necessary to be afraid? What reasons should I have to prevent me from doing this or that? Is there something to lose? Is there really a danger? Why shouldn't I be able to do this?" If eventually a diffuse, queasy feeling remains, it would be better if you really stayed away from it for the time being. It does not matter if you can explain your decision or not. If you don't completely agree with something, it eventually comes to nothing anyway.

Fear Starts in the Head

ith the advancement of civilization we have forgotten to listen to our gut feelings. We still have our intuition, but as we are logically thinking beings, our minds continually cut the connection to our intuition. Often our inner voice would like to make a decision that goes against the logical mind. For this reason, we (beings blessed with logical minds) prefer to follow the voice of logic. As I already mentioned, every being, every incarnated soul has its own life plan. Even if a decision seems paradoxical for the mind, it can play an important role in the life plan of the individual because without it one would have to make a certain experience later. The more often one evades a hurdle, the more often and persistent one will be confronted with it until finally one has no choice but to face the challenge.

Whenever we feel doubts and fears, thoughts preceded them. These thoughts might have developed right in the moment before the fear arose, or they may have already settled in us years or decades ago. Such thoughts are already so deeply rooted in us that in certain situations they are not thought consciously. Instead they are spontaneously expressed through a feeling. Therefore, letting go of such fears is difficult because they occur so suddenly and unexpectedly.

Just as we can generate positive feelings through positive thoughts, we create negative feelings through negative thoughts.

Based on our environmental conditioning and an alleged safety thinking that had been instilled in us sometime in our lives, it's much easier for us to let negative rather than positive thoughts settle in us. In case of spontaneously arising fears, the negative thought patterns can often be traced back to our childhoods. Hence, those thoughts had a whole life to calmly settle down. These thought patterns could have developed through experiences or through the influence of our surroundings. Overprotective mothers can fuel the biggest fears in us. Because they are so worried that something could happen to their children, they warn everybody and everything. To the child, the whole world seems to be a single major threat. It should be recalled that those mothers acted according to their convictions and that they had good intentions. They just wanted the best for their children. I would like to firmly point out that there is no negative judgment from my side. I only use this as an example for an explanation. I already mentioned it in a previous chapter that we choose our parents. They help us complete our program. It is so important that we don't judge! Everybody acts out of his or her own conviction, and this is absolutely all right. In fact, it's the only right thing to do.

A little child must follow the guidelines of his or her parents. That's clear. Of course, the intuition of a child is not worse than that of an adult, but a child cannot evaluate real threats yet. On the other hand, children have a much better link to their intuition than adults. The intuition of children is not silenced by deep-seated thought patterns yet. That's exactly what we should learn again. We are adults, and we are able to evaluate real dangers. Therefore, we are capable of making distinctions. But where is the danger when we do something we have never tried before? It might be inestimable what comes out of the experience, but can this really be considered as a danger? Here our minds are playing tricks on us. Let's say we feel driven to learn a new profession. We might still have our old one, but we don't feel satisfied with it. Either it never did satisfy, or our attitude has changed throughout the years. Eventually we think that it would be wonderful to absolve a training as landscape gardener. Although we get a feeling of euphoria and joy when we just imagine the idea of working in and with nature, we have to deal with a little troublesome voice in the back of our minds. *Will I find a job? Will I earn enough? Am I able to invest enough time and energy into the training? What if it isn't so much fun as expected? Would it be better to let go of this idea and stick with what I know?*

What does this voice try to tell us? It tells us that we have no control and no experience over how things might develop. Again, it's the ego that wants to keep us small. Naturally it's something new and unknown at the same time. But only because we don't know it yet, it does not necessarily mean that it is harmful for us. Why do we think, *Who knows if it will go well?* instead of *Let's see how it goes?* Something we have never done before bears the risk of not pleasing us. Certainly! On the other hand, it bears the same chance that we really enjoy it. It's always a risk to try something unknown. But the fact that something is new to us does not doom it to failure.

If we have a good feeling and if there are no obvious dangers, we should try it. Our intuition shows us the way we should follow. It is not always necessary to know where it leads to. It's only necessary to make the first step in order to find out. It is the turn of our thoughts when we have to deal with practical planning and executing. But our thoughts must not determine our path.

A lack of faith in one's intuition causes the thoughts to take over leadership. However, this leadership is based on the mental level only and is oriented toward and adapted to the outside world. Faith in our intuition—in ourselves—allows our thoughts to work on our behalf and on the behalf of our targets.

... AND WISDOM BEGINS IN THE HEART

When we hear an inner call directing our views in a certain direction, we should take this call seriously. Our souls know the plan for our current lives in detail. Every call, every wish, and every dream points us to what our life plan contains and to what we want to get accomplished. It doesn't matter what kind of experiences we will make when we follow our hearts. Because they are parts of our journeys, they will exactly correspond to our life plan. There are some experiences that we only have in order to know that something is not a part of our path—perhaps to prevent us from getting in an even worse situation at a later point or to help us recognize the right door when it's ahead of us.

When we follow our hearts, we can be trustfully confident that everything will be in perfect order. When we listen to our inner voice, we remain on our path and are always supplied with everything we need. Fear is unnecessary.

However, the same applies to the reverse. When we want to do something specific after careful consideration but have an uncomfortable feeling, although our rational minds can see that everything is all right, we should reflect a moment.

Perhaps our inner voice wants to tell us something we have not taken into consideration yet. Maybe it wants to warn us, or perhaps the experience that we are going through does not belong to our plan and could cause an unnecessary detour or might teach us something the hard way. In any case, we should listen. We will definitely experience what we are supposed to experience. But if we follow our intuition, we will remain on our path, and our experiences will be smoother than those if we listen to our thoughts, which are unable to know something better than our True Selves.

The brain is useful to find practical solutions for acute problems but not to determine our path. If we allow our minds to determine our path and if we act contrary to our feelings, inner tensions will develop. Our heads pull in one direction, and our souls pull in another. These tensions cause insecurities leading to a loss of faith and the feeling that one is a lone fighter, for nobody can understand us. If we really want to find answers to our real questions about why we are here and what our fate is or if want to simply think about a current problem, then we must switch off our minds and stop their continuous flow of thoughts. When the mind does not interrupt, it is silent enough so that we can perceive the quiet voice of the Higher Self. Only in the silence will we clearly understand it and receive the answers to our questions. Our souls point us to the way we have chosen for ourselves. As long as we are faithful to our path, no matter what our environment thinks, nothing can go wrong. We are unified with ourselves and satisfied because we live in harmony with our fate and don't act against our convictions. Nothing can frighten us, and we can accomplish everything and anything.

As Wayne Dyer puts it, "Banish doubt. When doubt is banished, abundance flourishes and anything is possible." At the same time when you banish the doubtful voice in your head, the filter between you and the abundance that life has in store for you is resolved. Then you have become a true match with your intention. There is nothing blocking your path anymore, and you can drive directly on your highway of life to its fulfillment. You already feel the clear connection with what you are about to become. You and the extended you, which you are intended to become, are one. Banish doubt and listen to the loving and wise voice of your heart.

Discovering a new path and opening a new door is always an adventure. That's the special part about life. Life is so exciting, and there is so much to discover. With our entry into this world we have signed up for a lifelong lucky-bag subscription. We are not forced to use the things inside the lucky bag, but at least we should look inside and find out if it contains something useful for us.

Is Suffering Really Necessary?

> Words really do not teach. Your true knowledge comes from
> your own life experience. And while you will be a constant
> gatherer of experience and knowledge, your life is not only
> about that—it is about fulfillment, satisfaction, and joy. Your
> life is about the continuing expression of who you truly are.
> —Abraham – Esther and Jerry Hicks

Despite of our connection with our True Selves and our Source, despite all positive thinking and faith, and despite our full conviction of being on the right path, events will happen to us, many of which are not pleasant. No matter how safe we feel on our path, we will always have to deal with some inevitable experiences because we keep approaching new hills to climb that we have set up for ourselves in advance but have not yet mastered.

We compiled the program for this lifetime long before our births. It contains all the emotions we want to feel, all the realizations we want to achieve, all the persons we want to meet, everything we want to experience together with these persons, everything we want to learn *through* them, and much more. This program is like a red thread running through our lives so that we can stick to our plan. Therefore, some of the suffering we experience we have deliberately chosen before we came into this body so that we can remain faithful to our route and experience certain emotions and insights. This might be the moment when some of you indignantly shout, "Hey, I am not making my own life hard on purpose. It was not my choice to have these neighbors, this ex-wife, this illness."

I can only say, "Sorry, but that's how it is!" Some things had obviously been packed into our life plan right from the outset, and some things happened unconsciously because of our way of living. Through straying from the ideal line, we pulled these things into our lives so that they make us aware of the places we don't want to go and so that we realize where we should go instead. Whether we draw unpleasant circumstances consciously or unconsciously into our live, the final result is the same.

Although we had already spun out our red thread of life, our free will remains intact. This free will enables us to make all our planned experiences when and how we want. But as we, through entering our physical bodies, have forgotten what we wanted to experience, we fight against challenges because we don't understand why we meet them. Yes, it even goes so far that we feel disadvantaged, treated unjustly, or cheated by God. We generate opposition and make everything more strenuous than necessary, although we ourselves chose the experiences in order to achieve the necessary realizations. Resistance causes even more unpleasant feelings and pain. By concentrating on circumstances we don't want to have, we draw even more unpleasant situations or unwanted people with uncomfortable attitudes into our lives.

Of course, we have decided to experience not only unpleasant feelings and occurrences in our life but also many beautiful ones that lead us to insights. When we understand that we have chosen all these things ourselves because we derive a deeper meaning from experiencing them, then we will cease to struggle and are able to also go through the dark hours of our lives with a little bit more ease. There is always light at the end of the tunnel!

BENEFIT FROM CRISES

We learn from pleasant as well as from unpleasant confrontations. But we benefit most from the crises we go through. Every single crisis can be considered as an intense training that we complete. Every one of us stands on a different rung on the development ladder and is confronted with those challenges that lead us to climb to the next rung. What is not difficult at all for one person can be an almost insurmountable hurdle for another. Again, everyone has their individual life path, and no one, except for themselves, knows it. Hence, nobody should ridicule the problems of another person because they cannot assess the situation from their points of view.

As long as everything proceeds like clockwork, we will not make an effort to look for what might not be all right. We don't even have the idea that something could *not* be all right. When something hurts with our bodies, we go to the doctor. Here we need warning signals because only when we feel pain do we recognize that something is wrong. In order to achieve certain realizations, we must go through a crisis, as we would perhaps miss the more pleasant learning options. Or perhaps they would not have the necessary effect because they would not cause us to reflect thoroughly enough. Therefore, it is never a punishment to be confronted with painful situations. They are simply necessary for us to learn certain lessons and to really integrate those lessons into our lives. Together with the essence from this realization, we are well prepared and can successfully move on to the next intermediate target.

Even the most spiritual people have to go through different crises. They have not stopped learning either. Every person on earth has to fulfill their mission. Perhaps some only came here to help us learn. For this very reason, they must often walk through the deepest valleys in order to be living examples for us and to show us how all difficulties can be overcome.

Everything that happens to us is sent with love so that we

successfully fulfill our mission. This realization enables us to regard every crisis we must go through with different eyes. When we accept every challenge with gratitude instead of turning away from them, when we take the opportunity to face them, then we will be much better able to deal with each one. Then we are aware that the time has come again to make the next big step on our tour through this life.

Yes, unfortunately we have to experience pain and suffering as well so that our learned lessons can be strengthened and so that we can integrate them into every fiber of our being. Only then can these lessons really become parts of us as deep inner knowledge. When we immediately respond to every challenge instead of continually trying to avoid them, we can handle them much more quickly. Through turning away, we get the feeling of being lost and lonely. The more often we avoid facing a challenge, the more diffuse fears become. Because we don't want to look closer, we don't even know anymore where our fears eventually come from. Now the reason for the fear is only our lack of faith because we don't know anymore what's behind the veil. As long as we close our eyes to the tasks we ourselves have chosen for this life, we will be confronted with them over and over again until we finally look closer, roll up our sleeves, and approach them.

Let's face our challenges. There is nothing to fear. Everything we encounter is a part of what we planned before this incarnation. Everything we have determined for this incarnation is a part of our fate and our path. We are guided by our Higher Selves at all times, and we are always supplied with everything we need. We are never alone. At the appropriate moment the right tools and persons are placed at our sides so that we successfully master our tasks and grow. Doubts and fears only disappear when we face them. With the awareness that we only have to master tasks that are specifically tailored to our own development, any fear will immediately dissolve. When we are ready for it, we will reach the next fence to get over. Everything is as it should be, and everything comes at the right time. Through inner growth the preconditions for realizing the dream of all dreams can emerge out of the biggest crisis because that's the only way to reach the required maturity.

When we have really learned a lesson, we grow in maturity. A lesson can be called learned when it has become a part of the inner self. Grasping it mentally is not enough. It must become a deep conviction, an inner knowledge. As long as this is not the case and the lesson remains hanging on the mental level, we will be confronted with it over and over again until we have reached the self-set target and until the realization to be made has become a part of us. A meaningful lesson is learned when we are able to be wholeheartedly thankful for the unpleasant episodes of our lives without even thinking about it because we have anchored the knowledge that any kind of occurrence only happens for our development.

Ascending through Letting Go

Our feelings are like a measuring station that cannot be cheated. When we feel good, our thoughts and activities and the generated vibrations are in accordance with our True Selves. However, when we feel bad, when we suffer from the emotions we experience through certain circumstances, situations, or the presence of certain persons, then the vibrations of our thoughts and activities are not in accordance with our True Selves. Through our feelings we can determine at any time if we are in harmony or not.

Our darkest hours can turn out to be our greatest blessings. When we, through certain circumstances on the outside, reach a point that throws us into complete helplessness, disappointment, frustration, desperation, or self-doubt, we are given the chance to look into the deepest depths of our souls. Therefore, we get the opportunity to realize what is not but what should be in harmony with the vibration of our True Selves. When we are in danger of losing our footing, there is often no other way but to let ourselves fall into the depths! This exposes to our sight what we were not able to see before or what we did not want to see before. Then we have the conscious choice whether we want to ignore this flashing neon sign or to make use of its warning, turn around, and become aware of what we really want.

When we cling to our negative feelings and therefore to the corresponding vibrations because we don't realize that we are not the victims of circumstances but the creators of our lives, then we continue to be confronted with circumstances and persons corresponding exactly to these vibrations. But when we make use of these negative emotions by facing them and becoming aware of what's not all right, we transform them into something positive by concentrating on what we really want. And what we *really* want comes from our inside—from the True Self that have gotten the chance to speak up. When we give attention to these positive thoughts and to the corresponding feelings, we draw exactly that kind of circumstances and persons into our lives that are in accordance with these vibrations. The chapter titled "The Law of Attraction" will give clearer information on these correlations.

When we feel the pressure of extremely painful emotions in us, there is nothing wrong with completely and consciously sinking into them for one or maybe two days. Hence, we feel ourselves with every fiber of our being and might realize some aspects that were hidden before. Only through the tool of negative emotion can we become aware of this yet undiscovered but nevertheless existing part inside us. As soon as we have found out what the crux of the matter is, we usually see a light at the end of the tunnel and start inevitably to ascend from the depths. Understanding the reasons behind this pain makes us realize aspects of the solution, and soon we see the solution itself. This realization strengthens us in such a way that our frequency increases. Those who have once experienced this know the feeling of happiness that arises through ascending from the floods of powerlessness. Through the realization that we acted unconsciously against our own selves, we have gotten things moving again. Illusions and distortions of this unconsciousness dissolve, and we get a clear view. It probably counts as some of the most wonderful experiences when we rise to the surface again through inner strength gained through a realization. These kinds of realizations can never get lost again.

We need this inner alarm system because it helps us see that we are unconsciously and ignorantly fighting against ourselves. As already mentioned, our bodies use the same principle on the material level. Through pain we realize that something is wrong. Once the body is switched on, it's a sign that we have ignored the alarm bells of our feelings for too long. If even our bodies make the sirens howl, negative feelings were able to spread for a long time, and they threaten to manifest on the physical level in the next stage.

> Don't run from lessons; they are little packages of
> treasure that have been given to us. As we learn
> from them, our lives change for the better.
> - Source unknown

Don't condemn what you have suffered. Honor what you have learned from it.

CHANGES

All changes, even the most longed for, have their melancholy;
for what we leave behind us is a part of ourselves; we
must die to one life before we can enter another.
—Anatole France

Most people have difficulties with change. It can start with
the ending of a television series, continue with a change
in the management, and might end with the death of a
beloved friend or relative. Many people have a hard time dealing
with the prospect of possible change because it makes them insecure
not knowing what comes after. However, apparent continuity gives
them a sense of security.

However, there is no standstill. This would be absolutely
impossible. As I have already mentioned, we continually and
mutually influence one another's circumstances. We have our life
plans, and these plans also include that we touch other people's life
plans to help them, to support them in their development through
our presence in different kinds of ways, etc. Therefore, there is
always movement. Through movement things change, and only
change causes development.

Hence, it is easy to understand that change is the driving
force because otherwise living this life would make no sense at
all. When we have understood this, we don't fear changes in our

lives. We know that they only happen so that we don't stagnate in our development. By understanding and accepting that things are subject to permanent change, we will also cease to cling to these things. Therefore, we free ourselves from dependencies. We also automatically free ourselves from the fear that is connected with the loss of apparent belongings. When we understand that continuity is just an illusion and that change is reality, we will be much more conscious in here and now. We take every moment the way it is and act accordingly, as only what's in the now is real.

We always stay the same. "*There is something that stayed the same throughout all these years, while everything else changed. This is the constant feeling of presence, the knowledge about your existence. This sensation or 'I am' feeling has never changed,*" *Sri Nisargadatta Maharaj* has said.

Everything is subject to constant change. Nothing is permanent, even if it makes the appearance of being safe. Relationships develop and break up. Savings accounts are opened and banks go bankrupt. Children grow up and leave their parents. Jobs change, and people are born and die. Changing circumstances are the most normal thing in the world. That's exactly how we should see it, as it's always only the circumstances that change. We, however, always stays the same. We are always ourselves. We have existed since eternal times. Sometimes we are stuck in physical bodies for a moment, and then we leave it again. During the time when we inhabit our bodies, we experience one adventure after the other to feed ourselves with experiences and knowledge. However, the True Self never changes. It's only the circumstances that come and go and support us in our growth.

We should not struggle with decisions we have once made in our lives. Because things are different now, it does not mean that a previously made decision was wrong. At that point in time it was absolutely right and led us to exactly where we were supposed to go. Circumstances can change. Yes, they must change. Otherwise there would be a standstill, and a standstill means a step backward.

Changed circumstances don't mean that we did something wrong. They only require a new decision, a next step.

Change brings progress. Without change, there would be no movement. There would be no development, and we would still have to freeze because we would not know how to make fire. Yes, nobody would ever fall in love because this would cause changes. In short, if there was no change, there would be no life. Without change, our wishes and dreams would never come true. Strangely enough, nobody has anything against this. The amazing thing is that we don't have to actively do something to advance and develop. When we follow the perceived feeling of our path, we are automatically in accordance with our life plan and make all necessary experiences. Changing circumstances helps us to progress the way we are supposed to.

Unfortunately we also have to face unpleasant changes. They help us to have those kinds of experiences that are necessary so we can get ready for the realization of our biggest dreams. Change often means that we must finish something so that something new can begin. However, as long as we struggle against finishing the old, we cannot move one step closer to the new. Therefore, we are often really compelled through outer circumstances to perceive these changes that bring the new into our lives because the old is finished and outdated. This simply means that we are ready to open a new door and to gain new insights.

Divorces and separations are very painful changes. But how many times has it happened that both partners—after they had went through all the pain and difficulties connected with their separation—eventually found the love of their lives. The quote in the beginning of this section said it clearly. We often have to bring an end to one phase of our lives so that we can enter a new one. I like comparing this process with a room. I can only enter a room when I have already left another. Whenever big, small, lucky, or painful changes are likely to occur, they are tools to gently push us forward so that we don't forget where we originally wanted to go.

Changes in Relationships

Relationships are also subject to permanent movement and change. We get to know each other and use what the other person sets free in us for our change and our development. As soon as both partners have given each other everything they needed for their individual development process, the relationship changes again. This is mostly the moment when they part again so that further development is not blocked. Therefore, it is not useful when two people only stay together out of habit or moral beliefs, although they have nothing to give to each other anymore. When they stay together anyway, they might block their own and their partner's development. This may sound very hard and factual, but it's a natural law. The purpose of every relationship is to learn from each other. When the learning process is finished, the relationship changes. If this is impossible, the ways separate, and new people come into our lives. All these arrangements have already been made with each other before this incarnation. Even if we have no conscious memory about this, this fact remains.

It can also happen that one partner wants to separate but the other doesn't. Often the one who wants to leave enables the other to make the last learning step in this relationship, including everything that happens before, during, and after the separation phase.

Of course, this does not necessarily mean that there are no lifelong relationships anymore. Naturally they still exist, and this is wonderful. But one should not consider oneself a loser or someone who is unable to have a partnership just because he or she was not able to experience a marriage until the death of the partner. For some people lifelong partnerships right for them, and for others life holds other variants in store. There is no universal rule that works for everyone. The only rule we have to apply is to go with the flow of life and to not hinder our own development as well as that of our partner through purely rational thinking.

This also explains the increasing divorce rate. It does not

necessarily have to do with the fact that marriages generally are more easygoing than they were in the past. Above all, we all develop at a higher rate. Let's consider the computer industry. How much technical development took place between 1950 and 1970 in contrast to the period 1970 to 1990? There is an enormous difference in the speed of development between these two decades, but compared to all the changes between 1990 and 2010, both traveled at a snail's pace. Likewise personal development is moving as if it is on the fast lane. Relationships fulfill their purpose much faster, and therefore, many more couples separate at more frequent intervals than sixty or more years ago. Furthermore, it's not considered a social taboo anymore when two people decide to go separate ways after their time together. There are also many consensual unions without a marriage certificate. When they separate, it's in principle nothing else than a divorce. But this is not so noticeable because there is less bureaucracy involved.

DEATH

If we are able to accept changes as that what they are, namely normal and unstoppable parts of life cycles, we can welcome them as gifts—gifts that are presented to us so that we can climb to the next rung of our ladder of life. In the ideal case it even goes so far that we lose our fear of death. As I already said, we always stay the same. Only our bodies change until we leave them. What changes within us is the gaining of experiences, our spiritual growth. But we ourselves and everybody we love and know remain existing. Many people have a fear of death. For them death is the opposite of life. But the opposite of death is not life. The opposite of death is birth. We are life, and we never die. Only our bodies, which are our temporary homes for physical existence, are born and pass away.

Life in a physical body is just a short excursion to gather knowledge. When we have reached the point where we don't consider death as an enemy but as a normal part of development, we realize that there is nothing to fear. He who is not afraid of death is not bound to anything. He who is not bound to anything feels free. Nothing can stop us from pursuing our target with joy and enthusiasm so that we can realize our dreams with passion and appreciate every day as a wonderful gift of God. When we are not afraid of death, we realize that there is no "too late" anymore because basically there is no end of our existence. Death has lost its sting.

It has certainly become clear that nothing in this physical world is permanent. If we remained in continuity, we would be unable to develop. Even apparent continuity is subject to change. Sometimes when a blockage has become too strong, change might (subjectively perceived) suddenly enter our lives as an enormous discharge to allow us to catch up.

The only thing that stays the same in the physical world is change. The only thing that exists forever, for it is not subject to time and space, is the "I Am."

Pressure from Outside

Many people think that the wishes of others come first. They are good-natured, helpful beings who can't say, "No," because they think it is their duty to give others what they want. This kind of giving though is not a giving from the heart but a giving from the mind. It's a giving out of obligation. It is giving in. Therefore, two things are achieved. On the one hand, we don't get the wonderful feeling of joy through giving, but instead we get a feeling of force and pressure. On the other hand, this kind of giving is not appreciated either. From others we are perceived as what we emit—as easily to be manipulated. Through this inability to say no we are constantly being abused, and this creates additional dissatisfaction and disappointment.

Of course, it is hard to resist the pressure of a guilty conscience that we may feel. There is often a lot of talk about responsibility one should recognize, or one is given the feeling of "being the last hope." It is also very popular to put pressure on family members under the cloak of traditions and religion. It's often one partner putting pressure on the other, being sure that he or she will certainly give in for fear of separation. Additionally fear of conflicts in general can prevent one from standing up for oneself.

If we allow ourselves to be put under pressure, we sink into the deepest of our depths a bit at a time. We literally hide inside of ourselves so that we cannot be seen anymore and are left alone.

Unfortunately this does not work because if we do not communicate, our environment does not know that we feel that we have been put under pressure. Often there are only misunderstandings that can be clarified with one single sentence. Precisely because people do not clarify situations, sometimes even bigger misunderstandings develop. The victim thinks that the others should notice his or her tortured feelings. If nothing is clearly communicated and covered up, the misunderstanding cannot be cleared up. If we continue to play this game, hoping that the others read between the lines, nobody notices that we are acting against our own will. As nobody knows what's going on inside of us, everybody will face us in the same way, presuming that everything is all right, as otherwise we would certainly communicate it.

Now how shall the outside world know that there is something we don't want, that we partly even feel cornered when we don't communicate it or even cover it up?

These people believe that their surroundings make use of them and that they are unable to free themselves. They think that their environment must stop asking them for favors. They themselves cannot say no, so the rest of mankind must take the responsibility for them. They consider themselves the victims of their circumstances. The more they see themselves as victims, the more convincing they play this role and the more they are overloaded with orders and expectations. Through the law of attraction, the pressure from outside is getting bigger and bigger. As time goes by, these people can even find themselves in a state of shock when the telephone rings because they are afraid of being pushed around and used again. When specific persons get in touch with them, their stomach spontaneously tenses up, as they fear that they will be drawn into something again that they absolutely don't want. They know in advance that they will play along again. Very often these people suffer from eating disorders and digestive problems. In acute situations they have no appetite but rather stomach pressure and diarrhea. Hence, they suffer from acute stress symptoms, which, in the worst case, can manifest as a gastric ulcer or even cancer.

I think it's pretty obvious where the error lies. Nobody can be put under pressure unless he or she allows it. Pressure always comes from the outside, never from the inside. When we open our doors and let the pressure in, it blows up inside of us. We can only be taken advantage of when we allow it. This does not mean that we should not be cooperative anymore, but we should be cooperative consciously. Whatever we decide to do, we must do it from our heart with the full consciousness that perhaps we will not receive thankfulness. But this will not disturb us because we do it out of love with our hearts. We will also be able to express it with love that we could not provide help in this or the other situations. There will be a big astonishment when for the first time we stand up for our true convictions and say no with love and clarity. What will happen then? In most cases, it will simply be accepted. Many people will even ask with amazement, "Why didn't you say that much earlier? We would have understood you." One does not understand why one has been so submissive for such a long time. Then we see that our heads have talked us into something that does not exist.

Even if somebody does not agree with our no, that's all right. Because of the individuality of all human beings, we cannot keep everyone happy anyway. If somebody does not want to reconcile him or herself to our decision to live according to our own convictions and if the individual is unable to accept that these convictions don't necessarily correspond to the ones of our counterparts, this person will likely not fit into our lives anymore. Perhaps we have experienced enough pressure through exactly this person so that we are now ready to learn from this period of our lives and liberate ourselves from our own wrong thinking. Either this person (or a whole circle of persons) will withdraw from our lives, or through our changed frequency a transformation with our relationship to our environment takes place.

When we change our thoughts and therefore our behavior, our frequency changes as well and only attracts all that corresponds to this new vibration. As I was very insecure when I was younger—among others because of my fears—I was automatically susceptible to dominant persons. I radiated the corresponding vibrations that told these people, "I am insecure. I am unable to compete with you. I don't stand up for my wishes and convictions. If you want to force something on me, I will reluctantly agree with you." I was just what others were waiting for. One day, however, the pressure became too much, and I internally exploded. Through blasting away all old thought patterns, this explosion revealed my real truth. I realized that it was absolutely right to say no without having to justify it or explain myself. It was as if I had discarded an extremely heavy load. I felt indescribably relieved. Within this feeling of liberation, I felt love for that person through whom I had experienced this pressure because she had brought me to my senses. Additionally I did not have the least bit of fear of this person anymore because now I knew that I was my own boss and that only I had the right to decide for myself. Above all I understood that I myself had put pressure on me. The other person was still the same; however, something had changed in me, and this change took the pressure off of me. In reality, I could have put an end to this at any time. It is never the world that has to change to make my life happier. It is always me that has to change, and it's only an attitude.

In principle, it does not matter at all who puts pressure on us and why. When we notice that we don't act out of an inner conviction but out of the convictions, wishes, and demands of others, then something must be wrong. As soon as we recognize that we are in a state of shock when we are confronted with an opinion or a request, we should ask ourselves this question: "Do I really want to do this?" We should listen to our inner voice and be honest with ourselves. It is also possible that we say, "Yes, this is what I want to do." Then we feel this yes in our hearts, and when we act, it's not from of a resigning habit but from a conscious decision. But if we cannot identify with what is brought close to us, then we should leave it alone with a clear conscience and honestly communicate this. It would never fulfill us anyway, as this kind of giving is without quality and does not fulfill its real purpose. Dr. Wayne W. Dyer has a good affirmation for this. "I would rather be loathed for who I am than loved for who I am not."

When we are authentic, we are also satisfied with ourselves. We are free from pressures and emanate this to our outside world. We are therefore taken seriously by our surroundings and treated with the respect we deserve. When we think, speak, and act according to our inner convictions, we are not only able to speak no with clarity, but above all we can also give a wholehearted yes.

Nobody can make you feel inferior without your consent.
—Anna Eleanor Roosevelt

Inner Tensions

There are times when we are nervous, tense, and driven by an inner restlessness. In many cases we don't even know why, and we can't find an explanation for these emotions, which makes it even more unpleasant. If we don't know why we feel an inner turmoil, we also have no idea how to help ourselves. So we feel helpless and at the mercy of these arbitrary emotions.

Inner tensions develop when the head and the heart are not in balance with each other or when we have to do something we don't really want to do. It's an inner defense against an outer influence that the mind follows blindly and habitually but with which the soul cannot identify. This inner turmoil is an alarm sign, and it tells us that we are not acting in accordance with the True Self. It does not matter at all if it happens consciously or unconsciously. Our inner voice immediately notifies us when we are at a distance from ourselves. When the mind with reason or logic drags us in a different direction than our inner voice, this is marked by nervousness, insecurity, self-doubts, aggressiveness, and extreme sensitivity, and it is often also accompanied by physical symptoms like digestive problems, breathing and heart issues, headaches, etc. Our feelings are a guidance system, and they give us a clear feedback whether we still comply with our Source or not.

The inner turmoil can be enhanced by outer influences like changes in the weather, stress, or the moon. The moon especially has an influence on our energy balance, a pull that should not be underestimated. If we are in resonance with this, the full moon can strongly enhance what's already in us. If we are relaxed and easygoing, it can make us high-spirited. If we are sad, we can also become depressed, and if there are already tensions and aggressions in us, they seem to get even more intense. However, this does not mean that the moon or other outer factors are the causes for these tensions. They only make it obvious that something is not in balance. We can make use of these enhanced feelings because through them we can figure out the reason for our inner turmoil much easier. So it's best to do some soul-searching first and to find out what kind of situations or persons we currently have to deal with. Usually we know pretty well what makes us lose our balance, but if it's not enough to simply think about it, we should meditate on it. Another option would be to take a time out and put distance between ourselves and the situation or person if possible. This does not necessarily have to be a holiday for several days. An extended walk in the forest or some relaxation at the waterside or in one's own garden may be sufficient. As soon as the cause is found, we must consciously decide whether to we leave the situation as it is, to set certain limits, to clear the air through a clarifying talk, or to simply continue to allow everything to carry on as before.

1. Moving Away or a Change of Direction

When we feel that a certain constellation, a request from somebody, an assumed task, a relationship, or something similar causes an inner tension, we should follow our feelings. In this case, the rationally thinking head acts against our inner voice. This does not necessarily mean that our feelings show us the easier and more comfortable way to the solution. They only point you in the direction that conforms with the frequency of your True Self. Sometimes this might mean that we go different ways, that we refuse to accept certain invitations, that we change our job or our place of residence, etc. When we have finally managed to make up our minds in favor of our own being, inner peace will be restored.

Sometimes, however, we don't want to decide against something. The situation or relationship may principally be in order. Often it's only a slight change in direction that has to be made. Or it's some detail that worries us. It may also be an insecurity or uncertainty about something unspoken that is unduly burdensome. There can be feelings growing in us, and these feelings can be of a very positive nature. Out of the fear of being rejected, these kinds of feelings can make it very difficult for us to confess. The fear is so big because we are afraid of destroying something with talking these things out instead of creating what we are longing for. Equally a confession may cause a surprising and positive change—the beginning of a wonderful new period of life. Yes, a discussion may bring pain to the surface, but at the same time we gain certainty about a situation and can proceed with the new information.

The only thing that matters is that we clarify the situation for ourselves and that we don't allow ourselves to be intimidated by possible consequences. Eventually we regain our inner balance, but this can only happen when we are honest with ourselves and with our environment. Otherwise we will continue to nourish our inner dissatisfaction.

2. Conscious Acceptance

Often it's inevitable that we have to face the issue of unpleasant situations. It may come through discussions with our boss or a person close to us that we have not taken up ourselves. It can also come from job interviews, visits from relatives, court hearings, or whatever. In many cases, we cannot really evade these situations, as that would aggravate them. We should never blindly escape all situations. Each of our actions should be consciously chosen and carried out. The sky remains blue even when we close our eyes and don't see it anymore. Sticking our heads in the sand does not mean that everything vanishes into thin air. Whenever we postpone something that's inevitable, we will encounter it again and again until we finally turn our attention to it. The more often we postpone it, the more troublesome it becomes every time.

We should meet inevitable situations with openness. We can't avoid them anyway. Now we have the choice whether we deal with these situations unwillingly and with negativity, which will have the corresponding result, or we face them with conscious optimism, make the most of them, and visualize the desired outcome. Then we will achieve a result that we can embrace.

However we act in a situation or whatever we express toward a certain person in order to restore our inner peace and harmony, we should do it with love and a clear consciousness. It is important that we do what gives us a feeling of inner peace even if it means that we have to change the way we approach the problem. This step can be difficult and painful. However, inside of us we know that it's necessary. We can only find our inner peace when our hearts and heads pull in the same direction. This harmony has to be created so that we have our bundled power at our disposal and constructively pursue and realize our targets. When our hearts and our heads are in harmony with each other, we are automatically in harmony with the Source. And if we are in harmony with the Source, we are at peace within us—peaceful, loving, and satisfied.

FEAR: CAUSE OR SYMPTOM?

Now here is the crucial question again: What came first—the chicken or the egg? In many cases we don't even know why we are afraid of something. At a certain incident, a key word, or a gathering with one or more persons, we can suddenly flip an inner switch to alarm us, and an uneasy, negative, oppressive, fearful feeling arises. So fear seems to be a symptom arising from our old polarized thought patterns. As long as we don't finally reflect on why in the world we think these thoughts, we don't realize that we are unconsciously accepting outer or inner restrictive thoughts that reduce the potential of our individual talents to a minimum.

But can't fear also be a cause? Let's take the case of a depression. People who suffer from permanent anxiety states can with time develop depression. They feel powerless and helpless and at the mercy of their fears. They shut themselves away in their shells and possibly avoid everything that could remotely activate their fears. Thus, they withdraw themselves and get lonely, and this then leads to depression. So is fear the cause? When it comes to depression, yes, it is one possible cause of many because the depression may really be caused by the fear.

But even if the depression is an effect of existing fears, it does not mean that there is not something already underlying these fears. More specifically, the depression is the symptom of a symptom. It's just another cause.

Fear does not simply arise out of nothing. Fear is not a primary feeling that is given at birth. Our primary feeling is well-being. We were born out of love, and we always carry within us where we are from. We are a part of what created us. A piece of wood always remains a piece of wood. It does not turn to plastic all of a sudden. No matter how it is colored on the outside, it remains wood. It's the same with us. God is love. So we derive from God. And as God is love, our whole existence is based on love. Thus, we are love because we are born out of love. So when our whole existence is based on love, all other feelings that we feel inside of us must come from a different source. And this source is called unconsciousness. When we really consciously go through our lives and realize who we are and why we are here, we will recognize the wrong truth of our unconscious thoughts and distinguish them from our true nature. As long as we allow ourselves to be guided from a mind feeding us with negativity and counterproductive thoughts rather than from our primary feelings happiness, well-being, and luck, we will continually experience tensions, insecurities, fears, and blockages.

When we live our lives consciously, our True Selves, which are connected with the Source at all times, speaks to us. Unconsciousness, however, lets the ego to speak. The ego permanently feeds us thoughts that then take us far away from the truth so that we don't realize that we consist of love only. It talks us into perceiving anger, resentment, insecurity, desperation, disappointment, humiliation, and naturally fears. These feelings are caused by thoughts we have stored in our ego, and our ego delightfully supplies us with them whenever the opportunity shows up. As long as we don't see this, we will continue to turn to the ego for help so that it confirms our thoughts and feelings. What a vicious circle! But as soon as we are conscious and see and hear clearly, we will find out that we not only don't want this negativity but also don't need it anymore, for we can dissolve the illusion we have created through it. We will find out that negativity is not a part of our true nature but a parasite that we had permitted to successfully nest in our heads throughout the years.

Through our unconsciousness we stir up counterproductive thoughts and feelings of diffuse fears that cause various problems on the physical, social, and soul level. We don't even think that we have produced these problems ourselves through false thinking patterns. If we convince ourselves long enough of something, we believe it, and when we believe it long enough, it becomes a part of our belief system. We may already be so deeply identified with certain fears that we are not aware of all the previous negative self-suggestions anymore. This brings us salvation. We have not helplessly surrendered to these fears because it is our free choice whether we want to perceive them or not. When we are able to allow a constant stream of negative thoughts and feelings, we can do the same with positive influences as well. In the beginning it may seem to be somehow strange or even difficult to reprogram ourselves, as we are used to our negative imprints. Just as we can make our lives hard with negativity, we can make them a heaven on earth through positivity.

Hence, fear is basically a symptom, namely a symptom that arises from the unconscious stream of thoughts in our heads, and this is the result of old thought patterns far away from our True Selves. As body, spirit, and soul are one, our unconscious thoughts (as well as our conscious negative thoughts) can trigger various psychological, mental, and physical side effects and health issues, such as the previously mentioned depressions. This can mean susceptibilities to infectious diseases, digestive discomforts, headaches, tensions, etc. But also chronic diseases can occur, such as respiratory disorders, gastric ulcers, high or low blood pressure, heart problems, skin diseases, allergies, cancer, etc.

When we perceive unpleasant feelings, it's an obvious sign that we are not aligned with our True Selves. Consequently inner tensions emerge, and we feel bad and unhappy. Now these feelings will sooner or later manifest as health conditions or diseases. It is not possible to separate body, spirit, and soul from one another. One influences the other, or one supports the other if properly applied. If we carry a burden, even if only thoughts that cause bad feelings within us, depending on the duration and intensity, it will eventually find its reflection in our physical bodies. Whatever we perceive as negativity cannot correspond to our true nature. Our true nature is positive and based on well-being. So if we chose positive thoughts and therefore trigger good feelings, we enhance our energy level. Through these positive vibrations we automatically influence the condition of our bodies. This goes even further. If our bodies feel fitter, more agile, more powerful, and free of pain, this in turn has an effect on our feelings and thoughts. So we can simply transform a negative spiral into a positive spiral.

If we want to say good-bye to diseases, feelings, and behavior patterns resulting from fears, we must begin with the cause. We must become aware of our thoughts and control them. We can think what we want. Nobody can dictate to us what to think. It is solely our own free decision. Therefore, it lies in our own hands whether we want to feel good or bad. For many people this may sound like sheer mockery, which I can understand very well. I myself once stood at the point where I had to decide whether I should go on to pursue my target or keep being afraid of my path. I decided on behalf of the target and immediately noticed that there was nothing on my path I really should have been afraid of. The more I practiced to produce only constructive thoughts, the more experienced my new way of thinking became and the easier the path toward my target consequently became. I moved forward more rapidly and recognized many connections I was not able to see through the fear in front of my consciousness. Supporting people and circumstances simply fell into place. As time went by, I was reflexively only thinking in a constructive manner. Whenever I was erroneously about to fall back into my old thinking behavior, I noticed it immediately and changed my thoughts.

It's all about taking the first step. If this is taken, we immediately perceive positive changes that motivate us to proceed in this direction. The more experiences of this kind we have, the deeper the realization that we ourselves are the architects of our own fortune. The deeper and clearer this realization gets, the more we become what we believe. The more we are at home in this belief, the more positive and confirming occurrences show up in our lives. And this will enhance our new belief even more, and it becomes a deep knowledge eventually.

We will still be confronted with situations where we think that nothing makes sense and that despite of all the work on ourselves, everything goes wrong again. That's normal. Changing circumstances call for new actions, which is also unknown territory for us. At first we have to find our way through these new situations and the corresponding emotions and occurrences. As when we are on our way to a new level, we must pass the appropriate intermediate exams in order to be prepared for the further route. A once-won realization does not mean that we have discovered the philosopher's stone. It's just one of many realizations needed to reach our goal. The more we are aware of this, the more motivated we will be when we encounter all these crises and challenges. Therefore, we will be able to walk through them with more strength and confidence. With growing consciousness, we will never fall into the deep holes again like we had before. Our conviction to not allow any more suppression but to instead remain in charge of ourselves has already been planted deep within us. Hence, small stumbling blocks cannot stop the upward spiral any-more.

Fear is just a symptom. The cause lies in our thought structure, which we can control according to our own will. We have the power in our hands if we, through the choice of our thoughts, allow the manifestation of positive or negative symptoms in the form of emotional and physical conditions.

... BY DISCOVERING WHO YOU ARE NOT!

PART 3
JOURNEY TO FREEDOM

Freedom means feeling good, regardless
whether others like it or not.
- Erika Kind

The Principle of Duality

e were born into this world in order to experience ourselves through the world of opposites. We immerse ourselves in one quality, move through it to its opposite, and eventually absorb it into our being. There are certain emotions that can only be experienced through duality, and the achievement of desired knowledge in connection with duality is only possible through entering a physical body in this space-time reality.

If we, for example, came into this life with the wish to experience the feeling of liberation, we must experience imprisonment at first. If we want to experience tolerance and generosity, we must first go through jealousy and stubbornness. Naturally the experience of the opposite may have been our wish as well. Perhaps we even jump from freedom to captivity in order to really understand and appreciate the feeling of freedom and to integrate its true meaning into our being. We wanted to come into this world of opposites because we can create and awaken the most intensive feelings here and anchor them within us irrevocably. An incarnation on earth is like a crash course in development.

Balance

The duality also embodies the oneness of all that is. We don't have to be particularly attentive to notice that everything has two sides in our world. Every one of us knows that there is light and dark, hot and cold, good and evil. This information is not new. But what's not so obviously clear and what many don't want to realize is the fact that both sides are necessary. As we have acquired the habit of looking at things unilaterally to analyze them and to cut them into pieces, there must be an opposite of everything we see so that the circle is closed again. Duality is necessary in order to ensure equilibrium. If there was an overhang of positive or negative vibrations, everything would fall out of balance. As long as we are unable to see everything as one, we need the opposites so that the balance in every situation and in every circumstance is assured. Everything that exists is energy and was created from the same energy. Therefore, it is integrated in one and the same energy. This energy is pure life. The pulsating forms change, but in itself it all stays the same and is in perfect balance and harmony. Hence, no imbalance can ever emerge. All is one and will remain one forever. It does not matter whether we understand this or not or whether we like it or not. That's how it is. We experience it daily. Within this energy, everything is inseparable and connected. Every action, every circumstance, and every thought finds its balance. That's where the following saying comes from: "When a butterfly flaps its wings, a sack of rice falls on the other side of the world." Herein lies the law of cause and effect. When we have understood this, we also understand why there are no coincidences and why there are only natural consequences from this law. This also includes the law of attraction.

The universe is in perfect unity. Everything together is a whole. Every single thing, every stone, every living being, every word, every feeling, every thought has its opposite. The wider the gap between these two opposites is, the more extreme each of the opposites shows up so that both sides eventually can combine to one unity in wholeness again. To understand this, we only have to take the number ray. (I am surprising myself at the moment. Throughout my whole life I have hated mathematics, and now I use it as an aid for understanding, and I am even happy about that.

This is another example of the fact that everything has two sides and that one never knows what something may be good for, even if one dislikes it at first.)

The zero point represents the perfect unity. The higher something is in the direction of the positive numbers, the deeper the opposite must slip into the minus so that balance is assured. This means that the positive and the negative are perceived less drastically the closer they approach each other. This can be compared with a seismograph. The higher the amplitude on the one side is, the more the needle swings out on the other side. Success may be a good example too. The more successful we are, the more jealous people will show up in our lives who want to make our lives appear in a negative light—no matter how justified our success may be. We all know the saying, "Where there is sunlight, there is also shadow." This comparison gets to the heart of the effect of duality. The lighter and brighter the sunlight is, the darker and stronger the shadow gets. If the sun getting weaker—maybe because clouds are getting in between you and the sun—the shadow details will get softer or disappear completely.

Who has not experienced this yet? We are exuberantly happy and on cloud nine, and shortly afterward something happens. It may be a little something, and we may slide into the cellar. Perhaps we just pulled off a particularly lucrative job and are delirious with joy. So that we get our balance again, we may soon afterward step into a big pile of dog mess. We could get a flat tire, or our partner could be a pain in the neck today. Because of all these delays it may become too late. Through all this, our previous delighted mood sinks far under zero because we are frustrated and are not able to truly enjoy our business success anymore.

Exactly the same thing can happen the other way around as well. Certainly everyone has already experienced this. When we feel extremely bad because we are sick or because we must accept a disappointment or a loss, all of a sudden hands are held out to us, mostly from people we don't necessarily expect kindness from, which makes the balancing effect even bigger. Balance always takes place—both in the small as well as in the large.

A divorce is mostly a very traumatizing matter that saps one's energy. But when it's over, we may find the right partners for the rest of our lives or start successful careers, and that might not have been possible without the separation from the previous partners.

Not everything is positive and friendly. Everything has two sides. Let's look at the following opposites—love and hate, luck and loss, mistrust and trust. They seem to be completely different emotions. The closer both sides approach to each other, the calmer it gets in between them. When they fully connect with each other, something unbelievable happens: They unite and dissolve at the same time. To get back to the number ray, plus and minus approach each other until both reach the zero point. When they have reached the absolute center, what arises now? Zero equals nothing! To express it more comprehensible, indifference arises, and this means that everything is equally valid. If a matter is neither positive nor negative, it simply *is*. It is not subject to any judgment anymore. The compulsion to judge disappears. Peace arises from the realization that all is good the way it is. The circumstance in question is simply accepted the way it is, without feeling the urge within oneself to divide it into good or bad. What we then perceive is the feeling of an unbelievable inner contentment as we are not searching for good or evil. It's all in order because it is in perfect unity. We can have this experience every time we are able to dissolve a blockage inside of us. Negative and positive disappear by connecting with each other and forming a perfect whole. Dr. John F. Martini calls this the quantum collapse. I warmly recommend his book titled *Breakthrough Experience.*

However, there is nothing wrong with experiencing both sides. Positive and negative don't have the meaning of good and bad. They only describe the two opposites. We are here to learn. We all must learn to balance both opposites. We first must understand them so that we are able to do this. Who would know what hot meant if he or she had no idea of cold? Who would appreciate the light if he or she did not know the darkness? Who would know what hunger was if he or she was permanently full? Who ever felt compassion for somebody if he or she did not experienced it him or herself in various situations? Who would receive help if he or she was not in need of help? Somehow it's pretty easy to understand why we have to make experiences at all. Remember the story about the ego and the unconscious self. We want to go through all experiences again and again until we can see everything as one. We cannot accept only one side and exclude the other one at the same time. Only both together help us to gain insights. In principle, we only have to accept that everything we experience as negative is equally important and necessary, and the same thing goes for experiences that are positive. When we stop fighting one or the other but see everything as a part of the whole, accept it, and learn from it, we do ourselves a great favor. Resistance only causes more pain and suffering. On the other hand, acceptance and surrender cause inner stillness and enable us to thankfully integrate all occurrences as necessary steps on the way to our target.

When we are in this awareness, we start to see circumstances, persons, and also inner conditions as a whole without dividing them into good and bad. Then we know we are not treated seemingly at random by life and used as a yo-yo. Then we are not up one moment and down the next anymore. At this point we stop pushing against something inside of us, which is the first step to dissolve inner tensions, fights, and lacks.

I bring an example from my own life in order to highlight this aspect more practically. As already mentioned, I was a very insecure girl, and this did not really cease as an adult, not even as a mother.

At the age of sixteen I met my husband, and we married seven years later. Like I said earlier, I had very little self-confidence. I left it to my husband to defend me against the outside world. I even believed that it was my husband's duty to protect me and to demand respect for me, particularly because he knew that I was unable to do this for myself. The only problem was that he did not do it! Whenever I approached him about this, he just blocked. Later I started to consciously walk my own spiritual path, and little by little I came to understand that I couldn't give the responsibility for myself and my soul's peace to another person but that I had to accept it and take the responsibility for myself. I recognized that I am the only human being on this planet who can solve my problems, for only when I solve them myself are they really solved. Hence, I learned to accept others the way they were, and I learned that it had nothing to do with me when they confronted me with negativities or tried to manipulate me. This had nothing to do with me. I only reflected those kinds of characteristics. They had to work on themselves and the things they did not like about themselves. Furthermore, I accepted that everybody had their own history and that I could not know what led to their current behavior. By accepting that, I myself had to cope with my own problems. I was able to accept this for others as well. Hence, I could dissolve judgment in some areas, and I hardly took things personally anymore. Instead, I was able to show love and understanding. In the end, the one who emits negativity suffers much more from it than those who should be affected. This inner process clearly caused an interesting turnabout. Those people who belonged to the previously mentioned group suddenly seemed to face me with respect, consideration, and tolerance. They did not put pressure on me anymore and accepted my opinions even when they differed from their own ideas. I was met with much warmth, and it was not necessary to defend myself anymore. As I was steadfast in myself and emitted this charisma now, I was not a target anymore. Instead of absorbing negative frequencies from others, I was able to radiate my understanding and neutral views.

Moreover, I did not show any resistance toward others and their opinions anymore. I just let their viewpoints be subjective truths. I also let every person be the way he or she was, for I could not estimate what was right or wrong from their points of view. With this attitude, I did not offer a platform for arguments.

The two opposites in this example are not difficult to see. For a long time I felt disappointed, hurt and rejected and not taken seriously because my husband did not come to my defense. But because he did not do it, I was forced to eventually assume responsibility for myself. Of course, my husband's ignorance of my fears and sorrows was not a conscious action from him. All this was a learning process for him as well. Through his intuition of not dealing with *my* problems, I learned that only I myself could solve them and that I could not give the responsibility for myself to anybody else. A lesson is only learned when one passes the exam oneself.

On the one hand, I was deeply hurt by my husband's behavior. However, the positive contrast was the resulting development of my self-confidence and my realization that I had the right to live my life according to my own standards. This newly created basis was the starting point for an unbelievable transformation process within me. Many years later my husband was able to see the situation that had been such a burden for me before from another viewpoint arose. Not only did I stand up for myself, but my husband backed me as well. In fact, he was right not to do this earlier. If he had, I would not have had the chance to learn this lesson.

If you find yourself in a situation where you feel uncomfortable, immediately watch out for the positive elements behind it. There is always something positive. Every single situation always contains both sides. It's often the case that we perceive the negative elements first and that the positive arises out of them. Mostly we can only realize all this in hindsight. Therefore, it's important to simply be aware of it and to optimistically pass the exam, to take the moment as it is, and to act according to our own intuition.

My father's background is another example that shows there is a positive element behind every negatively perceived occurrence. As a child, it was not easy for him in his family. He was the third of three children. His sister had died years before his birth. He had an older brother who was fortunately very much supported in many areas. My father himself, on the other hand, was not treated lightly. As far as I know from stories, he was not a child who was easy to care for. During his school days his parents were constantly summoned by the school director, for my father would not refrain from playing tricks. Of course, he was always afraid of being caught or betrayed when something went wrong. He could not give everyone a little bit of something to keep them happy. Therefore, he was caught in a vicious circle. Eventually he was always blamed for everything. On the other hand, nobody ever stood up for him even when he was innocent, as no one believed him anymore because of all the mischief he had already caused. As time went by, he developed feelings of inferiority, which were about to pull him further down into this negative spiral. But already as a teenager he had started to wake up. He realized that things could not continue like that and decided that he had a choice—either to be broken by the circumstances or to break out of them. He chose the second option. Although he was not the brightest at school, he enrolled himself into a secondary school at a very young age. His parents were very astonished, for they did not believe him capable of successfully passing the exams in this school, but nevertheless, they let him go. Now the tide turned. My father noticed that indeed he was able to get something accomplished. It was especially motivating for him to see that he had success when he pursued his path with total commitment. After he passed his exams at this school, he took a job and began studying as well. He was able to cover the costs himself. At twenty-eight he started his own business, which he successfully ran until he died at the age of sixty-five. But that was not all. My father was a very successful businessman who said,

Certainly, my parents may have done a lot of things wrong, well, then again perhaps not. If they had not behaved the way they did, I would not be at the point where I am. That's what I am thankful for. My inferiority complex was necessary to get me going and to find out what I can do myself and what I am capable of getting accomplished.

So he clearly realized that out of the negative experiences his future success, including all of his changed thought patterns, developed. The positive development was only possible because he got to know the opposite pole beforehand, and that made him think. We need contrast to grow.

Dr. Wayne W. Dyer has said, "Appreciate everyone and everything. Look upon every experience you've ever had, and everyone who's ever played any role in your life, as having been sent to you for your benefit. In this universe, which was created by a divine, organizing intelligence, there are simply no accidents."

Search for the opposite when you feel uncomfortable in certain situations or in the presence of certain people. Do this when you feel too happy, for when you fly too high, you will land with a smack on the hard asphalt soon. Always search for the opposite in order to bring stillness and balance into the situation. When you master this, you become aware of the spread of peace inside of you and realize that you have freed yourself from more fetters. With this feeling of inner peace, love, and safety, you are ready to take the next step.

EVERYTHING RESULTS IN COMPLETENESS

Opposites must exist so that the balance remains intact, for everything together results in a whole complete in itself—complete in both the detail and the superior sense. With this knowledge we are now able to understand something very decisive, namely the huge differences in the world population's consciousness and in their way of living, acting, and thinking. Let's just observe ourselves and the environment.

If a man stubbornly lives according to his physical mind or gets emotional, he loses his inner balance. In order to restore balance, the exact contrary effect in the form of a person or an incident will appear. It does not matter if the emotion is a "melting away in happiness" or pure desperation. For the moment we can exclude those people who are in inner peace and in balance with themselves and with their Source. Because they are centered, they don't influence the opposites. However, as most people don't permanently reside in a state of balance twenty-four hours a day and seven days a week, they keep the poles moving when they are off-line just like our contemporaries who are still living in control of their ego-driven minds.

As an example for the balance of the energy field within a population, let's look at the wars in Afghanistan or Iraq. How fanatic were the initiators who started these wars! With how much enthusiasm they were able to convince the American citizens of the idea of patriotism! And how many massive countermovements arouse in Europe and later in the United States as well? Environmental pollution and animal cruelty attract organizations like Greenpeace, and political parties originate whose goals are aligned on environmental protection. The more men who have died in wars, the more boys who were born. The more spiritual teachers arise, the louder the voices of doubters become. When people experience great suffering, waves of helpfulness wash over them. The lighter a side is, the darker the other side will become. That's not frightening. It's just a law. Balancing will always take place. Within itself, everything is always in order, and we will never be able to bend this law. If we try to get it under our control—and this sounds unbelievably ridiculous—we will merely feel the effects of this law.

The more we are in tune with the Source, the more we

automatically connect with one another. Each of the approximately seven billion human beings on this planet contributes to the whole with their ways of living, thinking, speaking, and acting. When there is overwhelming generosity, there must also be cruel stinginess and hard-heartedness. It's the same with talents and abilities. We share them with one another. Somebody else contributes that which I don't have. But instead of competing with others or declaring their talents as wrong or inferior—just because we are jealous, we don't have the same ability, or their talent does not meet our personal taste—we should accept it with gratefulness and concentrate on contributing our own part. It is not meant to be that one individual alone is proficient in everything because it would be unbearable for that person.

The more we follow our feelings and align with the source within us, the more persistent we stay centered. Then there is nothing more to balance. Harmony resides—true harmony and not an affected, enforced, and false harmony. When everything meets in the middle, all is equally valuable, and there is nothing more to balance. Now stillness arises within us and outside of us. We are all one. Every one of us is an expanded particle of the Source, with which we are connected at all times and where we all eventually return to after we have left our physical bodies. When we return to the Source again, we melt together with it. Every being on this planet is a part of the big whole ... forever! No being is inferior or superior to another being. We all origin from the same Source, and we are all proceeding toward the same target—to become one again with all that is. In order to reach this goal, we must work together. Develop peacefulness within you first and share it with everyone. Only when the last opposites are resolved will the illusion of separation disappear.

The existence of all that is can be visualized as a huge puzzle. An individual piece of this puzzle is small and, when looked at separately, is meaningless. However, if one looks at this piece of the puzzle as a part of the whole and puts it into its appropriate place, then it connects, and the complete picture is seen in absolute perfection. This image also illustrates how important it is to take up one's own place instead of trying to live the life of somebody else. There is only one specific place for each individual piece, for every piece is shaped and colored differently. Of course, it can torture itself and allow others to force it into an apparent correct form, but it does not belong here. The piece would disturb the whole picture and stand out unsightly. Disharmony would arise. Additionally the real place would remain empty, for only one piece fits exactly into it. If one piece of the puzzle was missing at all, the whole picture would be worthless.

Each of us has his place in this world, and everyone is equally important. Let's take our predetermined place and contribute our part to the completion of the universal puzzle!

GIVING AND TAKING

Giving and taking are two complementary energies that have to be in balance so that everything is in the correct relation.

We incarnate here on earth to make experiences, to mature, and to develop so that we are eventually one with God again and no further incarnations are necessary. We receive as many chances as we need in order to learn everything we have to learn. No matter what we do and no matter what we don't get accomplished, there is never a "too late" or a "not possible anymore." We may come back as often as we need to until we have completed our task.

Hence, these excursions to earth are real gifts. Everything is arranged for us so that we can have exactly those experiences that bring the required learning effect. We learn what we need to approach our final target—to be one with God again. So we *receive* something here—the gift of experiencing and realizing.

Here the law of duality comes into force again. We also must *give* something so that everything remains in balance. This happens automatically through our presence on this planet. Just through our existence we have an influence on the circumstances here. A newborn baby, for example, can neither walk nor speak. Nevertheless, it has an enormous influence on its environment just through its presence.

Edwin Elliot stated, "By being yourself, you put something wonderful in the world that was not there before."

Everyone who comes to earth in order to receive the gift of experiences also leaves something behind. Sometimes it's obvious and visible for everyone (e.g., the legacies of composers, singers, actors, philosophers, inventors, doctors, scientists, etc.). Their works are famous all over the world. But humans who have not been at the center of worldwide interest also leave their traces. Let's think of the newborn baby again. Holding her baby in her arms is an experience that a mother could not have made through anything else. The newborn baby has not really actively done anything, but still the child already has given something. Great talents would probably never have had the chance for a breakthrough if they had not had somebody who believed in them and perhaps even actively supported them. There are also fathers and mothers living modest lives and enabling their children to pursue big careers.

Poor and needy people give very impressive examples. They place themselves at the disposal to give other incarnated souls the opportunity to help. Who except for fans of the *Sissy* trilogy would know the actor Karlheinz Böhm today if he had not founded the aid organization Menschen für Menschen (Humans for Humans)?

Everyone here on this planet creates havoc and devastation. We received this planet as a gift so that we may make experiences. In the course of this incarnation we also leave something behind, and this makes it easier for other incarnated souls (also future incarnations) to reach their targets faster. We leave tips and hints that they (and we ourselves as well) can build on. Through history we learn what has proved to be of value and what should rather be avoided. Everybody leaves his or her personal imprint behind— everybody without any exception!

THE DUALITY WITHIN DIFFERENT CHARACTERISTICS

Just as we find a positive and a negative pole in all situations, this phenomenon also exists in opposing characteristics and even within these individual characteristics.

If we, for example, speak about ignorance, jealousy, ruthlessness, arrogance, anger, etc., reflexively we perceive these characteristics as negative.

As an example, let's take a deeper look at ignorance. Of course, we find the negative aspect of closing one's eyes to something new or different in it. On the other hand, it also includes a positive aspect. Ignorance helpfully stands at our side when things would be overwhelming for us. We ignore many things unconsciously because they would overwhelm our receptivity. Ignorance is a part of our instinct, helping us stay on our path and protecting us from things that would distract us. It can also protect us from psychical violations and harmful influences. This ignorance is developed to varying degrees in every person. To categorize it as a negative or a positive characteristic depends how it is expressed. However, this is a purely subjective perception. For one person ignorance might be necessary as a protective function so that he or she is not distracted from pursuing a consciously chosen direction out of profound conviction, and to another person, he or she might use it as an escape. Again everyone can only know for him or herself what's individually right for the person.

Thus, the ignorance can be enormously helpful to ignore disturbing or interfering conditions. There is a very matching statement by Lao-Tzu, which says, "To eliminate negative influences, simply ignore them." Furthermore, ignorance helps us to make use of the law of attraction by only giving attention to what we want and ignoring what we don't want to pull into our lives.

If we were standing in your physical shoes, we would not
let the reality of something be our basis for attention; we
would let the feeling-vibration of it be our basis. So we would

start saying, to anyone who was interested in knowing what we were about, "If it feels good, I give it my attention; if it doesn't, I don't look at it at all." You can and will create the essence of anything that you are giving your attention to.

– Abraham – Esther and Jerry Hicks

Likewise, we can split the example of ruthlessness. If we use it to realize our plans by listening to our inner voice instead of giving attention to disturbing voices, ruthlessness helps us to not give up easily at the first sign of difficulties. It's negative though if one deliberately does harm to others with one's behavior.

Now let's take a look at the seemingly positive characteristics like compassion, helpfulness, gratitude, positive thinking, understanding, tolerance, appreciation for others, etc. As an example, I would like to take the often misunderstood word *compassion*, for it can transform into pity. On the first glimpse, feeling pity for somebody seems to be something unbelievably compassionate and altruistic. In the end, however, pity does not help the person in need, for nobody gives the individual courage, and the sympathizing person will often also drift into the same bad condition. On the other hand, if someone turns toward us with compassion, we normally feel understood and cared for. Compassion allows trust to emerge, and thus the compassionate person with positive power is able to pull the suffering person out of his or her hole without letting him or herself fall into the hole as well. However, wrongly practiced compassion can result into a patronizing, overprotective, narrowing, and even possessing behavior.

The negative aspect of helpfulness is reflected in self-abandonment, obedience, exploitation, martyrdom, and hypocrisy, and it can even result in the experience of becoming a victim of abuse. When helped in dishonorable intentions, helpfulness is often used as a cloak for the wish of being loved, missing self-confidence, the fear of rejection, the search for appreciation, a bad conscience, etc.

Hence, it is obvious that one cannot categorize a characteristic as positive or negative purely by the word. I would even go so far as to say that opposing characteristics don't exist—stingy and generous, sad and funny, sluggish and adventurous. Of course, in the original sense of the words they do, but everything depends on to which extent the characteristics are expressed and when and where they are acted out. Each of us carries within us all aspects. Likewise, it's the golden middle that everyone has to find for him or herself. Sometimes one must express the negative aspect of a characteristic to finally be able to expand one's knowledge. Every quality within us can be of an enormous advantage for us when we learn to adequately express it. Stubbornness—adequately lived out—helps us to have great powers of endurance in order to reach a target. Let's make use of the potential within us! Let's become aware of the gifts we have brought with us, and we will conquer the world.

There is positive and negative in every circumstance, in every event, and in every person. Both poles are totally subjectively perceived and categorized as positive or negative. To the same extent, even the biggest catastrophe and the hardest stroke of fate have their positive sides or at least the seeds of something new growing out of them. However, the more intense we are affected by an incident, the more difficult it is to see the positive aspect and to balance it out with the negative. But the balance exists at all times and everywhere. All opposing emotions and mood swings approach one another more and more during our spiritual evolution. The difference is getting less and less. When two opposites are becoming one, they dissolve, and something new emerges—space. This space is then filled with pure divine energy which we truly are. We gain space so that the True Self can unfold.

Let us not forget that everything is subject to a universal law and that the mind is not capable of having a clear conception of this perfect universal order; however, we all have a knowing feeling within us. The mind arises from the brain, and the brain arises from the body, which was born out of matter. Our True Selves, however, arise from the universal Source and dive into these bodies for a certain period of time in order to learn with the help of matter. The Source stands above matter. It creates and organizes matter. As it was the Source of creation that created us, the knowledge of the Source is in our souls and not in our heads.

PRACTICAL EXERCISE

Like I described above, every situation and every occurrence contains positive and negative aspects so that they all stay in balance. Now think of a special situation that is somehow burdensome for you and contemplate the following questions:

- Which positive aspects have arisen from this unpleasant experience?
- What has changed?
- What did I learn from it?

Take enough time and write everything down that you can think of, even the slightest detail. Try to understand the situation and illuminate it from every possible point of view. Think of all the people you met in that moment or shortly afterward, and remember how they encountered you. Try to become aware of every little aspect that eventually has proved to be positive.

Now think of all these positive occurrences and experiences. Remember them with all your emotions and feel the gift you have received. Realize that all the unpleasant events were necessary so that the positive occurrences and beneficial gifts were able to appear. Feel the balance between giving and taking and between the negative and the positive. When you have realized that and when you are able to feel gratitude for this specific person or situation, then you have connected the oppositions within you and brought them into balance. You have understood now which gift you have received as a result of the previously frightening situation. Maybe you feel the rising of tears of emotion, of releasing, and particularly of love.

When you are able to feel these emotions, the time has come to make peace with this past trauma. Now you can see it as an aid to progress in your development. If a person is concerned, express your gratitude toward him or her—either personally, in writing, per telephone, or simply with thoughts. Become aware that you have learned an important lesson and that you can now continue to pursue your path with new strength on the basis of new information. Thank God that you received the grace to be able to absorb this new realization into your experience and that you came a little closer to Him as a result. Remember all this when you encounter the next challenge in your life.

The Opposite of Fear Is Love

Fear is nothing else but the absence of love. Where there is love, there is no fear. Love fills us with power and inner stability. Fear can only arise when we feel alone and separated. It's our ego that tries to talk us into these feelings, for this is its only way to bind us to it. In reality, however, we are never alone. Through the divine spark within us, we are connected with every living being not only on this planet but also in the whole universe.

Your Source wants you to experience everything you chose. By focusing your attention on something, you emit the intention to go through it. The universe will actively support you and provide you with everything you need. However, because we have forgotten how to consciously apply the law of attraction, we are often confronted with circumstances we don't really want. Anyway, by giving them our attention, we attracted them. The consequences of confrontation with things we don't want can make us feel misunderstood or left alone with our true wishes and longings. In reality, this is not the case, for if we were really alone, nothing would happen to us at all. Because we are loved, we are given everything we desire. As the Source never interferes with our free will, we are also given unpleasant occurrences. The love of our Source is so big that it provides us with everything we ask for. Yet it never leaves us alone. We will become aware of this at the latest when we have reached a particularly low point in our lives.

In our darkest and seemingly loneliest hours, we are suddenly offered a helping hand. When we feel abandoned by God and the rest of the world, somebody always stands beside us and pulls us out of the quicksand. We are never alone. We never were and never will be. It's not only people who are sent to us when we are standing with the back to the wall. Sometimes we can also have flashes of inspiration leading us to the solution of a deep-seated problem. All this is sent to you because you are loved. The universe loves you and wants you to reach everything that you have set up for yourself. The universe does not want you to be sad. It does not want you to feel lonely, for this feeling is only a distraction of your mind. You are love, and you are loved. Everything we perceive on the outside is a perfect reflection of what is going on inside of us in the first place. Through the duality of the physical world and the results in the outside world, we are shown the effect of our radiation. This is a wonderful gift and a signpost that helps us (if we are open for it) to turn our attitudes around for our well-being.

The contrary of fear is obviously love. When we are filled with love, there is no room for fear anymore. Doing something out of love immediately resolves fear because it loses its basis of existence, namely the feeling of being isolated. When we feel love, we feel the connection with our Source, which is the Source of the love we feel. Whenever we are consciously connected with our Source, we have the power to accomplish everything we desire. Actually nothing can then stop us anymore. We are creators and co creators in every single moment. We have the power to manifest whatever we feel inside, whatever matches our inner conviction. The only things that might stop us are blocking, counterproductive thoughts that cover this consciousness like dark clouds. Only the belief that what we wish for is not possible suffices to disconnect us with the power of intention—and so it shall be. But when we are filled with love, then we are connected purely and are really connected to our Source since our Source is pure love. Fear and doubt are dissolved, and we are free to follow our path to its highest purpose.

The love of what created us is immense and unimaginable. God's love inhabits every single living being and fills it with life. Each of these living beings emits this love again even when it is not conscious of it. Love comes out of every bird's twittering, every being, every air draft, every blossom, every snowflake, every breath, every embrace, every friendly word or glance, every sun ray, and every raindrop. All this exists, for it was created out of love. As we all were equally created out of love, this love essentially resides within us. True, real love originates inside of us. In reality, it does not originate: Love was always there. We just did not perceive it. All that ever manifested in the outside world has existed in our inside before. It's the same with love. Through us, the divine spark radiates to the outside. It never functions the other way around.

Sometimes an idea of love awakens in us when we fall in love. But this is really only an inkling of divine love. When we are in love, we often hope that the other gives us what we don't have. We hope that the other makes us happy. However, this means that we are looking for luck in the outside world. Outer circumstances are subject to change, and when we realize that the other person does not embody what we originally saw or intended to see in him or her, our love for this person looks and feels quite different again. Everything we are looking for on the outside—be it love, luck, protection, belief, etc.—will never fulfill us. These qualities lie inside of us, and we only have to set them free. We are only able to be happy when we have realized that happiness can only be found within us. We are only able to give love (and to receive it) when we have discovered it inside of us and when we love ourselves. We are only able to feel protected when we have understood that nothing can ever really happen to us because we are immortal, infinite beings and only inhabit perishable bodies. We are only able to believe when we have realized that true belief is a conviction that needs to be felt within ourselves and that cannot live according to rules that other people have pulled from their individually perceived conviction.

When we feel these and many other qualities inside of us, we cannot lose them anymore, as they are a part of the True Self. In contrast to all outer forms of appearance, the True Self is imperishable. We can never lose them. The love that actually encompasses all that we are still looking for—protection, belief, courage, optimism, etc.—lies within us always and forever.

Love is the energy that makes us the image of our Creator and that is the connecting link to our Creator. We can feel this connection and God's love when we become aware of the truths that we are immeasurably loved, that we were allowed to come here in order to make experiences, and that all we need is always at our disposal. When we are aware of this oneness, we know from the bottom of our hearts that there is not one single moment that we are alone and on our own. God's all-encompassing love is always inside of us, and that means that God is always inside of us.

Love is not created. Nor does it arise. The only reason we think that love needs to grow is that we often only discover a small part of it and uncover it little by little in the course of time. But in reality, love has always been there in its all-encompassing greatness. Love is always there—even when we are not aware of it. Just like the sun is there even though we cannot see it during the night, love is always inside of us and around us. It always was, and it will always be. In her song *Liebe ist*, Nena (99 Red Balloons) sums it up by saying, "Love does not become, love is!"

Fear is darkness, and love is light. Where there is light, darkness cannot exist. By nature, we are light.

THE EVALUATION OF
SUBJECTIVE REALITY

Objects are really the perceiving of them. Conversely,
therefore, the perceiving of them is what the objects are.
—Sri Nisargadatta Maharaj

Reality is what you see. *What* we see depends on *how* we look
at it. The same thing or situation can be perceived completely
differently by two people. Every perception is totally
subjective. What one person likes, another categorically rejects.
One person loves the sun, the beach, and the ocean whereas another
feels better in the mountains. A snake may cause a feeling of disgust
in one person, and another is totally fascinated by it. We look at our
reality with our physical eyes, but our minds decide what we make
of it. Perception and sight are not always identical when our mind
gives us a brain-controlled answer to the seen image.

How we perceive an image or an occurrence depends on our
thoughts in the first place. These thoughts are reflexively retrieved
by outer influences and by our past experiences (which can also
come from a former lifetime). However, we do not only perceive
from the views of our minds but at the same time from the views of
our life plans and our feelings. If we, for example, want to make the
experience of standing and singing on the stage, we will continually
feel drawn to it (unless our minds interrupt) and will spare no

effort to put this into action. If this experience is not listed on our life plan, we would probably not even be able to comprehend this passion, let alone present something, and we would thus probably sit in the audience.

We all see the same things; however, each of us perceives them differently according to our level of consciousness. For this reason, it would be presumptuous to put a label on other people's opinions and to judge them. When we judge something, we also must set a standard. But how should such a generally valid standard be, as each person has a totally subjective perception, an individual story, and a point of view? Everyone measures from his or her own point of view. Therefore, a different evaluation scale counts for everyone. It's interesting that we apply this scale not only to others but mainly to ourselves. Our perspective is compiled of a mixture between our own view, the view of our surroundings, and mainly the media. We take over the belief structures of others and make them our own. For this reason, we don't perceive ourselves with our own eyes but with the eyes of others. How often do we look at ourselves in the mirror and criticize ourselves? We may consider that our bodies are too heavy, too thin, too big, too small, or whatever. Who determines how the ideal body measurements must be so that it is perfect? How does one define *perfect* anyway? Everybody is perfect because everybody is a complete mini universe in him or herself. That's how it is, and it is good. That's what makes life on this planet and the interaction between its inhabitants so colorful. Everybody is perfectly correct just the way he or she is—both internally and externally—and everybody contributes exactly that what would be missing without him or her.

When we judge, we ignore the individuality of others. Based on ignorance, genocides, wars, racial hatred, suppression, and religions (claiming that they alone possess the only truth) develop. I want to clarify that I don't judge or even dismiss religions. Every religion has its convictions and focal points, and those people whose own beliefs are in accordance with the contents of the respective religion should deal with it. In this context, I just want to point out the fact that religions include clear guidelines according to what one must live to reach the target. There is little or no room for the uniqueness of each person's individuality within these guidelines.

What others say about us can never be objective statements. They see us from their points of view, out of their own reality. Thus, we may not take their opinions personally, neither the positive nor the negative ones. They are always subjective and have nothing in common with our True Selves. If the statements were objective, there would be no evaluation at all. Instead everything would simply be perceived the way it is without dividing it into categories. When something is meant to insult or even to hurt us, we should not take it personally anymore when we have understood that it is the expression of one person's subjective perception, which can be totally different from the perception of the next person. When we believe what others say about us or how they judge us, then we absorb the subjective belief structures of others, which have nothing to do with our true nature. Likewise we should (know that we have this knowledge and) use our own words and thoughts with care, for they are just as subjective and can only represent our viewpoint and not an objective perspective. With our subjective statements we can hurt those people who are not conscious of this subjectivity.

With the realization of this information, it is practically impossible to feel hurt or insulted by somebody.

EVERYTHING IS PERFECT IN ITS IMPERFECTION

The same counts for illnesses. When somebody is ill or handicapped, in the minds of the general public that person is considered to be imperfect in some way. He does not correspond to the image of normality. But why should somebody who was born with Down syndrome, who suffers from cancer, or who lost a leg in an accident be less perfect than someone who, in the prevailing opinion, is considered to be healthy? What's normal, and what's not? What's perfect, and what's not? Who determines when something is perfect and when it can be judged as inferior or incomplete? Moreover, people with a physical or mental weakness mostly have different characteristics and capabilities than healthy people. For example, it is well-known that blind people possess a more distinct sense of hearing, an excellent tactile perception, and very large memory functions. When one sense is removed, the others become more developed. How now can this be integrated into the evaluation scale? Only the one who created us can evaluate whether his creation is perfect or not. What God creates is perfect, or else it would not exist, for everything is a part of the big whole—every tiny detail.

The flower is blue. That's how it is. Whether it's grown too small, too big, too pale, or too strong, who can really assume the right to decide that? Sure, we can say, "I like it more when—" but this does not mean that the flower is inferior just because it does not meet the standards of one single person.

When we understand that judging and criticizing are inventions of our minds and that everyone perceives reality according to his or her state of consciousness, then it is only logical that really nobody can decide on the correctness of another one's action. When somebody has a big dream, that person ought to pursue it. It is the individual gaze that he or she throws in a certain direction with longing and passion. No one can objectively evaluate whether a person should pursue the realization of dreams or not—except for the individual. Only we ourselves know through our intuition where our path shall lead us. We may not allow ourselves to be confused by possible negativity and ignorance in the outside world. Our environment, no matter how well-intentioned it may be, always sees everything through its own eyes. Just because somebody else would not walk our path, that does not mean it's not all right for us to walk it. Likewise we should not let others talk us into accepting their point of views when we have the feeling that they don't fit into what we perceive ourselves. The only thing we really have to do in order to bring harmony into all the different legitimate perspectives is respect them.

In his book *Pointers*, Ramesh S. Balsekar writes the following about truth: "One cannot seek truth as an object, nor can truth be described. It can only be suggested or indicated, but not expressed in words, because truth cannot be conceived. Anything conceived will be an object and truth is not an object." As Sri Nisargadatta Maharaj puts it, "You cannot 'shop' for truth, as something which is authoritatively certified and stamped as 'Truth'. Any attempt to find the proof of truth would involve a division of the mind into subject and object, and then the answer could not be the truth, because there is nothing objective about truth, which essentially is pure subjectivity."

Absolute truth exists. A single true reality doesn't. Reality is perceived by every being subjectively—at anytime and anywhere—just the way it correlates to these beings' attitudes and sights. Therefore, we cannot judge it, for there is no scale for classification. Truth is always subjective.

Let things be how they are. Let's simply accept that each of us has the right to *perceive* things from a different perspective. By stopping to judge and evaluate, we get rid of the enormous burden of having to classify everything into categories. As I have already explained in the chapter titled "The Principle of Duality," it is essential for us that everything has its opposite. Therefore, opinions that seem to be totally contrary must exist as well, possibly just to give us the opportunity to view things from a different perspective—provided that we are already open enough. We all do what we do because we don't know any better, and we believe that we do the right things. You don't have to take what others throw at your feet. If you don't want it, leave it, but don't judge them. All we need is available, and every one of us embodies an aspect of the whole. Hence, not everybody can play the same role: There must be the chambermaid and the bank clerk and the baker and the butcher. This is what makes life so miscellaneous, and it is so fascinating to get to know the multiple sides of another human being because he or she is so differently programmed than we are.

What we all have in common is our heritage and the nature of our true being. What distinguishes us is only the different roles we play. When everyone respects and accepts these different roles without judgment, everything results in a harmonious whole. A peaceful cooperation with room for individuality develops, and a person is able to contribute the whole potential of his or her talents and capabilities.

By evaluating and judging, we curtail our range of vision and set unnecessary but massive limits to our own horizon. We don't allow ourselves to experience the complete spectrum but only concede a small excerpt to ourselves and our environment. Our programmed thoughts reflexively explain to us how we have to look at an occurrence or person, and quickly they leave their mark on the object. Thereby, we limit the possibility of perceiving all facets because we close ourselves off.

When we evaluate, we take away from ourselves the opportunity to make new and wonderful experiences. We miss many beautiful moments that could bring us new and wonderful people, many unbelievable experiences, and self-awareness. When we classify everything into self-invented categories and block our view for the complete picture, we close many doors and exclude the light. However, when we open ourselves and simply look at the things the way they are, we recognize their true beauty and the gift that is hidden in every moment and in every encounter. We can learn so much through the diversity around us.

LIVING WITH VARIOUS REALITIES

The more convinced we are that our minds are the measure of all things, the more the ego speaks and thinks through us. It will always try to mislead us, telling us that our own reality is the only truth. It will cause us to believe that only our sight of things is real.

If we identify with what our ego talks us into, we will permanently be tempted to convince others of our own truth. But what is truth? Consider this excerpt from the book *The Fifth Agreement* by Don Miguel and Don José Ruiz:

> For centuries, even millennia, humans have believed that a conflict exists in the human mind – a conflict between good and evil. But this isn't true. Good and evil are just the result of the conflict, because the *real* conflict is between the truth and lies. Perhaps we should say that *all* conflict is the result of lies, because the truth has no conflict at all. The truth doesn't need to prove itself: it exists whether we believe in it or not.

Hence, all disagreements, arguments, and wars don't occur because it is all about a fight between good and evil people but instead occur because everyone claims to possess the truth. As long as we allow the ego to determine that our personal truth is the only valid one, peace can never be. Every person lives according to a different truth—a truth that we subjectively perceive through our own reality—and so the mind will always try to claim its right for this truth.

Truth, however, is what is. It is *what* we see and not *how* we see it. Truth is not what we want to see or how we might bend it. Everything other than that what really exists is subjective messages created by the human mind. Ultimately these messages are the results of our fantasies and have nothing to do with conscious perception.

A bee *is* a bee. Whether we like it or not, it's a bee. That's *what* we see. In our subjective view of *how* we look at the bee and out of the fear of being stung by it, we also can make it a monster. We can accuse it of being dangerous because it has a sting, and we can also talk others and our children into this belief so that they equally pit themselves against the bee. Nevertheless, it's *just* a bee. The truth is that flying animal with yellow and black stripes *is* a bee. However, it's a lie that it is dangerous just because we are afraid of being stung by it. That's an invented story and has nothing to do with the truth. Something that doesn't exist is read into it. The bee itself, however, exists.

Conscious perception does not evaluate. It simply perceives what is. As soon as we evaluate, we classify things in good or bad, pretty or ugly, etc. So the mind doesn't have anything to do with conscious perception. If we really want to perceive what exists without evaluating it, the mind must be still. If this is possible, the truth of the individual may remain the truth of the individual, and nobody questions it because we know that it is just a subjective perception just like we all have. When we stop believing that the real truth is determined by the human mind and when we realize that our truth is subjective and allow others to have their subjective truth as well, disagreements and eventually wars will cease to exist. When we have integrated this kind of acceptance, we have come pretty close to the real truth.

Through what we read as the basic truth and through what we make of facts, our way of life arises. The more conscious and nonjudgmental we look at the things, situations, and persons around us, the easier it is for us to deal with the resulting circumstances. It is very liberating not to compulsively feel the need to evaluate and judge everything. I will quote Don Miguel and Don José Ruiz again. "We don't have to die to go to heaven or hell. Heaven is all around us just like hell is all around us. Heaven is a point of view, a state of mind and so is hell."

What we create as truth in our minds decides whether we live our lives in satisfaction and happiness or in dissatisfaction and bitterness. If we at least understand that each person brings his or her own truth into the world, it's easier for us to respect those truths instead of reflexively refuting it, for we are aware that we would only react out of our own subjectivity. By realizing this, we can save ourselves at least this aspect of a self-created hell.

THE CREATION OF ONE'S OWN REALITY

You were born with an innate knowledge that you do create
your own reality. That knowledge is so basic within you that
when someone attempts to thwart your own creation, you
feel an immediate discord within yourself. Still, within you
today lives the knowledge that you are the creator of your
own life experience, that absolute freedom exists as the basis
of your true experience, and that ultimately the creation
of your life experience is absolutely and only up to you.
– Abraham – Esther and Jerry Hicks

Abraham puts it very clear. Each man lives in his own reality.
The decisive factors are different opinions, points of view, ways
of thinking, experiences, and preferences. As we are all individual
beings with unique qualities and as we all have come to earth with
completely different motivations on what we want to experience,
there are as many realities as human beings.

We are here to self-actualize ourselves and to experience what
we can only experience in physical bodies. However, this does not
change the fact that we have creative powers and that we ultimately
are these creative powers. That's what we all have in common.
When we entered these physical bodies, we have forgotten our
divine abilities. We can manifest anything we wish through the
energy of our emotions and preceding thoughts. "The world is how
we see it," a song says. That's exactly how it is. Our convictions arise
from what we feel is real. If someone is convinced that the world is
sad, dark, unfair, and dangerous, it will reflect just these qualities
to this individual person. He or she will basically only search for
these aspects, and the person will plentifully find them to confirm
that things are really how he or she sees them.

There is, however, also a different possibility in seeing the
world, namely as a gift, as a chance, as friendly, as filled with many
little and big daily miracles and filled with helpful and open hearted

people. We can feel surrounded with love. That's how the world will then be for us. Everything presents itself as how we want to see it all. Consequently we experience our individually created reality. This is the law of attraction. We create ourselves and our environment through our own perspective.

In a statement Abraham shares the following information with us: "It will not satisfy you when you allow others to try to create your reality for you. In reality, it is indeed absolutely impossible that others create your reality." (This quotation has been retranslated from German into English, as we could not find the original. The German version is as follows: "Es wird euch nicht befriedigen, wenn ihr zulasst, dass andere die Realität für euch zu erschaffen versuchen. Tatsächlich ist es sogar völlig unmöglich, dass andere eure Realität erschaffen.")

It is not possible that others create our reality. Often this impression arises because we let others dominate us, we see ourselves as victims, or we consider certain circumstances as punishment. This is never the case. It is entirely in our individual hands what we want to experience, what we make of our experience, and how we deal with the results. When we think of tolerance, we feel tolerance, and then we are tolerant and receive tolerance. When we think of jealousy, we feel jealousy. Then we are jealous, and we will experience jealousy from the outside. We get what we emit. We create our reality according to our conception of reality. Accordingly, we receive what corresponds to the vibrations we emit. Our world is just like we see it in every detail.

If a person's perspective does not correspond to our own,
we should not condemn it and call it wrong, but instead
thankfully make use of it in order to expand our own focus.

This is what I mean with my own quote in the previous sentence: As long as we erroneously believe that our reality is the only one, it is hard for us to accept that other people experience a completely different reality. This is most evident in different culture groups, but with the knowledge that people have their own points of view exactly corresponding to their vibrational rates, it should be easier for us to respect their reality just like we want others to respect ours. With this tolerance toward ourselves and others, we are automatically more open to see certain situations, persons, or ourselves through another person's eyes. We are therefore neutral in our perspective and give ourselves the chance to learn a lot. These other points of view can help us find new approaches to solving problems and a different or/and expanded view.

Through our own point of view (consequently our actions), each of us is responsible for the kind of people and circumstances we let into our lives. Many people may dislike this statement, and others may indignantly shout that they never wanted to have this person or that occurrence in their lives and that they were not able to help that this or that happened. Unfortunately I must say that it was indeed their own fault. The responsibility for what happens to somebody always lies within them individually. Their viewpoints together with the corresponding thoughts and emotions attracted what those people focused their attention on. If we dislike our current reality, we are able to simply change it. We are free to see in our environment what we want to see just like we may ignore what we do *not* want to see. When we are sitting at the doctor's and have to wait, then we should not be annoyed and think, *Now again I have to wait so long. It will certainly take even longer than the last time, and I will come back home late. And then I have no time any more to get this and that accomplished. Everything is going to be hectic again. Blah, blah, blah.* One already feels stressed before there is even the slightest reason for it, and then one emits nothing but stress and negative expectations and so an increasing aggressiveness. Alternatively we can also make use of this waiting time. We can read a book, meditate, visualize beautiful things, or just be happy about this compulsory break. Hence, we automatically have a positive charisma. We are relaxed and in a good mood.

As soon as we change our point of view, the corresponding thoughts and emotions change as well. Circumstances will change. New people will enter our lives. Others will leave, and still others will approach us differently. All this happens because of the vibrations we emit. The precondition is opening. It is the openness for other viewpoints. It is the openness for the truth that our reality is not the only one and that we can learn a lot from others' realities and their perspectives.

We are the creators of our own experience of life, and we have the power to create everything we want to experience. "As Within, So Without." What we develop within us will appear in the outside world. If we want the world to be colorful, joyful, and bright, we first have to look in that direction and see the bright and the beautiful in everything we encounter. There is something bright and beautiful hidden in every situation and person, and we can see it if we want to. We are the creators of our reality—each of us individually.

> Be the change you wish to see in the world.
> – Mahatma Gandhi

You yourself are colorful to no end. Everything you are supposed to become, to achieve, or to experience already lies within you. Allow your uniqueness to be spread all over the world. Be the person you feel you are and let your brightly shining light illuminate every corner in this universe and everybody's heart. Don't be afraid of the opinion of others. Others' opinions of you are none of your business. Don't doubt the burning fire inside of you. It is there because it is meant to become a part of this world and an extended expression of your divine nature. This fire is patiently waiting till you let go of the belief that you *must not* or *cannot* and let it flow through you to the outside world to share your gift and passion with others.

Heal yourself and you heal the world.

CONNECTION WITH THE INNER LIGHT

To be within the inner light means to be connected with the Higher Self and with the Source. The Source is nothing else but the universe or God. It doesn't matter what one may call it. Out of this oneness, everything can be accomplished. Through connection with the Source, everything will always be for the benefit of the individual and his or her surroundings because everything happens in harmony with the universal laws.

There are many different ways to become aware of our True Selves so that the associated consciousness is then perceived as the connection with our Source. It happens when the stream of thoughts stop and the heart opens up. Mostly it happens unconsciously and without us recognizing it as a connection with God. It can happen through a traumatic experience but also through an unexpected and positive occurrence. Very often it may also happen in a moment of stillness and relaxation. It can come from the observation of a sunset, a relaxed moment in a deck chair, or a time on the couch in front of a burning candle. It can happen through listening to special music or profound words. Or it can happen by realizing that a dream has come true.

Very often we feel it around Christmastime. Hence, I like calling it the Christmas feeling. During that time of the year different vibrations dominate, which makes it easier for us to open our hearts. We are more approachable, more cooperative. We have a natural joy of giving and sense a feeling of warmth and an emotional kind of love. Those who have already experienced this will immediately recall this feeling, for it is absolutely wonderful and one would always love to have it.

To not only be able to *consciously* recognize this condition but also to be able to *consciously* precipitate it, we must *become aware* of some cornerstones that we have put into a drawer and forgotten. The magic word is *consciousness*.

LIVING IN THE HERE AND NOW

One of the most common causes why we develop fears, self-doubts, and blockages is that we either cling to things that have happened in the past or long for something in the future. The only bad part is this: The past is over, and we will never reach the future because it is the future. Real life happens in the present and only in the present. Every moment we experience is in the here and now. Neither can we experience a yesterday or a tomorrow but only the present moment. We must make use of the present moment, as within it lies the possibility to create something or to get something started that will become the present moment at a later time.

PAST AND FUTURE

The reason why we cannot or do not want to concentrate on the current moment is often that with our thoughts we cling to something in the past. That can be episodes on which we contemplate with wistfulness, or others which pursue us, for they have changed our lives. Sometimes these feelings come from actions in the past from people we are unable to forgive, and sometimes we think that we have made a big mistake. Whatever the reason for looking back may be, it prevents us from what we could change or make better today. As long as we are stuck in the past with thoughts and emotions that cannot be changed anymore, the moment when we are really able to change something passes unnoticed.

When we understand that the past is simply over, then we will begin to see it in a different light. There was a time when the past had been the present. In that present we had experiences. It is essential that we integrate these experiences in our lives in order to profit from them in the here and now and to initiate something for an experience in the future here and now.

We are often afraid of the future. We are afraid of things that may (possibly) come and that cause in us an unpleasant feeling. Whatever it may be, it is the future. What is in the future does not exist in the here and now. So why should we wreck the present moment or let it pass while all our focus is on the future? Sometimes we have fearful or simply negative expectations toward bad news, lectures that we have to give, job interviews, an upcoming discussion, an examination, or whatever. But why are we afraid at all? Why do we focus on the negative? As we cannot really know how something is going to be, it can just as well turn out very positive.

With three children, most afternoons are extremely crowded. One has a music lesson. The other has to go to his therapy. The third has his sport program, and maybe a birthday party or an appointment at the dentist's comes up at short notice. Mostly everything accumulates in one single afternoon when school is over, of course often accompanied by some other things which join on short-notice. The smooth execution of all these tasks is a logistic master stroke for one single person who is not able to bi-locate. In earlier years I seemed to enter a state of crisis days before when I just looked into my calendar. I was edgy and nervous. I could not get anything done and got on everybody's nerves. I always kept thinking about how exhausting and stressful everything was going to be! Of course, that's how it eventually was. When this afternoon in question finally came, I was already completely worn out. Instead of completing what I was just doing with calmness,

I was always three steps ahead. In the end, however, everything always turned out well. But because of my attitude, I felt wiped out in the evening. Through the stress that I generated myself by visualizing how hectic everything was going to be, I wasted a lot of energy. Retrospectively I thought every time, *Why did you put yourself down before? It was totally unnecessary.*

Today I enjoy taking the children from place to place. I insert a CD with hot music, and away we go. Even when time is almost running out, I don't get stressed anymore. The children know that they may have to wait for a little while when time is getting short. That's the way it is—step-by-step! It is all going to work out— one step after the other. Since I think like that, very interesting things happen. Sometimes something was suddenly cancelled or postponed, or surprisingly the mother of one of my children's school friends would give my child a lift because he or she had the same destination. The knot was untied as if by magic.

In this context, the example is fitting because I used to panic when one of my children got sick. If I had stayed in the here and now, only the moment would have counted. I could have focused my attention fully on the situation instead of panicking and worrying about how difficult it could become. I was frightened of an imaginary future in my head.

Why do we drive ourselves crazy with something that could happen in the future? All we can do is to prepare ourselves as well as we can and wait until the moment comes—if it comes at all.

If you are once again afraid of an incident that might happen in the future or if something that happened in the past still burdens you, then make yourself aware that neither the future nor the past exists. And if there is anything that you are able to do in order to have a positive influence on possible occurrences in the future, then do it now, for you can only do it in the here and now. You cannot do anything yesterday or tomorrow because when tomorrow is there, it is again a new here and now. It is always here and now.

WE DON'T GO THROUGH TIME. TIME PASSES US BY.

We are not heading toward the future. The future always remains the future. We ourselves are always and solely in the present. We always stay how and where we are. We are not moving toward the things. The things are heading toward us. What we call the future is heading toward us by becoming the present moment. And what we call the past was once the present. We are! We were! We always will be! We can sit there all day long and do nothing, and time passes by itself. The evening is heading toward us without us heading toward it. We don't move toward the things, but the things move toward us. We ourselves are in the center of the action in the flow of life. While time passes by supplying us with encounters and realizations, we always stay the same. We exist in the present only, and in the present it is essential to act so that we maintain a present we feel at ease in.

A happy life is just a string of happy moments.
But most don't allow the happy moment, because
they're so busy trying to get a happy life.
–Abraham - Esther and Jerry Hicks

Every single moment in life brought us to the point where we are today. Every single moment was important—every single one! Life consists of sequences of moments. If only one of these moments had been different, maybe we would not wear exactly this piece of clothing or would not have this state of consciousness, this profession, this house, etc. Every moment that continually approaches us brings us someday to the point we wanted to reach in this life. Every single moment! A moment, however, cannot be captured and stored. It comes, and right away it is history. It is impossible to cling to the here and now. All we can do is dwell in the present state of being and to consciously perceive the episodes of life and how they are passing us by like a film.

Such episodes arise from every moment. They can be a very moving and touching ones, or they can be almost unperceived ones. Nevertheless they approached us specifically. Every moment of calmness is an episode as well and can be a very important one, for it helps us to come back to our senses. Mostly, however, we underestimate the effect of such a calm moment because it *moves* us less than the more exciting ones that may put us in a state of turmoil. It is the calm moments that lead us back to the core. In those moments we can file the documents of life into their corresponding folders.

Silence

Only in silence our mind is getting clear.
The clearer our minds, the smaller our fear.

In conquering fears we are progressing our lives.
Satisfaction and love are about to arise.

With love as the base a new power is felt,
a power with which everything can be dealt.

So go into silence, drift into your light,
and feel your true power as the source of all might.

—*Erika Kind*

Every moment is a precious gift. Hence, we should consciously witness each moment with open eyes. They are not matters of course but treasures that enrich our lives in every instant.

Awareness

Live everyday as if it was your first and your last at the same time!
– Source unknown

There is a magic word with which we can enter our inner light within one moment. The word is *awareness*. To act and perceive with awareness transfers us to the status of unity. As soon as we are conscious, we hear, see, and feel more intensely. We perceive more aspects of what surrounds us. Children live in the here and now by nature. They don't worry about yesterday or tomorrow. There is only the here and now. And children discover while they are in the here and now and are not detracted from thinking of the past and also thinking of possible future happenings. That means that we mostly think of illusionary occurrences. Hence, the current moment with all that it includes simply passes us by. If we pause and only care about what is happening right now, we perceive everything with all our senses. We do what is important in this moment and only what can be done now. If we do it with awareness, we do it with all our passion and give priority and our full attention to the current project. We connect ourselves with what we do, and we do it in accordance with the current moment. As soon as we are attentive and awake, we are conscious as well. As soon as we are conscious, we are in the here and now.

Anyone who has children themselves or who has much to do with them can tell you a thing or two about them. With children at our sides, we discover the world with open minds. A kid examines every pebble from all sides and can follow an ant along its path for hours. Let's think of the first snow, flowers along the footpath, wind, rain, sand, or water. Let's do it like the children and let's walk through our lives with the same open eyes and ears. Let's discover everything new just as if we saw, smelled, tasted, and sensed it for the very first time. Through consciously experiencing everything with all our senses, we see our world and ourselves in a new way. We recognize the wide variety of miracles that surround us and really begin to see our world through the eyes of a child who respectfully gazes at everything from all sides. Through this kind of awareness we see more, and we perceive more intensely what we see, which makes us see even more.

By opening ourselves through consciously perceiving our world, we consequently perceive ourselves in a new way as well. Now an expedition into our own inner world begins.

ACCEPT AND LET GO

One of the biggest problems most people have is the ability to accept and to let go of things, occurrences, happenings, and people. The main reason why we have problems with the acceptance of what is mostly lies in the concept that we must have everything under control. However, this is impossible. As precise as an agenda may be, nevertheless, somebody may fall ill, or a train may be late. Then nothing fits anymore. It does not make sense either to believe that control gives security. If we suddenly realize that there are certain things that we really cannot control, we easily lose our footing. This is one of the main reasons for the development of fears and nervousness.

When we get into a traffic jam, we often keep looking at the clock, become more and more nervous, and talk ourselves into a rage because actually we wanted to be entirely somewhere else. Or we intended to give a garden party. And what happens? The forecast says it is going to rain cats and dogs. Many people complain about the bad weather at every opportunity and get completely caught up in their negativity.

Does this make sense? No matter how much one is normally affected by such a behavior, objectively seen, everybody should be able to admit that lamenting and complaining does not change anything. The traffic jam will not dissolve faster, and it will not stop raining earlier. We are wearing ourselves out by thinking about something that we cannot control anyway.

When we make ourselves aware of the fact that we cannot change these occurrences and we accept them the way they are, at first we get calmer and more relaxed. Then we can seek a solution. Maybe we take an alternative route and drive around the traffic jam, or we organize a tent and let the party take place just as planned. Above all, it takes pressure away from us when we stop feeling responsible for something that we should consider an act of God. Let's make the best of things that cannot be changed. Mostly new options and discoveries appear, for we are compelled to be creative and to be open to different paths.

The best thing about conscious acceptance, however, is that we remain positive no matter what happens. Perhaps we can even make use of the traffic jam and develop a special business idea to achieve a breakthrough. We have arrived at the subject of duality again now. Everything has its opposite. All that we call negative carries just as much positive in it. We just have to focus on the positive, although we might not always see it right away in any situation. We often see many positive aspects only when we look back. However, there are also occurrences that will never make sense to us because the seeming negative situation was actually a positive one for us. Let's say, for example, that you miss the bus and you have to take the next one. Hence, you are about ten minutes late. These ten minutes may have been necessary to prevent you from leaving the bus right in that moment when a truck started to skid, almost hit the bus, and caught you. You will never get to know this in detail, but the delay was your blessing. How many people had cursed on September 11, 2001, because they missed the subway and thus were late for work in the World Trade Center? They were just late enough to not be buried underneath the rubble.

Everything has a positive side without any exception! The belief in knowing that there is something positive in any situation and that nothing happens accidentally can help us to accept what is without quarrelling. Sometimes a door only closed because of the ventilation that an opening door caused. But as long as we brood about why the one door might have closed, we don't turn around to see the one that's openly waiting for us to enter. It is not that one door closes and another one opens up. To me it is the other way around. One door opens up, and only when we don't notice it, the other one closes to make us more aware of the open one. A closing door is not a punishment or a mean game God is playing with us. It simply says, "You are ready for more!"

There is a reason behind everything that happens, and this is to keep us on our path. To realize this helps us to deal better with many unpleasant situations. As we are continually confronted with things we have to learn, it makes no sense to try to get away from them or to even offer resistance. Resistance makes everything more difficult and painful. If we simply accept the things the way we experience them and move forward with ease, we stay in the flow.

Change what you can change, but accept what cannot be changed.

At this point I would like to clearly state that accepting does not mean that we have to put up with everything. Of course not! In this context, we are concerned with things that cannot be changed. It does not make sense to lament about occurrences and to talk and think oneself into bad feelings, anger, depression, or fears because that does not change anything about the situation. It could even get worse. We should surrender to unchangeable things, integrate them into our lives, and walk on. If we, however, have to deal with situations that disturb us and that are changeable, we should do it. It would be a mistake not to change anything in a situation that could be changed but to go on complaining. In other words, if we feel disturbed by circumstances that we have an influence over, we should change them. Resistance, however, against unchangeable things only causes suffering.

Dr. Wayne W. Dyer has said, "You can sit there forever; lamenting about how bad you've been, feeling guilty until you die, and not a tiny slice of that guilt will do anything to change a single thing in the past."

It is the same with guilt feelings. Every one of us has already done (or not done) something that we regret but cannot be changed anymore. This simply teaches us that we should learn from the situation in question but not bury ourselves in guilty feelings or wallow in self-pity. What happened happened and cannot be reversed anymore. Spoken words cannot be taken back or deleted. We can apologize, learn from them, and make the situation better the next time. Self-generated guilty feelings, however, can't help anybody. They only lower our vibrations, make us weak or even sick, and therefore emit signals that can have a negative aftereffect.

WHY?

There is not one single human being on this world that has not searched for explanations sometime in their lives. *Why did I have to lose my job? Why did I have to come across this person? Why do I have a sick child? Why did my big love leave me? Why did this person have to die so early? Why always me? Why? Why? Why?*

It is in the very nature of our minds to look for connections in order to understand what happens. If we understand why this or that situation occurred, we can live in peace or at least begin to reconcile with it. Often, however, there are simply no explanations the mind can grab, and we might not find answers for the question of why. There are reasons for that.

- With knowing too much, we could block our own path of development because we would hinder ourselves in pursuing it intuitively. We would anticipate the punch line. Before our birth we determined how we wanted to experience ourselves and what we wanted to experience. Hence, certain circumstances are given to us so that we can go through these experiences. Sometimes there are a couple of signposts on the path that lead to a certain experience. In order to gain self-consciousness, for example, we may get a very dominant, tyrannical husband or wife at our side. Through their presence in someone's life, they experience such a pressure that perhaps becomes so strong that they eventually learn to stand up for themselves. Who knows? Maybe they are getting divorced. The divorce may even be pretty dirty. Maybe they have hardly enough to sustain their lives. The question after the why may arise again and again. Why does this always happen to me? Why don't I get a reasonably well-paid job now? It would be too early if at this point the answer already came. "It all happened for you to develop self-confidence and strength because you will be able to live on your own." If it was clear that the man or woman of your dreams is already waiting for you—someone who pampers you and who loves you from the bottom of his or her heart—then the pressure would have never been big enough for you to step up and build up self-confidence. We can have these kinds of realizations only when the situations really lie behind us because otherwise this knowledge would block our development. We would not keep on following that path and would miss the deep knowledge that is only brought by the personal experience.

- Another reason why we might not get an answer to the why is that we simply would not understand it. We only receive the sort of answers that we are able to comprehend and put into action. Even if we received an answer to our questions, we would not be satisfied because at this very moment we could not grasp it. What happens does not always happen for our own advancement in the first place but for that of another person. We should not forget that we are all one and connected with one another. Every incarnated soul is connected with all other souls, and every action, every thought, and every word of a person makes waves. Our life paths constantly cross and are interwoven with one another so that we support one another in our development. Everything is subject to an unbelievably gigantic organization. It is really impossible to always understand every detail. Each is merely a part of the numerous wheels in the big whole. It is enough to trust that before this incarnation we precisely knew what we wanted to experience in this life and that everything we experience was chosen out of our own free will. Nothing happens coincidently. Absolutely nothing!

We are conditioned to think that we must understand the "sense behind" or the "reason for" everything. Nobody, however, has an answer to everything at hand. Even people who seem to have an explanation for everything often don't do anything else but mentally construct a possible answer in order to cope with the situation. By doing so, they nourish their own reality but not always to their own advantage. A dogged search for answers does not make a situation easier. If we cannot find an explanation, desperation and frustration seems to get bigger. Maybe we understand all connections someday, maybe not. We will not understand them better or faster by allowing our thoughts to circle around them all the time. The contrary is the case. If we are so focused on a certain direction, then we may overlook the direction where the solution could perhaps be found. Realizations cannot be forced. Realizations simply arise. They often arise when we have withdrawn our minds from the problem, accepted the situation the way it is, and proceeded on our way. If there is no explanation, then stop looking for it. Otherwise you wear yourself out.

It is a big relief to understand something completely different instead, namely that one simply does not have to understand everything. Maybe our environment considers this attitude complacency or even escapism because, as mentioned before, through our acquired belief structures we usually want to understand everything in order to keep life in control, but that is illusionary, of course. Our surroundings will demand things from us again and again, things that are not in accordance with our concept of reality. However, we do not have to go into that. We do not have to find explanations for circumstances we really cannot understand, and we do not even have to explain this.

If you understand, the things are the way they are.
If you don't understand, the things are the way they are.
– Zen wisdom

We can drive ourselves crazy by craving answers that we cannot comprehend yet anyway. We can simply accept the situation or circumstance because our questioning thoughts will not change it anyway. Until we maybe find an answer one day, we should accept the situation with the liberating knowledge that there is in any case a reason behind it. If a big dream bursts like a bubble in front of our eyes or if our plans lie in ruins when things have suddenly changed—although we were so sure that our previewed goal must become true—the reason behind it is that something much greater and more significant is still waiting for us. We will, however, not realize this as long as our concentration is focused on one subject that cannot be clarified at this very moment anyway. Of course, we can become passive, desperate, angry, and resigned, and we can stare at this one door that is now closed for us for the rest of our lives while we go on searching for the reasons. Alternatively we can simply turn around and see that another door has already opened for us. That will always be the case! Disappointments or broken dreams mostly point out something new and tell us that we are now ready to follow a new path. We just have to be still and turn around in order to discover the newly opened door. Nothing happens by accident or arbitrarily. There is a reason behind absolutely everything, and everything has a meaning—whether we understand it or not. With resistance and self-pity we are just treading water. When we, however, have confidence and go with the flow of life, we can pass through new gates. The less we search for the why and offer resistance against what's already there, the faster we recognize all the options and possibilities that life offers us. The most incredible and gigantic successes and developments arise from the deepest crises. Life is a big adventure filled with in numerous surprises and wonders. The art of living merely consists of *wanting* to experience them.

THE ACCEPTANCE OF THE INDIVIDUAL

Accepting not only refers to occurrences but also to other people. We often have to deal with people who vibrate at a somewhat different wavelength than we do. (By the way there are also people who dislike us too!) As mentioned, everybody has his or her own view on things. Everybody has his or her tasks, and everybody has been shaped by past experiences. We can never exactly know why people behave the way they do, and therefore, we should refrain from judging and criticizing them. Don't we wish that they also do not judge us? Simply let the others be. When someone encounters us unpleasantly, it is important to be aware of the fact that we don't have to take it personally. Often it is their own frustration or their fears and sorrows or simply their unconsciousness. Sometimes it seems to be easier to accuse others of what in reality is our own responsibility. Therefore, we must not assimilate insulting statements from others. What happens is that somebody tries to transfer his or her anger onto us to feel better about him or herself, but that never works. Additionally it may be that we somehow reflect the other person. That means that our counterpart discovers behavior patterns or whatever in us that he or she does not like very much in him or herself. Or the person is disturbed by aspects that he or she would like to have. Instead of realizing that, the other person tries to correct us. So be aware of that and don't necessarily take everything that is offered to you when it causes bad feelings inside of you. Bad feelings are a sign that what the other person offers is not in harmony with your True Self and therefore nothing you need.

But be careful. Of course it also happens the other way around. It is not always only the others. Our own unconsciousness causes us to play along in the same way. Hence, we should be even more tolerant as we experience ourselves through others as well. We mirror one another, those parts of our personalities that need to be improved in ourselves. So we should not react insulted or even angry but instead have understanding for the ones who have just discovered what they still have to work on within themselves.

Take the people how they are. Don't try to change them, for you cannot change them anyway, and it's not your right either. It is not our task to decide how another person has to be. We do neither know the other person's history or that individual's life plan. Furthermore, it is possible that the other person even has to face us just the way he or she does so that we learn something from this encounter.

We cannot change another human being, but we can wear ourselves out with trying to do so. We cannot control other people's behavior, but we can learn to control our own behavior as well as our attitudes and our thoughts. Like I explained in the chapter titled "The Evaluation of Subjective Reality," everybody creates his or her own reality and therefore sees the things through his or her own eyes. Although we may see and hear the same things, everyone perceives them individually. That's often a reason for misunderstandings but has nothing to do with mean intentions. What happened is that we approach the situation or thing from different angles and therefore see them from a different perspective. In reality, we can profit very much from this if we also try to see the things through the eyes of the other person. Conscious acceptance and the ability to give in then prove to be inner strength and provide true greatness. If we treat others the way we wish to be treated, they will return the favor.

ACCEPTANCE OF RESPONSIBILITY

Acceptance also means to accept the consequences of our decisions. If you made a decision, you acted out of the momentary situation. In this momentary situation the decision was right. Trust your inner feeling. As soon as you have decided something, accept the responsibility for it. You cannot blame another person, and you don't have to justify yourself either. Stand up for it without quarrelling. If you have already made a certain decision, don't ask yourself in retrospect if a different decision would maybe have been better. What's decided is decided. Now move forward! If circumstances change, maybe a new decision needs to be made. That does not mean that the other one was wrong. Thus, stand up for your decision—no matter what consequences it entails—and experience the inner strength you gain.

In order to really be able to assume responsibility for a decision, you must make it yourself. It is not enough to take over the decision that another person has made for you. Only because it may be the right one for that person, this does not necessarily have to count for you as well. You have to face the consequences for your decisions yourself.

By the way, not deciding anything is also a decision that you are also responsible for.

Making a decision means moving the circumstances. Not making a decision means being moved by the circumstances (and by the decisions of others).

BREAKING THE CHAINS

The more doggedly and tensely we hold on to something, the more we hinder natural development—whether it is a job, a promotion, a relationship that does not get off the ground, or whatever. The more we get stuck, the more we act out of our minds. Now the ego takes over and tells us, "You must get it. You must have it. You must win, and you must keep it." Therefore, we may cling even more to something whose time has not come yet. Or it is subject to change, and we do not want to accept that. Often it is also the not knowing that almost drives us to despair because we want to achieve a certain result so badly and think that nothing makes sense anymore if it does not occur the way we want it. In such situations, we are confined to a circumstance or a person, and it seems as if we cannot free ourselves from it, although we are aware of the heavy load that this attachment brings along. Even if we know that we should free ourselves from it and want it too, we do not know how.

Chains can be a symbol for dependency. A chained dog will go on trying to break away. Another dog that is not chained, however, lies peacefully beside his doghouse. The more imprisoned and boxed in we feel, the more intensely we try to break free of it. Now I would like to relate an example from my own life. At the young age of twenty-three, I married my puppy love. I can still claim today that I have a very tolerant and existence-conscious husband. Nevertheless, I felt dependent on his approval, his opinion, and his support when it came to external attacks. Yes, that's right. I *felt* dependent. In fact, he gave me my total personal freedom. Whether I wanted to do some training or if I wanted to go out with friends, he would let me do everything. However, because of my insecurities, fears, and old thought patterns, I would not allow myself to live out my own wishes with happiness and a good conscience. The tricky part in this was that I did not even notice it. I constantly tried to make it plain to my husband that I wished he would behave differently toward me. He did not do that. The more I became obsessed by the idea of what he did wrong instead of realizing that I made myself dependent on his attitude, the more dependent and desperate I felt. Throughout the years, however, I began working on myself and clearing out my internal thoughts. I learned to believe in myself and noticed the growth of my inner strength and self-confidence. Suddenly I realized the dependency in which I had maneuvered myself. It felt as if there was a chain tensely wrapped around me that would sometimes hardly let me breathe. Slowly I veered away from my husband who all of a sudden started to a new view of me according to my inner change. (The explanation for this lies in the principle of duality. A natural balance automatically took place.) I pulled at the chain, and after an especially insightful weekend, this chain was so tight that I could not bear it any longer. I asked my husband for the separation. Twenty-four hours later we decided to allow ourselves a reflection period of five days. After the expiration of these five days I gave the go-ahead for a new beginning. What had happened in this short period?

After I had asked my husband for the definite separation, the chain broke. I had made the step to free myself from the dependency, although I had no idea what would happen now and how everything would go on. The liberation and the step into the unknown were suddenly so much more important than the safe place I was used to and remaining chained in continuation of the same old story. So when I broke the chain, I immediately felt my freedom. I realized that it was me who had brought herself into a feeling of dependency, and I realized that it was me who had freed herself from that feeling. I also felt that that period in my life was finished. An unprecedented sense of freedom pervaded me. In fact, I was not even able to be dependent anymore. If these heavy words, "I want us to separate," would not have passed my lips, things wouldn't have changed. When I realized that and felt the strength to exist on my own, I saw my husband, myself, and the whole situation in a new light. Yes, throughout the last years I had changed, and I also had different ideas of living together than years before because now I felt independent. Thus, the foundation was laid for a new beginning of our relationship.

The whole situation had to come this far because then I was in a position to break the chains that I had put around myself. After this escalation I was able to return to my marriage without problems, but now I was an independent, free individual.

This occurrence did not only cause my liberation from

dependency. Through breaking the chains I was also able to see myself. Hence, this example will be beneficial in one of the following chapters again.

LETTING GO

This section deals with dogged attachment as well. In this case, however, we look at the attachment to something we don't want to let go of or the convulsive pursuing of an idea. I will again use an episode from my life to illustrate this. I always knew that I wanted to be a young mother, whereby *young* is a relative term, of course. As I was married at a pretty young age, I wanted to have children as fast as possible. Month for month I had obsessively been waiting for my menstrual cycle *not* to come. However, time went by, and I did not become pregnant. The more dogged I became, the more disappointed I was every time. Then my colleague seriously fell ill and was not able to work for one month. I already had had a lot of pressure at work, but now it was even getting harder for me. I only functioned and was afraid of the next day. Four weeks later she came back to work. I felt very happy, relieved, and freed. During that time I made the promise to myself that I would give myself time. If I didn't become pregnant, then fine. I just let go of this compulsion, and in exchange I received a feeling of freedom. Lo and behold, two weeks later I was pregnant.

The same holds true for the attachment to the past. Draw the lesson from what happened in the past and make use of the knowledge for your further life. Gone is gone and will never come back. Clinging to past occurrences prevents us from unfolding in the here and now. We are attached to things that do not exist anymore. While we focus our attention on a world that does not exist, the real reality passes us by. Clinging to things, occurrences, or relationships from the past is like hanging on a line. We cannot take a step forward. We are blocked and are unable to realize what we really want or ought to get accomplished. When we become aware of our attachment and notice the connected restrictions and hindrances, we are eventually able to accept the situation or person with our hearts and to let it go at the same time.

Dr. Wayne W. Dyer states, "What's over is over. You did what you knew how to do. It wasn't right or wrong or good or bad. It just was. But all you've got is today. You can't have it back."

We must understand that all past occurrences—no matter how strenuous they were—lead us to the point where we are today. Everything is subject to a divine order in which we develop. In retrospect we can understand much of it. Without the lessons we have learned from the unpleasant and the pleasant situations in our life, we would not be what and where we are today. The deep realization of this enables us to take all persons and circumstances through which we experienced pain in our hearts instead of struggling with what happened. It happened. It helped us, and it is over. When we have realized this, future occurrences that may be difficult will not turn out to be burdens for us anymore.

Letting go of illusions or past occurrences goes along with the acceptance of what really is at this very moment. By accepting what is, we become grateful for what we already have. Now we are also grateful for what happened to us. Gratitude promotes feelings of luck. When we are grateful, we feel happiness, and through these positive vibrations we pull new positive things into our lives. We will not cling to certain things, situations, or people anymore because if we did so, we would block the free flow again.

We all have dreams and wishes because they are parts of our lives, and we want to realize them. Sometimes, however, we get impatient. We think that we must determine the way to the realization of our intentions ourselves, and the more we wish for something, the faster, in our opinion, it has to become true.

The good news is that we should definitely follow our dreams, but we must know that we cannot determine how and when they can be manifested. If something does not work out, it is because the time is not right for it yet, because the conditions are not fitting yet, because our thoughts have not been in accordance with our goal, or because we still have to take one or more intermediate steps before we are ready. The magic word is *faith*. Have faith that everything is being organized at your very best and that everything will come as soon as the conditions are right and when the right time has come.

Tao Te Ching has said, "True mastery can be gained by letting things go their own way. It can't be gained by interfering."

Hence, don't interfere. Let the universe determine the way, as it can much better evaluate how and when something shall happen. If you commit yourself to only one way, you are blocking all the other hundred ways that might bring you to your target.

As soon as you are able to have faith, you can let go. After you have really let go out of the depths of your inner self, you are free, and something new can enter your life. One must often let go of old stuff in order to make room for something new. In order to gain new insights, old patterns of thinking and behavior must first leave. Just keep your eyes and ears open, perceive the signposts, and follow them. Consider every movement, every breath, every conversation, and every encounter as another step toward your goal. Through the learning process of letting go, you may have matured to the point so that your wish becomes true, for you then open up yourself and go with the flow of life again.

THE RIGHT MOMENT

Some things you're not letting happen right now because the
timing isn't perfect for you. Some you're not letting happen
because you are very aware of where you are. But all things,
as they are happening, are happening in perfect order. And
if you will relax and begin saying, 'Everything in its perfect
time. Everything is unfolding. And I'm enjoying where I am
now, in relationship to where I'm going. Content where I am,
and eager for more', that is the perfect vibrational stance.
– Abraham – Esther and Jerry Hicks

It is important to be able to wait for the right moment. Some things need more time than others. Some things, however, seem to be within reach, but somehow they do not really seem to arrive. It is very important to remain patient and not to start clinging or doubting and not to block our own way by building new obstacles again. Go with the flow of life! Everything that is supposed to come will come. It is supposed to come because you feel this burning inside of you, which is nothing but a reminder of your True Self. Your True Self knows what you intended to accomplish while you are in this incarnation. It knows your purpose and keeps whispering. Following this tender but pushing voice leads you on your path of life. And everything you feel as an inner call is part of this path— whether it is rationally explainable or not. You can precisely feel what this is going to be. The only thing that can block the flow and realization are feelings of doubt and fear. They are like a door you shut in front of yourself. What is behind the door is still there but cannot get to you. So don't worry. Your dreams are meant to become true. Follow that path, and your True Self will be revealed step-by-step. Let your inner being unfold to its highest fulfillment. The time when your dreams finally become true depends on your maturity and on the circumstances that are in accordance with the whole. Both aspects cannot be determined by you. If the fulfillment came too early, the manifestation would be doomed to failure. You would overlook the corresponding signposts, and you would not be able to understand them in order to act accordingly. Even if you were able to deal with the signs, you would still be overstretched with the realization of the wish, or the people who have to be involved would not be present yet.

Additionally there are factors that are simply beyond our knowledge. Don't try to force anything into being, for if you put all your energy into something that simply does not want to work out at the moment, even if you may already have reached your rudimentary goal, it will finally result in a disappointment. If your dream has not come true yet, don't worry. It is for your very best because the time is not right yet and further preparations are required. One thing, however, is sure. When the time is right, your dreams will come true. But only then! So remain patient. In patience you are in harmony and peace with yourself. In peace and faith no doubts can occur and hinder any manifestation since you leave the door open and let everything flow directly to you in its perfect order and time. Simply feel the anticipation for what is going to be, and you support the outcome! Consider the following from Lao-tzu:

To know harmony is to know the changeless;
to know the changeless is to have insight.
Things in harmony with the Tao remain;
things that are forced grow for a while, and then wither away.
This is not the Tao.
And whatever is against the Tao soon ceases to be.

Just as it is with the arrival of our cosmic orders, it is the same with the understanding of connections. We always only receive the information we are able to accept. Everything that exceeds our level of understanding dies out and remains unheard. Often we watch films or read books again that we had already watched or read before. It is not unusual that all of a sudden we gain insights we did not have before. It may also happen that occurrences we have been unable to categorize straighten out in combination with other realizations. It often occurred to me that I started reading a book and put it aside because of a lack of time or interest. When weeks or months later I took it in my hands again, I sometimes found explanations for things and occurrences with which I had just been confronted. If I had finished reading the book in a disciplined way beforehand, I would never have realized the meaning.

We communicate with you on many levels of your consciousness simultaneously. However, you only receive what you are

ready to receive. So you will not be able to draw everything that you need from this material, but always when you pick it up again and read it, it will help you to gain new insights"
– Abraham – Esther and Jerry Hicks.

(This quotation has been retranslated from German into English, as we could not find the original. The German version is as follows: *"Wir kommunizieren gleichzeitig auf vielen Ebenen eures Bewusstseins mit euch. Doch empfangen werdet ihr davon nur jenes, wofür ihr aufnahmebereit seid. Ihr werdet also nicht alle das Gleiche aus diesem Material ziehen, aber immer wenn ihr es wieder zur Hand nehmt und darin lest, wird es euch zu neuen Einsichten verhelfen."*)

There is something that you can do to make your dreams take shape easier and faster. You can have faith and belief. As I mentioned before, when your faith is firm and your heart is full of joy, you are able to make one step after the next because you trust that everything you do brings you closer to the fulfillment of your dreams, and you become more mature every day. Perhaps you learn on a different level from a lot of trivial things that help you get closer to your big goal—those trivial things that you would not normally even associate with the realization of your dreams. Has this not already happened to you too? You think and work in a certain direction, and after a short time you notice that it is not really what you had in mind. Simultaneously, however, you realize what you really want to focus your energy on. That was the case with me and this book. In the beginning I started to write about a completely different subject. It was a story about my life. Later when I contemplated what I had written, I suddenly noticed that it only dealt with a small detail. Everything circled around that which I had denied myself through my insecurities, negative thought patterns, and fears and how I started to perceive myself and to understand who I was and what I wanted. This detour was very important for me to discover the real subject of this book.

RESISTANCE

All of us already had to face situations or persons that meant great agony for us. We also experienced the dissolution of plans, which almost already had been realized. (That happens mostly with things over which we have no control.) Experiences like that can cause states of helplessness and impotent anger. The despair is always great when dreams seem to fall apart.

It is not so easy to accept a circumstance that shocks us and seems to hold us in its iron claws. Struggling against something we cannot change, no matter how much we want to have it otherwise, only enhances suffering and pain. With this attitude, one becomes deeply entrenched in the situation, and so it gets even more and more difficult to break free from the complementary psychic and physical symptoms. Often it is a long way to go until we are able to openly accept a certain condition or person. However, acceptance is the only way to free ourselves from the iron claw of despair. Throughout the course of our lives, we can always be confronted with these kinds of situations again. When we understand that everything happens because of its compliance with the universal order, we will be able to deal with it much better. If we, however, refuse to accept this truth and go on fighting against windmills, we will live our lives in captivity as prisoners of ourselves. A fight against an unchangeable condition can never be won.

In this context I would like to remind us of the already mentioned Zen wisdom again. "If you understand, the things are the way they are. If you don't understand, the things are the way they are."

To offer resistance, an enormous amount of energy needs to be invested. Acceptance, however, gives us energy and inner peace. Acceptance equals oneness with what is. Resistance strains our nerves and our health in general. Acceptance strengthens us. Resistance causes frustration, for one keeps running into a wall instead of making a step forward. By going with the flow of life, however, we feel the freedom of *not having to fight against* anything but of investing our energies *on behalf of* our true goals.

Slowly I was able to accept those persons who made my life difficult during the very unstable period of my life. I understood that through my resistance I only stirred up the disharmony between us. When I started to accept that these persons simply were the way they were, that I was unable to change them, and that changing them was not my business anyway, I was able to draw the most unbelievable lessons from their behavior. I was able to just let them be. By changing my own attitude, I pulled out the negative energy from those relationships, and hence, they became more peaceful and harmonic.

This does not mean that I allow others to force something on me. I just do not consider their behavior as personal attacks anymore but instead as parts of their development and as a form of assistance. Whenever I feel resistance to something, I realize this points to an aspect within me that is not in order. If everything was in order, I would not perceive resistance.

RESIGNATION

Accepting and letting go has nothing to do with resignation. Here we are talking about absolute conscious acceptance. Resignation means to give up, to act against one's own will. It means to do something that in reality one does not want to do, or it can mean not doing something that in reality one wants to do. One acts against one's own conviction. This attitude causes many of our fears and frustrations because we feel completely helpless. Involuntarily we leave the responsibility for ourselves to somebody else—somebody we do not even want to give control to. We accept the ultimate role of a victim and leave the design of our own lives partially to others.

Accepting, however, is the conscious decision to let situations and people be the way they present themselves, to integrate them into one's own life, and to proceed. It also means to only identify with what one truly wants to identify with. Sometimes it seems to be impossible for us to accept certain things, even though in our heads we know that there is nothing to change anyway. Deep within us, however, we struggle against accepting the unwanted situation with all our might. Don't judge yourself for it. In this case, accept at least the fact that you cannot accept the situation at the moment. This attitude alone can be an enormous relief. Anyway, be aware that the problem is only postponed. Through accepting, we become more relaxed and more patient. When you consciously accept what is, you express the gratitude for your own ability to have faith and for your understanding that everything that happens has been sent to you with love and that it is sent to you only because it helps you to follow the path that you have chosen for this incarnation. Send love and gratitude to every person, every relationship, and every occurrence, and you will achieve growth. Perhaps that is exactly what you have to learn from it—to accept without judgment.

It is most important to be able to let go before you are able to accept. When you are ready to let go of past or nonexistent things, to simply look at things the way they are without evaluating them, to no longer doubt your own decisions, to faithfully await the right moment, and to stop offering resistance against things that cannot be changed, you will eventually realize what true acceptance means.

Letting go of what is not real means accepting what is!

MEDITATION

> The light of the stars is only reflected in calm waters.
> – Tibetan wisdom

Meditation is one of the best ways to return to oneself and to feel inner peace. Through stillness and the silence of the stream of your thoughts, you get back to the essence. It takes some practice, especially if you are a more nervous type who cannot sit still for a long time. But the time you spend in bringing stillness to your thoughts—even if it is only five minutes per day—is a very good investment. More serenity and calmness will enter your life, and that has an effect on your surroundings too. They will be inspired by you, and you will automatically draw clarity, peace, and serenity into your life, for everything you emit returns to you.

The purpose of meditation is to stop our stream of thinking. By meditating, we leave the world of hectic life, sorrows, and problems behind us for a little while. We dive into a world of calmness and peace. By bringing stillness into our thoughts, we step back from the things that burden us. We detach ourselves from what is not part of us and at the same time realize that important point. By clarifying our thoughts, insights, new clarity, and solutions to our life situations may arise. With meditation we recharge our batteries. We gain new strength and resilience. The more we meditate, the more mental and emotional calmness flows into our daily lives. It is much easier for us to evaluate the things without judging them and then to not reflexively feel responsible or personally attacked. By meditating, one can reach a state of deep relaxation and stillness. In this condition, true happiness, real love, inner peace, and harmony with all that is can be perceived. It is like a reunion with the immortal part of us, the part that arose from the Source and that is the essence of our existence. This connection can lead to great realizations and wisdom. Meditation has also a positive effect on our physical health. Through the reduction of stress, the tendency of high blood pressure, tensions, stomach diseases, etc., decreases. Being in harmony with our True Selves and the Source has also a diminishing effect on depressions and anxiety states.

Choose a place for meditation where you feel comfortable. Wear loose, comfortable clothes and sit comfortably. For many people it is pretty hard to sit in the traditional lotus position. It is totally sufficient if you sit in an upright position on a chair with your feet firmly on the ground so that you can feel grounded. It is essential that you are not going to be disturbed. Switch off your telephone. You can also go out into the countryside. Whenever I have the possibility, I try to take advantage of the sunset. Depending on the outside temperature, however, this pleasure is mostly limited to the summer months. When I have the chance to be close to a lake, a river, or even the ocean, I use these opportunities optimally. The soothing sound of water and its energetically cleansing effect makes meditation a very special experience. Water can have an enormous inspiring and clearing effect. When I sat at the ocean and listened to the regular sound of the waves, I sank into myself and received the idea for this book.

There is an endless number of meditation techniques and ways to acquaint oneself with them. Whether it is contemplating a certain phrase or finding the solution to a problem through a visualization technique, there are countless possibilities. In the beginning it may be a good idea to attend a class in order to exchange experiences and speak about insecurities. There are also numerous books and guided meditations on CD. When one has dealt with this subject a little, it is very recommendable to use one's own meditation technique.

GO INTO THE COUNTRYSIDE

When I was a child, for me there was nothing better than sitting in the open countryside, listening to the humming of the insects, watching the bees flying from blossom to blossom, and simply enjoying the peaceful calmness.

There is no better place to get into tune with the universe. Plants, insects, and minerals have no free will on their own. They solely follow their fate. Nobody needs to tell a bee why it exists or what its task is. It simply does what is in accordance with its inner self and therefore follows its instinct. The bee does not question anything and lives in absolute harmony with nature. A tree does not question anything either. It is its purpose to provide animals with a space to live, to give food, and to produce shade and oxygen. The tree lets everything that is supposed to happen happen. It simply is. No matter what happens throughout the year, the tree begins to flourish. It develops leaves and loses them again, but it is always there. Whatever happens, the tree remains the same.

From this point of view, we can consciously observe and become aware of all these wonderful beings that exist, no matter if they have roots, if they crawl, or if they fly. There is an enormous diversity of living creatures, and each of them has their own fate. They perceive their fate, and by following it, they contribute an important part to our space of living. If the bees preferred lying in the sun instead of collecting nectar, soon there would be no flowers anymore, and consequently the living space of many insects would disappear. If the insects disappeared, it would become tight for the birds. Every single living being has a task to fulfill so that everything remains in balance. Sit underneath a tree and breathe in its strength. Listen to the rustling of leaves in the wind and be sure that the tree will still be there tomorrow, although you might be somewhere else.

Sit down in a flower meadow or at a lake, stream, or river. Observe everything that surrounds you without judging. Observe a butterfly landing on a flower, absorbing food while flapping its wings. Have a closer look at its design. Look very carefully at a daisy. Now look at another one, and you will notice that each one looks different. Still, none is less precious than the other. Even if one doesn't have as many petals, it is perfect.

Go into the countryside. Take your time and observe, observe, observe. It will not take very long until a deep peace spreads within you. The more intense you perceive inner peace, the better you fit into nature. You are a part of nature. Respect this gift, be grateful for it, and be careful with it. Every living being has a purpose, including us. Let's go into the countryside and allow ourselves to be inspired by its perfection. If we truly visualize this unbelievable, elaborate system, we perceive a deep respect for creation.

POSITIVE THOUGHTS GENERATE POSITIVE FEELINGS

"When you learn to consciously allow your full connection with the You that is your Source, your experience will be one of absolute joy. Consciously choosing the direction of your thoughts, you can be in constant connection with Source Energy, with God, with joy, and with all that you consider to be good"
– Abraham – Esther and Jerry Hicks

Your Higher Self, which is what you are, consists of love just like the Source from which you are derives. Thus, you are love. Love is your natural state of being. To connect yourself with your real light, it is essential that you are able to feel this love. When you feel it, you are automatically in the light, for love is light.

In our daily lives when we are occupied with preparing food, doing the housework, making appointments, working, etc., it is everything but easy to see ourselves in the light and also to perceive it. In order to achieve everything that we are aiming for, we must return to the state that we derive from. We must occupy and surround ourselves with positive thoughts and feelings so that we can connect with our True Selves again. It is through this power that anything is possible.

Whenever you feel irritated, nervous, anxious, desperate, angry, disappointed, etc., watch out for thoughts that cause positive feelings in you. As soon as you feel positive feelings emerge, you are able to look at the previous emotions from a distance. It may be that you suddenly start laughing about your own negativity. It is possible that the negative emotions simply dissolve or that solutions appear right in front of your eyes. In any case, you will be able to view the situation with positive feelings from a higher perspective, and this change in your attitude brings you back into the here and now.

True happiness can never be found on the outside. As long as we bind our happiness to other people, possessions, or circumstances, we will be disappointed again and again because all these things are perishable. True happiness can only emerge from the inside, from the eternal within us. That is what we can always rely on, and we can never lose it. It emerges from the light that we are. We all are precious divine beings, and happiness is our basic right. To be happy is a decision we make on the inside. Opening up to the joyful beings we are and radiating these vibrations connects us with the same energy in the outside, which clears the way between to become what we already feel inside. Life does not mean you must stay who you are. It means you decide who you want to be. Only when we perceive happiness and luck do we ignite the energy with which we can achieve all our goals. When we feel happiness within us, we are able to deal with unpleasant situations, changing circumstances, or losses in a way that encompasses the whole picture and not only single aspects. Positive feelings, luck, and inner peace are not gifts that we might receive one day. These inner conditions, however, result from our way of thinking, our way of seeing the world, and how we face it. We are what we feel, and we feel what corresponds to our thoughts.

If we want to live content lives, we must start with consciously focusing our thoughts. Thus, it is up to us whether we want to live lives in the light or in the shadows. We must only become aware of that. At any time, we have the free will to choose what we want to think. We should make use of this power.

Most people are searching for happiness outside of themselves. That's a fundamental mistake. Happiness is something that you are, and it comes from the way that you think.
—Dr. Wayne W. Dyer

Acting out of the Inner Light

No matter what you would like to manifest, no matter what you are doing right now, no matter what you want to achieve, no matter who faces you, whatever you want to work on or what decisions you have to make, act out of your inner light. Whether you are going through difficult or happy times, remember to connect with your True Self. Thus, you will always act in accordance with your inner voice. When you are balanced within yourself, you avoid overreactions toward the upper as well as the lower level, and your thoughts and actions are aligned with your inner wisdom. Connecting with the Source of wisdom means that you think and act in the same energy frequency as the Source that it comes from. The Source of wisdom is God, and with God all things are possible.

The Law of Attraction

You may already have heard or read about this subject. Esther and Jerry Hicks published several books with the focus on this law, and it has consistently been a part of books and lectures by spiritual teachers. This universal law permeates all aspects of our daily lives and works at all times.

It is the secret to creating our own lives and anticipating the consequences of our acts. The basic principle of this universal law is that we attract everything we emit through our thoughts, emotions, and beliefs.

Primarily this law states that we draw into our lives whatever we focus on. It does not matter if our thoughts are busy with things of the past, the present, or the future. It does not matter either if the thoughts are pleasant or unpleasant, positive or negative, constructive or destructive. It would be wrong, however, to assume that we design our lives through our thinking process only. Thought may be the first step; however, as already mentioned, thoughts arise from the head, and the head is of physical nature. Our physical nature has great potential too. Our thoughts derive from matter, and that is how it should be because we are supposed to experience ourselves through the world of matter. Thoughts, however, are only the starting point in a process that can have a big impact on our lives. It is important to be aware that our thoughts influence our emotions. Eventually our feelings release the energy that creates everything we experience within us and consequently through our external world as well. Our emotions emit vibrations, and these vibrations attract persons and circumstances with equal vibrational patterns.

Often it is said and written that if you wish for something, you should imagine that you already have it. Think good thoughts that let positive feelings arise. Thus, your wish can become true. That is absolutely right. However, there is a risk that we orient ourselves on external factors instead of listening to our inner voice. We try to draw luck into our lives from the outside. When following that route, we separate ourselves from our True Selves. And at the same time we make our luck dependent on outside circumstances and the good will of other people, which never brings happiness but frustration, desperation, and disappointment. By intensely looking outward, we lose contact with our inner voice. When this has happened, our heads are in charge again. The tricky part in this is that we usually do not realize whether we act from our feelings or from our egoistical minds. When we are acting from our egoistical minds, our feelings are suppressed or pushed aside. We only see the charming glitter world of illusions and believe that they arise from our inner selves. So how in the world can I manage to prevent myself from falling into this trap? How can I strengthen myself internally so that I act according to my True Self and not according to my ego? I did not ask myself this question till I realized that I had already found the answer. Again and again I fell into this trap, and mostly I was not aware of it. I knew that I had to get rid of certain things, and for a long time I thought this would concern persons, circumstances, or activities. I felt some kind of inner tension that used to always arise when my imagination would not develop the way I was hoping. Sometimes there are intermediate stages necessary before something is ready to manifest, and for this one needs faith in one's own belief and the target. However, my impatience used to cause the opening of an abyss within me that blocked my path. This abyss—this discontentment with the way things developed—triggered exactly those feelings and vibrations that blocked the fulfillment. I meditated continually or tried to find hints in oracle cards about how to detach myself from those persons who apparently were the causes of my tensions and negative feelings. Finally the moment arrived when I understood what it was really all about. Automatically an intermediate step on the way to realizing our dreams is made. In particular, this method is useful for those who have already understood the principle of the universal law of resonance but who are not truly connected with themselves yet. Through this lack of unity and inner alignment, pure intellectual thinking develops, and consequently the fulfillment of our wishes is blocked by doubts emerging from our minds as well.

It is not about changing on the outside what we want to be different, not as the first step. All persons, circumstances, and occurrences that surround us are reflections of what is going on inside of us. We feel how we think. We emit vibrations according to what we feel and therefore draw the corresponding circumstances into our lives. It is never the other way around. Even if something that happens on the outside hurts us, it is nothing but the reflection of an imbalance inside of us. Otherwise it could not hurt us, or the hurtful situation would not have arisen in the first place. The solution is as clear as day. At first we must wipe the slate clean before we can be the cause of an imagined effect in the outside world. We already know that! This is an absolute logical process when one is familiar with the law of attraction. But how do we manage to wipe the slate clean within us?

I always believed that letting go meant letting go of ideas, imaginations, and even people. I thought that I had to let go of certain persons to release new capacities, and that letting go of them was an important step into a necessary independence. At the same time, however, I had trouble with letting go of them because within me (and here I really heard the voice of my soul) I felt absolutely uneasy with this thought. Hence, I was torn until, through a couple of successive events, the penny suddenly dropped.

The point is not to let go of something on the outside in order to create new space on the inside. The point is not to visualize things one wants to have and to thereby draw them into one's life. Actually it is totally unimportant and unnecessary to bother with this visualization work. The one and only point is that we let go of negative feelings. All of a sudden the scales fell from my eyes. By putting myself under pressure for such a long time and believing that I had to get rid of external conditions and persons, I had created my inner tensions myself. On top of these tensions, I visualized what I really wished from life. Through these tensions, however, I emitted the wrong vibrations. I did not receive what I was longing for and was disappointed. The tensions grew, and I visualized again.

Now finally I understood that it was not the persons or circumstances I had to let go of but my inner bad feelings. I realized that when I was able to release these feelings, the blockage would resolve simultaneously. I would automatically emit the vibrations corresponding to the remaining positive feelings within me. These vibrations are identical with my True Self and all the *real* targets I want to achieve. The achievement of our *real* targets is the key to fulfillment on earth. When we, after having let go of our negative feelings, emit our positive energy, which is in tune with our True Selves, our external world organizes itself automatically, and we do not have to control anything. Now everything can unfold the way it should. As I already mentioned, our external world is a reflection of our inner conditions. Negative feelings block us and therefore hinder or prevent manifestations. It is not the other way round. As long as we perceive negative feelings on our path to manifesting an imagination, it signals that we do not stand in our own light.

So when we are able to let go of these negative feelings, we are ready to visualize constructively. Now we are guided by our soul. When we do not perceive doubts or impatience anymore, we can be sure that we are on the right track. Further signals are our newly won serenity of leaving the way open and simply enjoying any occurring incidents that might be somehow connected with our wishes. These are the first buds bursting. When we are observing them, our emotional barometer tells us whether we are still in harmony with our True Selves or we have lost ourselves to the ego again.

Originally I intended to add some kind of manual for successful wishing to this chapter. Because of the previously described realization before I wrote this book, I decided to refrain from doing so because it would dilute, block, or completely hamper the basic requirements for the development of our inner being. There is really a big risk of drifting off into egoistic thinking. I myself ceased to get lost into wishing too much. When we are able to get rid of blocking negative feelings and a path opens up in front of us, we will notice it because of its resonance with our inner being. Automatically we follow our determined path while we have faith and serenity, guiding us to our goal.

The Risk of Repressing

It is wonderful when we are able to only think positively and live lives without any kind of suffering. Positive thinking, however, does not mean that one can close one's eyes to facts. Ignoring facts has nothing to do with positive thinking. It is denial. It is turning away from what is. Thinking positively means one can extract the positive out of a situation and therefore consciously focus one's attention on the desired aspects connected with it while he or she accepts the unpleasant aspects as facts without giving them weight. Positive thinking also means one can realize that absolutely everything includes positive and negative aspects. Everything is always in perfect balance, which, as a whole, is always good.

When we are able to think positively out of an inner conviction, our thoughts truly enable us to live in peace and harmony. The point is that these thoughts really have to be in accordance with our inner conviction. The risk of choosing the wrong path or ignoring should not be underestimated. Searching for positive thoughts when one does not feel well might be a kind of first aid in acute cases. However, it can also be a trap—a trap called repressing.

Inner tensions always arise when the mind and heart do not vibrate in the same rhythm. Now if we just whitewash these tensions by ignoring them, we repress them. Repressing has nothing to do with letting go. Before we are able to let go of something, we realize the point. Consequently we release the tension causing negative emotions because we understand that these emotions are not part of our true being and therefore superfluous. We understand that they do not help us but hinder our path.

The motivation why one wants to let go of depressing feelings is irrelevant. Trying to convince oneself that one lets go of these feelings by distracting oneself from them does not lead to the liberation of tensions. On the contrary, one just buries them deeper within oneself. We can notice this when the same negative feelings are activated in the same situations again and again. In our erroneous belief we cover them up with thoughts of happiness. A vicious circle is created, and one day the pressure gets so heavy that it leads to an explosion, the discharge of pent-up emotions. Often the discharge is triggered by a small thing. If one really had released the emotions, they would be gone and would not appear again. These unnoticed, repressed burdens are the blockages that distract us from achieving our goals.

The release of heavy emotions causes new feelings of lightness and freedom within us. Through these pleasant feelings, we open up to our Source. Now that we emit the same frequencies as our Source, which in its essence is pure well-being, through the law of resonance more feelings of well-being flow into our lives. If we, on the other hand, whitewash our negative emotions instead of really letting them go, they are still there and draw situations and persons into our lives that resonate with them. At the same time we keep the realization of our wishes at a distance. The wishes may sometimes even be right in front of our noses, but through the blocking emotions, we keep circling around without seeing them. That's because we are not truly aligned with them. We must stand still, look, and allow them to happen.

For the conscious creation of our world in tune with the True Self, it is essential to let go of negative feelings. Hereinafter I would like to shine a light on some of the many aspects connected with the law of attraction. Primarily it is about the many unconscious creations we draw into our lives through our thoughts.

THE EFFECTS OF BELIEF PATTERNS

Simplified, one could say, "We receive what we are. We are what we believe to be, to have, and to see." Thoughts that we repeat to ourselves for a longer period of time or that we allow others to make us believe will one day become belief patterns. A belief pattern is nothing else but a thought that first turned into a habit and then into a conviction. Many of our thoughts only turned into belief patterns because they became habitual. Because of this habit, we are not surprised about the realization of what we have focused our thoughts on. Through our repetitive thoughts, the same results occur again and again. Erroneously we believe that the occurred event confirms our belief pattern, whereupon the pattern anchors even deeper. The result, however, does not confirm at all that we are on the right track with our thinking pattern. Indeed, it only confirms the law of attraction. In particular, the result is a natural consequence of what we focused our attention on. No matter what kind of belief patterns we have, we always receive what resonates with their contents—be it constructively or destructively. Take a look back in your life and think of happy and unhappy occurrences. Now remember the convictions you had beforehand.

Let's take the simple example of a school exam. Supposedly you already messed up many exams, and now a bigger and perhaps more important one lies ahead of you. Let's also assume that you really learned diligently and that you mastered the material. Now the examination date is getting closer, and you are getting more nervous. *What if I mess it up again? What if I suddenly have a blackout? I will probably not make it. I have never mastered this school subject before, so it will certainly be a failure again.* Because of the deeply anchored belief pattern of not being able to manage this subject, you are convinced of not being able to manage it. You can learn as much as you want. With your inner conviction and the thoughts that continually feed this conviction, efforts cannot lead to the desired success. The bad examination result will confirm your conviction that you are a loser in this subject and that this is very unlikely to ever change.

Why in the world do we think like that? Just out of habit! If we step back a little and look at the issue from the other side, this is what we would see: "An exam lies ahead of me. I learned diligently and did my best. The subject has sunk in, and I feel well prepared for this exam." There is no reason to assume that it will not work out. Thus, our thoughts should better deal with an expected positive outcome that is much more realistic and desired. When we think and feel positively, we are much more motivated for this exam. With joyful feelings, we are able to see it as a chance instead of martyrdom. With this feeling or urge to get the exam accomplished and the knowledge that we do our best (because no one can do more than his or her best), the result may not be fantastic, but it will definitely be much better than it would have been if we had cultivated negative thoughts and feelings beforehand.

So if you are unhappy with recurring incidents, with one or more of your own behavior patterns, or with your life situation, contemplate the underlying concepts of belief. What do you think before certain things happen? Become aware of those and focus your attention on the results you really want to experience and match up with the outcomes. Exactly the same applies with everything that you perceive as enriching and uplifting. Contemplate the underlying concepts of belief and enjoy the realization that you created these pleasant occurrences through your own corresponding thoughts and feelings. If you focus your attention on desired results, you will achieve more of them.

The way we see ourselves determines who and what we attract into our lives. This is related to the desired results as well as the unwanted but also to those occurrences that, at first sight, seem to be secondary. When a woman is pregnant, all her thoughts circle around her pregnancy. She will continually and far more frequently encounter other pregnant women, whether in the supermarket, in the cinema, or in restaurants. You draw into your life what you think about and what you identify with.

So we attract into our lives what we create with our thoughts. It does not make a difference whether we want to add something to what we already have or if it is something new. The secret is to focus our attention on what we want and to identify with the feeling of having it. We must be what we want to be or to have.

In his book *The Power of Awareness*, Neville Goddard clearly expresses this point. "You must be conscious of being healthy if you are to know what health is. You must be conscious of being secure if you are to know what security is. Therefore, to incarnate a new and greater value of yourself, you must assume that you already are what you want to be and then live by faith in this assumption."

What Neville wants to say is quite simple. As long as we do not feel deep inside that we already have what we want to get, we will never get it. As long as we are not what we want to be, we will never be it. We must identify with what we want to have or to achieve, and we must completely be it. This knowledge must be anchored deeply within our being, and we must not doubt that our wish is already on the verge of being realized.

Elsewhere Neville writes, "The Truth that sets you free is that you can experience in imagination what you desire to experience in reality, and by maintaining this experience in imagination, your desire will become an actuality."

This is not about ignoring reality. In the now, things are the way they are. But by being aware of the universal law of resonance, we can express a wish and safely assume that right at this moment its roots are already growing down in order to manifest. It always works. The only things that can prevent it from happening are our own doubting thoughts. Let's think of all the things we did not consciously want to experience, such as illnesses, job losses, accidents, etc. Let's also think of all our wishes that became true because we never doubted their realization. So why not create our lives consciously when we know that it has everything we need and want? We only have to place our order and await the delivery. Creating our own reality is a secret that actually never really was a secret. We have only forgotten it and covered it up with our minds. Now we have to start practicing so that we can become the masters of our circumstances again.

THE FUNCTION OF OUR NIGHTLY DREAMS

Probably all of us know that we handle in our nightly dreams much of what we experience and deal with during the daytime. In our dreams we are confronted with the feelings and circumstances we were thinking about during the day or during the preceding weeks and months.

Dreams are helpful signposts. What we focus our attention on during the awake state, the thoughts we turn over in our mind and the emotions we feel appear in our dreams before they manifest in the physical. It is like a preview of what we might expect if we go on thinking the same thoughts and emitting the corresponding vibrations. We have the possibility to become aware of unwanted results in advance and to alter them into wanted ones by consciously changing our thoughts during the awake state and focusing on what we would like to achieve or receive.

A notebook right next to the bed is very useful. Whenever you wake up after a dream, make a small note. This helps you to recall it the next morning. If you do not wake up in the middle of the night, stay in bed for a short moment in the morning and try to remember your dream impressions. It is not about precisely remembering a whole story but the perceptions triggered by the dream. If the essence of the story was connected with feelings you do not want to experience, you have the possibility now to find out what kind of feelings you want to experience instead. By consciously focusing your attention on what you want, you withdraw the energy from probable manifestations of the unwanted situation on the material level and let it flow into something wanted instead.

At this point I would like to insert an example from my own life. For more than a year I wanted nothing more than to get pregnant. But as I mentioned in an earlier chapter, it was simply not meant to happen. Throughout that year I often dreamed that I was pregnant. In these dreams I was always full of joy about my pregnancy. A pregnancy was a great opportunity for me to bow out of work. My working life had become a heavy burden for me, and because of the daily time pressure, I was often at my limits. Now every dream in which I was pregnant ended before I gave birth to the child. Then my colleague fell ill. As she was absent for one whole month, I had to work even more. Occasionally I felt completely out of my depth, but I would not let others see how I really felt, and this did not make the whole situation easier. It was an enormous relief for me when my colleague came back to work after four weeks. My relief was even accompanied by a sense of euphoria that this energy-sapping time was over. Because there had been even more pressure on me during the last four weeks than there had been the time before, work was now not as confining and burdening for me anymore. Although I still wanted to get pregnant, it was not as important as before because I did not have to escape from work anymore. Now I really wanted to have a child and some time off from work. And lo and behold, soon I had another dream in which I was pregnant. This time, however, at the end of the dream, I held my child in my arms. Shortly afterward I became pregnant.

At that time I had no idea yet that my dreams were reflections of my inner attitude. After any of these pregnancy dreams, I merely felt frustrated. Somehow, however, I felt that their message said something like this: "No, no, you will not give birth to a child." I did not understand that my dreams were directly connected to my self-blocking thoughts. This example illustrates pretty well how my dreams changed after I was able to change my thoughts and feelings about becoming pregnant.

Night after night we also have wonderful dreams. Just as we can change our attitudes when we see an unwanted manifestation in our dreams, we can intensify our inner alignment when our dreams deal with something we have wished for. Remembering those dreamlike dreams and recalling the pleasant, happy, euphoric, and loving feelings connected with them helps us to push forward the manifestation of these truly desired results with more power.

Many of our creations are still unconscious manifestations resulting from reflexive thoughts and feelings. So if we are able to recognize our dreams as pointers to future creations, we will become more attentive about our stream of thoughts throughout the day. Through the power of thoughts that we consciously or unconsciously emit, we are continuously creating. Our dreams help us become aware of the creative power of our thoughts and emotions, and they make use of the received information. We are not at all at their mercy! If we can see our nightly dreams as advance notices, we are always able to change course in time.

In order to become aware of the development trends indicated by our nightly dreams, we can keep a dream diary. A notebook and a pen next to our bed invite us to write down impressive dreams— no matter if pleasant or unpleasant—directly after we wake up. Now we can realize which thoughts are currently on their way to manifest. If we do not like what we see, we can consciously change our thoughts and focus on the goal we want to reach instead.

CORRECT CHOICE OF WORDS

For the declaration of your wish, it is essential to visualize what you want and not what you do not want. You will always get what you keep holding on to. Fears are obstacles, for they always refer to what we do not want. If you, for example, are afraid of spiders and keep thinking whenever you enter your bedroom, *I trust there is no spider. I trust there is no spider,* you will only focus on spiders, and you will keep finding one in your bedroom. Fear is a very strong emotion. It can radiate much energy, and therefore, it has a great power of attraction.

I can show you more clearly the different ways of focusing attention. The negative, unwanted focus is this: "Do not think of pink rabbits! Completely ignore any thought of pink rabbits! Please not one single thought of pink rabbits!" So now what are you thinking of? You will not be able to save yourself from seeing pink rabbits in magazines, shop windows, TV programs, or playgrounds. In contrast, the wanted, positive thought is this: *Think of blue rabbits!* What do you think now?

The word *no* has no effect. As soon as we have the pink rabbit in our minds, our concentration is focused on the pink rabbit, whether the word *not* is connected with it or not.

Think retrospectively of what you have attracted into your life. Of course, we also attract what we do not want. If we are continually afraid of contracting an illness, we focus our attention on the condition of being ill. Although we do not consciously want it, our focus lies on illness. It will not take very long until the first signs appear. Here again the example of my sick children matches very well. I often had the spontaneous thought, *Oh, the children have not been ill for quite a long time. What if they get sick soon? Actually, it is time. Oh no, better not. Hopefully they don't get sick.* Usually less than two days later the first child would get a temperature.

CONTROLLING OUR THOUGHTS

All that we are is a result of what we thought.
– Buddha

Every thought in our head is a seed for the next creation. We create continually—consciously as well as unconsciously. It does not make a difference whether we want something to happen or we do *not* want it to happen. In both cases we focus on it and make it a part of our vibrations. We draw it into our lives whether we *want* it or *not*. All that we are and have today results from feelings we have radiated in our past. Below these feelings there were thoughts that moved our feelings in the according direction.

Our thoughts have a power that should not be underestimated. We attract whatever we think. If we turn on our minds and ask them to logically explain to us whether something makes sense or not, we may allow thoughts to enter our brains that are not in accordance with the wisdom of the True Self. Our thoughts are the decisive factors in deciding whether we feel good or not.

Thoughts always influence feelings. The crux of the matter is that by our thoughts we emit energy. This energy attracts those things that we focus on in our lives. Thoughts are reflectively followed by a compatible feeling increasing the process of attraction by a multiple. So we have to control our thoughts. On the first glimpse, this seems to be impossible because we are accustomed to a continual, uncontrolled influx of thoughts. In the beginning much discipline and self-observation is required, but it is possible to stop the unconscious stream of thoughts. We are able to think what we want to think. Always try to find positive words instead of enhancing what is not your choice anyway. By controlling your thoughts, you can automatically control your feelings. Feelings emerge through preceding thoughts respectively. They can be changed through the corresponding thoughts. Let's not put the cart before the horse. In order to make your dreams come true, you must feel good. The preconditions for good feelings are good thoughts. So the basic requirement for giving the manifestation of your dreams the right impulses is the control of your thoughts.

There are situations in which we automatically only know what we do *not* want. In the beginning it is very difficult to let go of unwanted goals. This mainly applies to recurring circumstances when we reflexively think, *Oh no, not again!* or for occasional circumstances that cannot be avoided. In these cases, negative concepts that reflexively flame up at the corresponding key word become reality. Feelings of anxiety play a very big role here. As already mentioned, all feelings emit vibrations, and these vibrations attract circumstances and people in accordance with them. The stronger the feelings are, the faster and more extensive the result will arrive. Feelings of anxiety even emit especially strong vibration because they are deeply and sustainably perceived. For this reason, things that we fear the most are very likely to occur.

The problem with fear is that we intensely occupy ourselves with something we do *not* want. The greater the fear of something is, the stronger the according feeling is. The stronger and the more capturing the feeling is, the more focused we are on what we do not want. However, as the universe does not distinguish whether we want something or not but only reacts on what we focus our attention on, the things we are afraid of are drawn into our lives with special intensity.

Now what can we do if our fear is so great that we are dominated by it and feel unable to get away from its claws? There is only one possibility. We must control our thoughts. As already explained in part 2 of this book, fear begins in the mind. So if we are able to get negative things going with our thoughts, we can do the same with positive things. All we have to do is attract different thoughts, namely thoughts expressing what we want. We must find a counterformulation. If we, for example, are afraid of getting sick, we should think, *It is marvelous that I am in good health*. If we are afraid of an interview and fear a certain result, then we should visualize the result we wish to get in the best of cases. If we are afraid of an exam, we should think of this affirmation: "Before my inner eye, I see clearly the solutions to the exercises, and I am happy to get my knowledge across." The knowledge of the law of resonance is essential if we do not want emotions that could have an unwanted influence on wanted results to arise. We may really trust that good feelings attract everything that causes more good feelings in us.

When you say, 'Yes,' to something, you include something you
do want in your experience. When you say, 'No,' to something,
you include something you don't want in your experience.
– Abraham – Esther and Jerry Hicks

Sometimes we feel bad because we are stressed. We may be negatively influenced by people or circumstances, or sometimes we are afraid of something. Sometimes, however, we do not really know why we are sad or uneasy. To get out of this trap, immediately find one or more thoughts that give you a happy feeling. Think of nice experiences, of people you love, of upcoming events. Think of things that give you a good feeling and do not give up before the unpleasant feeling has disappeared. Otherwise it is very likely that you will experience what resonates with your unconsciously developed negative energy.

I would like to remind you of the chapter titled "The Principle of Duality." There is something positive and something negative in every situation. Always try to become aware of the positive. You have already noticed the negative, so it is important to integrate the positive aspect. You get more of everything you emit—whether you consciously want it or not. So choose those thoughts and feelings that make your life easier.

Make a habit out of seeing something positive in any situation. Positive thoughts create positive feelings. Positive feelings create happiness. Happiness creates positive energy. The emitted energy attracts something positive. You receive something positive. You feel happy, and thus, you emit more positive energy that again attracts something positive. This continues endlessly until the moment when you become aware that this operation has become automatic. It is a matter of course, a law that cannot be broken. It is really so simple. It only seems to be wonderful and fantastic because we have forgotten it behind the veil of unconsciousness.

Search for positive thoughts so that the veil does not turn in the unwanted direction. We ourselves have the choice whether we want to be slaves to our thoughts and emotions or rule their lords and masters.

Kurt Tepperwein has said, "Thoughts that we don't get rid of, become our destiny!"

The law of attraction always works. What we attract in our lives is entirely in our hands. We always attract what we have felt before, and we feel what we have thought before. All that we are today and what surrounds us is a result of our energy vibration from the past. So if we want to change something in our current situation, we must focus our thoughts and feelings on what we want. We must become a match to what we want. This way we create a future now.

Leaving the Way Open

Wish for everything but don't get attached to anything!

In wishing and receiving, leaving the way open plays an important role. As I explained before, it is not up to us to determine the path. As the famous saying goes, "All roads lead to Rome." If you tensely hold on to a certain path because you think that this is the only way to reach your goal, you are blocking the other 287 ways to get there. The universe has its own means and ways of managing things, and it will find the perfect way for you. We would often choose more complicated ways, and we are astonished when something simply dissolves or happens easily.

So if you want a car, then wish for a car. Do not hold on to the thought that you first must win the lottery or come to an inheritance to be able to afford it. These two ways might be two options out of 199. However, it is not certain that one of them is designed for you. As soon as you have turned over your wish to the universe, simply follow the signposts, be attentive and open, and take your opportunities.

Relationships

Many wishes are concerned with relationships—relationships between partners, parents and their children, neighbors, colleagues, business partners, etc.—and with finding true love.

All those wishes are absolutely understandable, but what we must never forget is that we cannot change other people's fates and characters. What I mean is that we cannot change another person or group of persons according to our subjective concepts. Imagine that you have to change your character and your personality continually because everybody wants you a different way. We have no control over the behavior of others. The only things we can control are our own thoughts and feelings.

What we can do is express the wish to receive signposts to learn how to solve a particular relationship problem. We can also wish to meet our ideal partners. We can wish to finally meet our soul partners. As soon as we act out of our inner light, our wishes are clear before our eyes, and when we emotionally identify with them, our feelings have a positive effect on their fulfillment. However, never forget that everybody has free will. Just like others cannot control your behavior, you cannot control theirs. This means that as much as we may desire to be loved by certain people, we are never able to decide this for them and control their behavior.

Whatever we wish for, we must begin with ourselves. Whatever we emit, we will get back. If we emit mistrust, we cannot receive trust. If we emit ignorance, we will not be accepted. If we emit compassion, we will get encouragement. If we emit love, we will experience love.

You always attract people with personalities matching your current state of mind. Or people will show you aspects of themselves that match your current state of mind. Come out of your shell. Let go of illusions about yourself. Stop trying to be the person you think people might love and be the one who matches with the vibration of your Higher Self. Automatically people then will come toward you in a way that resonates with the divinity you radiate.

> I attract the cooperative power of the Tao when I release
> the need to control anyone's life, including my own.
> —Dr. Wayne Dyer, *Living the Wisdom of the Tao*

FAITH AND DOUBT

If you want your wish to come true, you must unconditionally believe it. The slightest doubt can destroy everything that you have built up with your belief, because you not only wish with your thoughts, but especially with your feelings and the energy you activate and emit through your thoughts. As soon as you question the manifestation of your wish—maybe because it does not happen fast enough or because you cannot visualize how it could become true—the operation can not only slows down but also become completely destroyed. Everything is going to happen when the conditions are perfect and when it is the right time. You have sent out your wish, and now it is processed. All necessary will be done to manifest it. It may be that you have to take one or other intermediate steps to put yourself in a receptive mode. Assuming you want to become a bank director, but you just completed your education. It does not make sense to send applications for the office of a bank director and to moan about receiving rejections. Begin with small steps toward your goal and let yourself guide. Apply at different banks as an ordinary commercial employee. Thereby, you leave everything open-ended. Perhaps you are only offered one single job. Perhaps you might have to choose between several acceptances and decide intuitively. Whatever the case, trust that the job you accept leads you toward your goal.

It is essential that we go on believing and working on the manifestation of our wishes. It often makes sense to take several small steps toward the realization; thereby, we can see little advancements again and again. If we want too much at a time and are fixated on big results, we are unable to overlook the situation, become frustrated, and think that nothing moves in the right direction because we do not notice the small advancements. The more conscious and confident we feel, the faster our dream will come true. Identify with your wish. Sometimes it comes to pass fast, and sometimes it takes a little longer. We will not necessarily understand why this is the case. It is only important that we accept it and regard every single step that we make as a step toward our goal.

Doubts may be clear signs that your thoughts are not in alignment with the voice of your soul. Listen to your inner voice and become clear whether your wish really comes from your heart.

If it has arisen from your ego or if you have adopted it from other people out of an insecurity or desire for recognition, you will not find fulfillment in it anyway.

Arising doubts can also inform you that the direction that you are moving in has changed. Reflect whether you still have the same feelings about your vision as in the beginning. As mentioned before, everything we experience is part of our life plan and takes us everywhere we are supposed go. A path is connected with every goal we locate, and we follow this path. Our goals, however, are only the signposts so that we take a certain route to have our planned experiences. So it is perfectly possible that while we are on the way toward our goal, we experience something that nullifies our original goal and lets a new one arise.

Doubts can make us rethink because our state of development has changed and readjustment has become necessary. If, however, you are still sure that you want to pursue your original goal, keep your faith up so that you do not prevent it from being fulfilled.

WE NEVER STOP DREAMING

We will always have dreams and wishes. Even if we believe that our biggest dreams have come true or that our greatest wishes have become reality, new wishes will arise because circumstances are involuntarily changing and new people are entering our life. At the age of twenty-five, it may have been our biggest wish to start families, to have children, etc. When we have reached this, we want to spend time with our families and to be good parents. When the children are grown or at least more independent, we may want to pursue our own ambitions again. It goes on and on like that. It has nothing to do with dissatisfaction if we go on to have wishes and experience their fulfillment. It has to do with progress and our own development. As we are here to develop and to gather new insights, we realized that achieved goals are parts of our development. They are the springboard to new dimensions through which new goals emerge in front of our eyes. It never stops. We intend to experience fulfillment after fulfillment. There is no limit to expanding ourselves. Dreams that we want to realize are the driving force to guarantee our progress and to live colorful and interesting lives. Every achieved goal is the foundation for the next project.

IF WISHES DO NOT COME TRUE

Despite the visualization of our wish and intense feelings connected with it, despite the corresponding emanation of vibrations and happiness we feel, it may still be that some wishes simply do not come true. In effect, our biggest wishes trigger our greatest doubts and fears at the same time. Sometimes we wish something so badly that we cannot turn our eyes away from it and we think of getting it day and night. We cannot think of anything else anymore and permanently try to find out whether the wish is on the verge of becoming true or not. We tend to fearfully interpret every little sign—fearfully because things often develop differently than we think they should so that event finally result in the fulfillment of our wish. Instead of giving free reign to the initial development with curiosity and faith, we allow desperation and hopelessness to overwhelm us. Now the fear that this wish might never become true is growing. As we know, fearful feelings are the greatest obstacles to success because fear causes us to focus on the failure of our wish fulfillment. It gives us the feeling and the related orientation of *not* having something. Even if our thoughts try to talk us into the contrary, as long as we feel these fearful doubts in us, we prevent the fulfillment. These doubts are unmistakable signs that we do not have faith in the universal law of resonance. If we had faith, there would be no doubts. With faith, we are free and open to receive the gifts that are already on their way to us. With doubts in our hearts, however, we close the doors again and again and therefore interrupt the flow. The law of attraction always works! Have faith and let yourself be surprised. Have no fixated expectations and time concepts. Emit feelings of joy and accept with gratitude whatever happens and flows to you step-by-step. Watch all the little signs condensing more and more until you are ready to receive your entire gift as a whole. There is nothing to lose but all to win.

It may also be that a wish cannot become true before you have taken one or more intermediate steps in order to be ready to receive the manifestation and its consequences for your life. So if you are absolutely sure that the fulfillment of your wish is part of your fate, go on following your inner call faithfully and regard everything you encounter as preparations for your goal, even if you are unable to understand how everything might be connected with the desired result. An open heart, an awakened spirit, and the strong power of a cooperative ego will always reach their destination.

There is another reason why some wishes cannot come true, namely because it simply is not part of your life program. Such a wish does not arise from the True Self but is built on the illusion that our happiness depends on something we need to attract from outside into our lives. A desire of the heart always belongs to our life program. A desire of the ego, however, belongs to our learning process and shall help us to return to ourselves. A wish that comes out of our heads is superficial, and therefore, it contains too many aspects we might not be satisfied with in case the wish comes true anyway. The good news is that then at the latest we realize that it has been a desire of our ego. Hence, we have gained another insight and have come closer to our original life plan. Nevertheless, I would like to explain in more detail why wishes that are not part of our life plans do not come true or at least not manifest in accordance with our concept of them. (Here again our heads speak.)

I return to the example of building a house. Before we enter physical lives, we design construction plans for the insights we want to gain and the associated experiences we need. This construction plan is the reason why we want to live this life in the first place. Hereupon, we begin to build the shell form. The shell form defines the framework conditions for our lives, which we cannot change during our incarnation. We can also call it fate. So if we construct a shell form with five rooms, we cannot add a sixth or seventh room after we are born into this life. The shell form—our fate—has already been determined. It helps us follow our original plan. As soon as we are born into bodies, we forget our original intentions, and our self-determined framework conditions continually remind us of the route we have to take. If we desperately tried to build an extra room anyway, it would not be possible because our house is designed for five rooms only. As long as we spend time on the sixth room, we will not make any progress until we turn our attention to the other five rooms again.

This does not mean that we have built a prison for ourselves in which we cannot freely decide anything. As mentioned, our shell form (our self-determined fate for this life) merely helps us to stick to our original plan. Now let's turn to the content of this fate—the five rooms, the cellar, and the attic. Every room contains its own theme. These central themes are directly connected with the insights we want to gain. The construction phase of these rooms until they are completely furnished (until the insight has been won) corresponds to the manner in which we deal with the challenges that life presents. It is up to us whether we oppose or welcome these challenges in order to develop one room after the other from the cellar to the attic. Developing and furnishing our rooms corresponds to accepting challenges, and that is what we call destiny. This means that we are subject to a fate but not to a fixed destiny. Designing our destiny is subject to our own will and how we deal with circumstances, situations, and people in our lives. It is up to us if we face life positively or negatively. We can make heaven or hell for ourselves out of everything that happens. It is not about what life throws in front of our feet. It is what we make out of what life throws in front of our feet.

To return to the nonfulfillment of a wish, if it is not our fate to have a sixth room, we can wish ourselves crazy. We will not get it.

By trying it anyway, we unnecessarily waste time and energy we could better spend on our true fate, namely on the rest of our house. As long as we feel that something is a hard nut to crack and simply not meant to be, we do not get anywhere. In the moment, however, when we let go of our fixed idea and turn elsewhere, our program continues, and all of a sudden we achieve one improvement after the other. We can compare this with a windup doll. When the doll arrives at an obstacle, it will continue to move against it because it is wound up, but it will make no headway. If we grab the doll and turn it around toward the open space, it will move forward unhindered again.

Open hearts coupled with clear minds enable the fulfillment of our contracts in all their beauty. Thereby, our five rooms, including the cellar and attic, beam in joy and glory. A trial to attach an unintended sixth room prevents us from designing the intended other five rooms. We will never get the sixth one, and at the same time we will not feel comfortable in the other ones because they are still in their unfinished states.

Let's design our existing rooms. Through our feelings the voice of our souls will always let us know when we are following our programs and when we are not. Who knows? Maybe we must be anxious about a sixth room from time to time in order to learn something specific, something that corresponds to the carpet in room number four, perhaps acceptance and letting go!

SUMMARY

In this chapter I have tried to illustrate as detailed and figuratively as possible how the law of attraction works and which blockages influence or prevent the fulfillment of our wishes and dreams. I believe that with these background explanations it might be easier to understand how simple this universal law functions. It can be summarized in simple terms and explain how we can always create the kind of reality we really want to experience.

We do not necessarily have to know what we want to do next or which decisions have to be made. All we have to do is let go of burdening feelings. When we let go of heavy feelings, we are authentic. When we are authentic, we feel good and are open to the flow of energy and life's abundance. When we feel good and authentic, only those things that correspond with our True Selves automatically flow into our lives. This is always what we truly wish for because it is not falsified by negative thoughts. The mere understanding that we do not have to do anything else but to let go of negativity in order to draw into our lives what we truly want takes an enormous pressure from us. Through our feelings of well-being we attract all kinds of circumstances, occurrences, and persons who bring us even more good feelings and help us develop. We must not forget that we have caused this pressure ourselves through our own mental concepts and expectations. Whatever a person creates is always up to him or her to change or solve through the change of the inner concept. Just by liberating ourselves consciously from these burdens, positive and joyful feelings spread within us and open the doors for universal abundance.

A wish that is not emitted through the pure self can never become true in the perfection we are hoping for.

So in order to make wishes come true, we only have to do one thing. We must be ourselves. We must let go of all negativity, burdening feelings, pain, fears, doubts, frustration, etc. Then comes to the surface what had been buried underneath all this negativity for years or decades, namely what we truly are. Now our true identities can finally expand to their full size. It is a feeling of absolute liberation. A previously unknown power, recognition, and deep trust spreads throughout our bodies and beyond them. This is the True Self—pure and authentic. When we are able to free our True Selves by dumping negativity, we know at the same time that we do not have to wish for anything. As we are now radiating what we truly are, only that can enter our lives. Whatever comes is what we want. Suddenly we understand that it is not necessary to have a concept of something. We only have to set free this felt love, this unbelievable strength and joy that we essentially are. Everything else organizes itself. We cease to struggle against outer circumstances because we turn to what we want. As soon as we have a concept again and try to determine which wish, which order, which occurrence would be most reasonable, we can be sure that our minds are talking again. It goes fast, and our vibration is not pure anymore. It is only about feeling good. If we only think beneficial thoughts and consequently only create beneficial feelings, circumstances are reorganized in accordance with the universal laws. All we have to do is go with the flow and hold on to our good thoughts and feelings. A reorganization of circumstances can certainly be a big challenge. That is why we must not visualize the way to a goal, as this can hinder or prevent us from reaching it. It is all about feeling good—nothing else. By feeling good, we create a frequency that makes it impossible to let unwanted things flow into our lives because it is a law that the same attracts the same. We really only have to care for our well-being since our true nature is well-being. In well-being, we are authentic. The implementation of our positive vibrations is organized by the law of attraction. Be good, and you will receive goodness. Be love, and you will receive love. Serve your surroundings, and you are served.

ACTIONS AND DECISIONS

Fear prevents us from following our path because it silences our inner voice. As soon as we have chased away the fear, our True Selves come to the surface, and we can recognize the difference. The True Self burst with boundless energy and happiness about being able to move and create something in this world. It is a pure zest for life. Our intuition helps us take exactly that path we are destined to take. When we follow this path, we feel trust, happiness, power, and love for what we do and for what we encounter.

All human beings act out of their conviction. Therefore, we

should never really be mad at anyone, even if it hurts us. That person only did what he or she felt was right in that very moment. The individual simply did not know better and learned something. Here again we can ask the question, "How can we know how he or she should have behaved better? What measure shall we take, and where shall we start measuring?" We all say and do things that others do not consider appropriate or correct, and nevertheless, we think we are right. We should not judge one another. Jesus even said, "Father, forgive them, for they know not what they do."

Everybody acts according to his or her current state of knowledge and consciousness, and that is always the best and only basis for what we do. Additionally the wrong actions of our counterparts may lead us to insights. Remember that we are all connected with one another and that our paths do not cross coincidentally. We continually help push one another forward on our path. This can happen in a really loving but also in a very painful or even threatening manner.

Here again your inner light comes into effect. You should only create wishes in accordance with your soul and express them through your vibrations, and it is the same with making decisions. Feel the oneness and harmony within you. Anything that is done, thought, and planned out of this oneness contains the essence of your soul and can therefore only be successful—no matter what the bottom line is. As long as your thoughts and feelings are in harmony with each other when you are making a decision, the result can only be promising. That means that the result will lead you to a needed insight. From your mind's point of view, the project may be a failure. But from your soul's point of view, you draw exactly the kind of insight from it that is necessary. The consequences will always be for the benefit of you and your surroundings— even if these benefits are not immediately recognized and you are criticized.

Sometimes you may not be sure how to decide, and you may ask others for advice. Thereby, a lot of different opinions and statements may approach you. Maybe you receive new information, or your own tendency is confirmed. In the end, however, it is important to do not what others think is correct but what you feel is best after you have investigated all available facts. This decision can completely go against all logic. Pay attention to your first impulse! It emerges from your inner voice. All thoughts that flow into you later are possibly already controlled by the mind, and these might be confusing. We must look inward to get clarity about our true feelings and motivations. An action that comes out of truth, love, and surrender will always be successful.

Every little step we take brings us forward. All these little steps, little occurrences, and little decisions that we continually make are necessary to generate the big picture. For every mile we want to leave behind us, we must walk 5,280 single feet.

WE DO NOT MAKE MISTAKES. WE GAIN EXPERIENCES.

Once a decision has been made, stand 100 percent behind it and move forward with it. When you later look back, you will often notice that an unusual constellation of situations was necessary in order to create a certain result. Of course, we often stand at a crossroads leading in two completely different directions. The only thing we really know at this moment is that the path that we have walked until now has come to an end and that something will definitely change. Now it is up to us to connect with our inner feeling and to move in the direction that is in accordance with our intuition. It is not always the easy way that feels like the right one despite everything. What is important is that it matches us, that we are able to identify with it, and that we can be 100 percent behind it. What is the use of lives in safety if we are unhappy? Sometimes we have to have the courage to take a risk. Deep within us, we know exactly when it is time for it, and then we can follow that path with curiosity and butterflies in our stomach but also with complete surrender and conviction.

There are no wrong decisions. Whatever decision you make,

it is the right one, and it takes you where you are supposed to go. All that we experience as consequences of decisions and all that we learn from these experiences correspond to our life plan. Even if we think that we made a mistake because we went through a—subjectively spoken—negative experience, this insight we gained was still missing in our collection, and it prepares us for an upcoming situation.

It is not about making the right decision. It is about making the decision that matches us and that enables us to learn our desired lessons through the constellations that have come about. The goal we want to reach is nothing but a signpost pointing to the path so that we can find and take it.

"We do not make mistakes. We gain experiences." Hence, every decision we make and every action we take are parts of our learning process and correspond to the divine order. Through every action and decision, we generate waves that in turn initiate actions and decisions of other people. Something is moving. Sometimes it may be necessary to make a wrong decision in order to meet a certain person who can give us the needed hint to manifest a wish or lead us to an essential hint to solve a problem. This means that our decision was not wrong because it helped us to reach the goal. Through our perception of making a wrong decision, we are even able to learn another lesson, namely that the wrong decision was absolutely right because it lead us to the solution.

Actually it is counterproductive to question a decision that has already been made. Though we would decide differently today, it does not mean that our decision was wrong at that time. All we can do is decide out of the present moment. We cannot decide out of a future moment. Of course, we will gather and evaluate all information available, but decisions can only be made in the here and now.

So do not be afraid of decisions and actions. No matter how you act, your action has just the right influence on your own development and on the development of your surroundings. Even if you change your mind at the very last moment, it is all right. It is not about what kind of result arises from a decision. It is about the experience you are going to have as the result of your decision.

FORGIVE YOURSELF, FOR THERE IS NOTHING TO FORGIVE

It seems to be very hard for us to forgive ourselves. We can forgive so many people, but it is difficult to do with ourselves. Perhaps it is important to know that basically we cannot forgive anybody as long as we have not forgiven ourselves. Every development in our lives begins with us—with our thoughts and the feelings arising from them. What does not come out of us, cannot be brought into our environment. "You can't give away, what you don't have," Wayne W. Dyer has said.

That's exactly how it is! We can only receive love when we have sent out love in the first place. We are only able to give love when we have realized love within us. It is the most wonderful discovery ever because when we love ourselves, we feel ourselves.

The good news is that we do not really have to forgive ourselves and others. As described before, every action and decision is part of the divine plan. It does not matter at all if the consequences are pleasant or uncomfortable. We have to deal with the resulting experiences only so that we can save them as further lessons in us and take the next rung on the ladder. Whatever happens happens in full accordance with the divine universe. Everything is wanted. Yes, everything! Whatever we did to someone, that triggered something in that person, activated something in him or her to take action in a certain way, to move into a new direction, to look inside, or whatever. Whatever someone did to us, however they triggered something inside of us, that had the same effect. Of course, there are situations in which we are impolite, aggressive, intolerant, unfair, etc. With this insight, we might feel sorry about our behavior. If we find out that somebody was hurt through our behavior and if we are hopefully able to admit this to ourselves, we should communicate it to the person concerned. Sometimes only a few words are required, perhaps only a gesture in order to break a chain of wrongful pride in us and to surpass ourselves. But we must never develop guilty feelings. Guilty feelings do not help. They slow down, block the energy, and do not allow positive developments. Whenever guilty feelings may arise in you, try to find the root and clarify the situation. You have nothing to lose. People who jump over their own shadows always win. Who has not yet made the experience of how it feels to let go of an unpleasant and oppressive issue that he or she struggled with and that made him or her heart heavy? It feels as if a heavy load falls off of the person.

An unbelievable love is required to construct this fantastic organizational network, which is the universal order in its absolute perfection. It is perfectly organized in such a way that every one of us is permanently supplied everything we need in order to experience everything we have come here for. This network is so perfect that it encompasses us all, and we are mutually sent to one another in order to guide us in our experiences, to support us, and to lead us. When we are able to understand and to accept all this, we will also understand that actually there is nothing to forgive because it is all well the way it is. Everything happens out of love. We are intended out of love and have come into this physical body out of love to send our love through our actions into this world and to everyone that is receptive of it. Love is our intention, and love is what we truly are. Whatever you do, do it with love. Love is your permanent companion in the outside world as well.

THE REALIZATION OF THE TRUE SELF

Realize your essence and you will witness
the end without ending.
—Lao-Tzu

The unbelievable discovery of the own forgotten self happens in most cases through particular situations or a constellation of certain circumstances. These circumstances are so perfectly aligned with one another that we cannot escape the confrontation with the next step of our development. These circumstances usually lead us into the deepest depths of our being. We feel that everything breaks down and that all our dreams run through our fingers like sand. Sometimes we think that we lose everything we have lived for. Often we really have to give up something or make a painful experience that forces us to open an inner door we had turned away from over and over again because now we must go through it. By going through it and listening to ourselves and letting ourselves sink down to the bottom of our inner ocean, the moment arrives when we start to understand. All this often happens within a short period of time. The situation is becoming particularly acute from all sides, and apparently a radical change is about to come. Then a straw breaks the camel's back. It feels like a gigantic explosion inside of us, blasting everything away that was compressed in us. It is like the tension between two tectonic plates discharging through an earthquake. All the accumulated, forbidden emotions and frustrations are like a helter-skelter trying to get outside. What follows is absolute silence and a feeling of deep peace. Within this peace a light quietly begins to shine, and it is getting lighter and lighter while it fills up the space with light and warmth. We recognize the essence of what we are and realize that all the negative emotions burst out of us because they have not been part of the True Self. And they never were. They were only artificial masks made of attachments to adapted thought patterns and belief systems. Now finally we are ready to let them go. We sense the immense life energy encompassing us, and we perceive a deep relief and an unbelievable feeling of security. An overpowering feeling of gratitude and happiness may be felt and seen as tears running down our cheeks. It feels as if there is something within us that is far bigger than we are and that hardly finds room in our bodies. All hindering thoughts and self-imposed prohibitions that had put us in chains and narrowed us are falling off like dried sludge. The wisdom within us and the love that we are fulfill us and flow into every corner of our existence. We literally feel as if we send out rays of light. We realize that we did not lose anything but that we still have everything. We realize that we can never lose anything at all, and we understand that everything on the outside is subject to transiency anyway. The false identification with things in our outside world begins to dissolve. All at once we can see what we are and what we are not. When we give up everything because we are forced to let go of things we cannot and may not hold on to, everything that covered our True Selves until now then automatically disappears. A strong force rises within us and gives us the knowledge that we can achieve anything we begin to tackle. With a previously unknown power, our exposed selves emit waves from our deepest and sacred insides. We emit waves of faith, belief, acceptance, and gratitude instead of vibrations of stubbornness, attachment, insecurity, and fear. This new emanation has so much more power than the old one because the blocking opinions about us have disappeared. With this new openness and consciousness, we know that we are given everything that we really need through our Creator's love.

At one or more points in our lives, it is inevitable to let go of something. We must lose it in order to realize what we really possess. Through the liberation of outer things—whether voluntarily (consciously) or imposed (by external circumstances)—we are becoming independent. We let go of things with which we erroneously identify. True freedom only arises through the independence from external things like compulsions, expectations (through us or others), and possessions. With this new independence, we are able to include everything in our hearts that we thought we would lose. We realize the grace of liberation and the glory of our unique being. I wish to recall Lao-Tzu's quotation from the beginning of this chapter. "Realize your essence and you will witness the end without ending." Whatever ceases to exist around us, including our physical bodies, allows us to experience that we do not cease to exist. By letting go of external influences, we remove attributes of ourselves that we are not and never were. Throughout our whole lives these attributes only covered what we really are because we allowed it to. These false attributes can be compared with a costume that, on the surface, helps us be somebody else. When we finally take it off again, our true apparition comes to light. This costume is woven from adapted belief patterns, acquired attitudes, the desire to satisfy others expectations, accepted guidelines we internally resist, the dependencies of persons, possessions, and circumstances. By taking this costume off, we expose the view to what we can never lose and to that which has provided us with the gift of our physical lives and the power of manifesting our dreams and wishes. We see what remains when the body perishes. We see and feel the wonder that we are. In that very moment we are absolutely free!

Putting this feeling of realization and liberation into words is incredibly difficult. Indeed, it is simply impossible because words arise from the mind and the mind is not able to comprehend this heavenly condition. We perceive it with our feelings and an inner knowing. In fact, it can only be grasped when it has been experienced just like every lesson can only be understood and assimilated when it is fully learned. Furthermore, everybody handles this experience differently. One wants to immediately share this wonderful experience with others, and the other quietly and thankfully closes it in him or herself. What we all have in common is the detachment from the ego. At the moment when we perceive the connection, the love, and the oneness within us, the ego is deprived of its livelihood because we have recognized and dissolved its illusionary distortions. I had the grace to experience all the above several times. Every time it has been a greater gift than before. After we have experienced this liberation for the first time, we want to repeat it again and again. It is a very familiar feeling. We feel the connection with our origin. Every time we uncover a part of the True Self, this connection is getting stronger. It feels as if God is personally embracing us. And actually he does because there is nothing between God and us. By freeing another part of us, we allow God to shine through us a little more. Everyone who has already experienced this knows what an uplifting feeling it is that encompasses every fiber of our being and makes us feel immortal and indestructible. In these moments we truly feel our connection with the Source.

Through the gift of such an incident we realize the grace of the universe that has organized and coordinated everything up to the smallest detail for us so that we may experience our self-realization. Although the preparation for an experience like that may take months or years and although indications may occasionally appear, such an inner transformation can eventually occur within a few days or even hours. The more abrupt and faster it happens, the more intense and deeper we perceive it.

M. Scott Peck says, "The great awareness comes slowly, piece by piece. The path of spiritual growth is a path of lifelong learning. The experience of spiritual power is basically a joyful one."

Everyone who embarks on a spiritual journey starts reading

books, attending workshops and lectures, and talking to like-minded people. We gather information and receive hints and pointers that point us in the right direction. However, as much as we might be able to identify with what we hear and read and even if we can accept such information as truth, it still remains on the surface. Even with the greatest conviction, all this knowledge is still on its way to become part of ourselves. We need time for this dry training so that we are prepared for the real showdown in order to classify the incidents and to apply what we have learned. After we have had such an experience of recognition and realization, that what we only believed by then has been transcended into a real deep knowing. The integration of knowledge can happen through many little aha moments or single but more intense occurrences.

It can be compared with giving birth. A woman prepares for it about nine months, but only when she has experienced how it feels to give birth to a child does she really know what the experience entails—with all emotions, ups and downs, and the final liberation and fulfillment. Indeed, it is like giving birth within ourselves, and we feel like a newborn baby. When we are open for it, we experience many births just like Peck's quotation suggests. Step-by-step we grow on the path we call life. Actually it is a joyful or even overwhelming experience.

When we come to this earth, we are born into small bodies—bodies that are so much smaller than our true existence. With the birth into this physical body, a veil of forgetfulness descends over us. There is a good reason for this, because how should we be able to slip into a role here in order to learn if we did not take this role seriously from the very beginning, if we were aware of this illusion? We need this forgetfulness so that we can work on our experiences. The bottom line is that there is only one goal to achieve. We must realize what and who we really are, and we learn this through our role-play and through the experiences we have. The reason why we incarnate over and over again is to transform from a caterpillar into a butterfly.

Realizing who we really are is the greatest realization, the most fulfilling enrichment, and the biggest grace. When we are ready to achieve this, it occurs because we have brought ourselves this far. Of course, we are provided with aids to help us; however, we must open ourselves up for these aids, and we must see and follow the signposts. Throughout all these incarnations it is our only goal to get back to the light where we originally came from. We get to the light by solving all the tasks we are given. This is what it is all about. The extent to which we are able to experience this, we will only know when we follow our path in faith and trust. There is nothing more and nothing higher that we can ever reach for ourselves. The next step is to share this realization with others, to infect other people with the light so that they discover their inner light themselves, begin to shine, and share their light with others as well. For that we do not have to be enlightened beings or have reached an especially high spiritual level. It is enough to follow our inner call, to go with the flow of life, and to live joyful lives in faith in ourselves.

The True Self and the soul are immortal. They come from eternity and are eternal. As we are all part of this eternity and therefore forever connected with one another, we can never be separated from one another. We all have the divine spark within us, and we are always connected with our Source through it. Nothing and nobody can ever separate us from it. We can never get lost either. We are connected, whether we live physical lives or if we have already left these behind us. We are equally connected with the souls in physical bodies as with those in the nonphysical realms. It was never different, and it will never be different. No physical death can change this. Therefore, you are always connected with your loved ones, no matter if they are next to you, if they live on a different continent, or if they have already left their physical bodies. What we truly are—our souls—always remains the same. We could compare this again with a costume we put on. We are not the costume that surrounds us but what is underneath. Hence, it does not make a difference if we appear in physical or nonphysical bodies. The True Self always remain the same. Therefore, our connections with one another always remain the same as well. It is only our perception that is dampened. If you enter your inner light, you can sense this connection. You are never separated from anybody, and consequently you are never alone. The deep knowledge that you are permanently connected with every human being and with every soul may guide you to see your inner light. Then you are connected with your Source, which is your home.

This earth is not our real home, and this life here is not the real life. The time we spend here is merely a short intermezzo. It is like attending a seminar, and we may creatively play on the playground earth for a while and experience ourselves in different roles. Here we are able to learn things we cannot experience in the nonphysical realms. Only here can we sense with our physical senses and experience emotions like grief, jealousy, envy, and anger. For these reasons we wanted to come here—to experience feelings and duality. However, our time on earth is limited, and so we should definitely make use of it. Who knows when our next opportunity will be?

As this physical existence is not our real existence, we do not have to be afraid of anything, especially not physical death, which only helps us take off our costume again. There is no other death but this. This is an important point, if not the most important point of all. There is no death. We can never die. We only alter our appearance.

Every living thing, animal, human, or plant, experiences that which is called death, with no exception. Spirit, which is who we really are, is eternal. So what death must be is but a changing of the perspective of that eternal Spirit. If you are standing in your physical body and consciously connected to that Spirit, then you are eternal in nature and you need never fear any "endedness," because, from that perspective, there is none. You will never cease to be, for you are eternal Consciousness.
    – Abraham – Esther and Jerry Hicks, from

When you have realized you are (only) here on a playground that God provided for your self-awareness, you become more tolerant, relaxed, and open to all that you are given so that you can fulfill your self-determined tasks. When you feel deep inside of you who and what you truly are, your ego dissolves, for you realize that it is only a part of your physical existence. As your true nature is spiritual and therefore superior to the ego, it does not interest you anymore what the ego wants to tell you.

You realize that it does not exist but that it has arisen from your own fantasy.

As soon as the ego is still, you will notice something very special. All of the sudden you hear your own voice again because you *hear*. On the outside things may have stayed the same. A stone is still a stone. A tree is still a tree. But you see everything in a different light, for you *see*. Also the people are still the same, but you perceive them differently because you *perceive*.

When you have found your True Self and realized the connection with all beings in the universe, the distorting veil of illusion falls, and you are able to see the true beauty and gloriousness of creation and the unbelievable gift we all have received. Where now shall fear exist? And where is there a reason for doubt?

As state in *A Course in Miracles*, "When the ego was made, God placed in the mind the call to joy. This call is so strong that the ego always dissolves at its sound. That is why you must choose to hear one of two voices within you. One you made yourself and that one is not of God. But the other is given you by God, Who asks you only to listen to it."

You come from God, so your inner voice is the voice of God.

RECOVERY OF FAITH AND CONFIDENCE

"Faith does not question—Faith knows," Neville Goddard has said.

When you are connected with your True Self, you have everything you need to pursue your journey through all experiences successfully and without unnecessary stops. You have been sent into this incarnation by your True Self in order to gain further insights so that you can grow. You are permanently guided by your Higher Self. It guides you like a navigation system so that you cannot get lost, and it gives you guidance through your dreams, wishes, longings, and inspirations. All these are flashing memories. Everything that you need to fulfill your task here is available for you. You only have to call it up. Here we can use the comparison with a power network again. Just flip the switch, and through the opening, the law of attraction will provide you with everything you need.

When you have contacted your True Self and perceived a feeling of "coming home" within you, you have realized that you are not alone and that you are protected and guided. With this knowing, a deep confidence arises in connection with a deep belief in yourself and in all that surrounds you. One thought enhances the other. It is like a positive spiral. With knowledge comes the belief in your own power and in the universal support that flows to you. Through the emission of this energy, you receive what you believe in, and you develop a growing confidence that strengthens your belief and continually supplies you with new insights through the new experiences you make.

Even if you are about to do something for the first time, you will be able to approach it without fear. You know that it is up to you because it is part of your inner path and because you are given a new opportunity to develop yourself. You will accept every challenge with trust. Even if a small portion of fear arises every once in a while, your faith in yourself will be strong enough so that you cannot be kept from facing the challenge because you know that everything you feel inside is part of your path. Your path is spread out in front of you, and all you have to do is to follow it. You are able to deal with everything you encounter because it matches you.

We develop an irrevocable safety within us, a safety we will not make dependent on external influences. We perceive this safety in the moment we realize that external safety simply does not exist because every form is perishable. We realize our invulnerability because we are imperishable. We were, we are, and we will always be. At this moment we play a role in a costume we call the physical body. This role is part of a film we have created for us in order to have experiences. When our mission is completed, we take off the costume, take a bow, and go home.

> For those who believe, no proofs are necessary. For
> those who don't believe, no proof is possible.
> —Stuart Chase

PATIENCE

One of the biggest problems in terms of belief is patience. When we want something, we want it immediately, or at least we want to have an immediate sign, a confirmation showing us that our visions and wishes are going to come true. But as we, in our unconsciousness, do not perceive all those small and big signposts, we are unaware that we are already heading toward our goal. As we have to learn again to trust and to believe in ourselves and above all in the universal laws, impatience in conjunction with doubts is an enormous troublemaker. It creeps in because we are so used to comprehending with our minds only. However, the universal laws are not comprehensible by the mind. So as long as we do not manage to switch from head to heart when it comes to spiritual issues, we will continue to stumble over and over again because we destroy or at least slow down the manifestation process through the arising doubts and thoughts like the following: *It does not work out anyway. I knew that it cannot function. It would have been too wonderful if it had come true. Why should I deserve so much luck?* The problem herein is that we try to decide on the form in which the wished result shall arrive. Stubbornly we are fixated on this unique option and let indications of the manifestation go by unnoticed. If we were patient and easygoing and if we had trust, we would be open for everything and would attentively watch out for all kinds of signposts.

Because of our habitual thought patterns, impatience can be considered as an understandable blockage we must first resolve. As long as we feel safe, we are patient—just until an irresistible need for confirmation makes us become impatient again. When we become impatient, however, it is a sign of doubt. When we doubt, we have lost confidence. Whenever you hear an inner call or you have a desire, an idea, or a vision, trust that it arises from your inner self, which wants you to pursue your path. No dreams or wishes come without reason. They are indicators showing you that you should make the next step toward your destination.

Wishes Fulfilled

My wish for you is that
your wishes get fulfilled.
To make this come true,
your doubts have to be killed.

A burning wish or dream—
reminder of your soul.
It says, "Please don't forget.
I am your wake-up call!"

It's part of your True Self,
which means part of your path.
Believe this inner voice.
Wake up. Don't doubt. Have faith!

It wouldn't be in you
if it wasn't meant to be.
Your wishes get fulfilled.
Believe, and you will see!

—Erika Kind

Follow your feelings and you will achieve your goal. When you feel your inner light, you feel confident at the same time because you know that all you ask for will be given to you. Your order has been placed, and the delivery is on its way to you. Now all you have to do is wait until you—you and the circumstances—are ready to receive. It may take a while, but it can also arrive the next day. Patience is the magic word. It is only human to be impatient, but nevertheless, impatience can block your way to fulfillment. Whenever impatience arises, go back into your inner light. Listen to your inner voice and connect with your Source (turn on the power), and you will feel that everything is in order. When you are connected, you have all the confidence you need, for you are one with yourself and with God. With God, anything is possible. You know that the fulfillment is only a question of time. When you know for sure that your wish can come true, how long would you wait? Just as long as it takes, right? Through the feeling of certainty that you perceive by your inner knowledge, you would have all the confidence in the world. Why should you not trust your Source? God sent you into this material world as a part of himself in order to experience himself through you. God loves you. He would never turn against you. He supports you in your development wherever he can.

I know that all my dreams and wishes arise from my True Self. This self is a part of the energy that created me out of love and goodwill. My self knows my path and guides me steadily to move forward with confidence. Through the all-knowing Source, with which my self is permanently connected, I receive everything I need, and I lose everything I need to lose to pursue my path. Through the divine order, everything is always unfolding at the perfect time and in the perfect way.

Joy in the Heart

All day long we are busy with all kinds of activities. Some activities we enjoy more, and others less. A lot of things we do not even think about anymore. Whether we like doing them or not, we just do them. However, things we do with joy succeed not only faster but also much better. It is often the things that we choose consciously. Nevertheless, we do not get around many things we not only do not like but that even trigger resistance in us, yet they need to be done anyway.

Let us think of the old topic of homework. Who does not look back on this subject with mixed emotions? Is it not the case that we did our homework much easier and faster when we liked the exercises and the subjects? Is it not true that it was harder for us to concentrate on the more unpleasant exercises? If we had approached all tasks with conscious joy and motivation, we could have spared some hours of boredom. What was the point that we did some exercises unwillingly and with bad tempers? This attitude was of no use at all. We were unfocused, and so we made more mistakes than necessary. And making more mistakes even prolonged the homework process, and we developed even more resistance. Anyway, our homework had to be done nonetheless. So if we already know that something cannot be avoided anyway, we might do it as well with conscious joy.

Whatever we have to get accomplished should be done with joy. If we approach a task that we usually tried to avoid with enthusiasm, we will notice that we find it to be no trouble at all. Therefore, we might like doing it from then on. The mere acknowledgment that something is done better and more easily than before and that a better result is achieved gives us a joyful feeling. With this joy in our hearts, we are able to also approach the next challenge with a smile on our lips and in our hearts. Knowing that we are able to perceive pleasure in something not so pleasant can even motivate us to proceed with ease because we know that we are capable of dealing with anything and feeling good no matter what happens.

This does not only concern activities that need to be done but also persons we have to get along with. Remember this and smile the next time when it comes to cleaning the windows, ironing, having a delicate interview with a customer, or visiting relatives. This is how it all begins. Smile! Consciously smile and you will feel a sense of pleasure or even enthusiasm. Your charisma is just as positive as you approach a situation. It is not about affected kindness. This would have the opposite effect because you would then only play a role. Playing a role, however, enhances your inner feeling of tension, resistance, and discontentment. It is about the conscious attitude of "I *want* to be happy." When we consciously feel happy, we feel love at the same time, and therefore, everything we do and experience is an adventure. Doing something with love means to fill the action with positive energy. The result can only be positive. Even if it ultimately does not meet our expectations, time was not wasted because we felt good while we occupied ourselves with this topic. Moreover, it can be rightly affirmed that we did our best because we did it with love. What is better than giving love? At any moment we can only do the best we can.

Often we cannot enjoy something, or we are even against it because we may have heard sometime that this or that is difficult, lowbrow, dirty, boring, or whatever. We have accepted this belief and have lived with it without ever having our own experience.

It is our real fate to experience joy, and this is the same for every individual. When we create an inner feeling of happiness with our thoughts, it is the best or the only way to achieve a satisfactory result. With open hearts and enthusiasm we recognize our true talents and abilities, which we brought with us into this world so that we could fulfill our potential. Whatever we do with passion becomes a part of ourselves because we leave marks corresponding to the True Self. The more intense we are able to experience the results of our positive attitude, the happier we are. Hence, we develop confidence in our abilities and are glad to assume responsibility for what we do.

TRANSFORMATION FROM "I MUST" TO "I WANT"

We are repeatedly confronted with situations and events that cause an inner resistance in us. We should always listen to our feelings and be aware that this resistance could be an alarm signal. Sometimes, however, we just have to face a situation we cannot avoid, such as a meeting with a person we do not like very much or an activity that is part of our job and cannot be ignored.

So instead of resisting, which increases our aversion and does not change the fact that we must go through a certain situation, we should consciously transform our thoughts. As long as thoughts like *I must do this* are wildly racing through our heads, we feel an aversion against what needs to be done, and this is resistance. However, if we surrender to the situation and consciously think, *I want to do it*, our feelings toward the situation change. We begin facing the issue and welcoming it. The feeling of resistance is changing into acceptance, and the insight delivered by this transformation is turning into joy. Therefore, the energy we feel, emit, and give into the matter changes. We will approach the matter with a neutral if not joyful attitude, and it will be successful. Most probably the task will be finished faster than expected. By transforming the thought *I must* into *I want*, real miracles are likely to happen.

"A woman asked me one time, 'What are the blocks to my happiness?' I said, 'The belief that you have blocks,'" Dr. Wayne W. Dyer said.

For being successful, happiness, enthusiasm, and passion are required. Happiness is our birthright. We should feel it with every fiber of our being in order to set those powers free and enable ourselves to successfully and joyfully pursue our fate. If we do what we do with joy and passion, we are opening a door to ourselves. This is the door to real inner happiness.

There is a simple rule we should particularly remember when we are facing awkward situations. "Do what you love and love what you do."

Happiness Is Our Birthright

Happiness is our birthright with which we have come to this world. Each of us is able to be happy. We all are part of what created us.

God created us, and God is love. Therefore, we are love ourselves. Where there is love, there is happiness.

Every human being wishes to be happy. Everyone wants to have a lighthearted life. And every one of us should have both. The problem is that most people search for happiness on the outside. Many people suffer from the delusion that their happiness depends on outside factors and that they either possess it or lack it because they either receive it or not. As long as we believe that happiness is something we arbitrarily get or do not get, we will continue to search for it. Happiness, however, cannot be found anywhere. Nobody and nothing can make us happy or unhappy. We ourselves decide whether we are happy or unhappy. We ourselves are responsible for our thoughts, for the consequent emotions, and for the reality that's created out of them. The fact that we ourselves can decide which feelings we want to feel proves that everyone is able to be happy.

No one is happy as long as he or she makes his or her happiness dependent on external factors. If we make our happiness dependent on special jobs, persons, or some particular circumstances, it is unstable and will easily dissolve as soon as something changes. Then frustration inevitably sets in because we have no influence on external factors. Let us take the subject of relationships. Assume that you meet a person who seems to match your ideal vision of a partner very well. Now you choose this person to make you happy. As time goes by, you notice that some things are not as perfect as you would like them to be, but you ignore them and think, *Well, this is going to get better. He/she will certainly change this behavior/attitude when he/she has been together with me for a while.* However, if the wished characteristic does not emerge or if an existing characteristic does not disappear, you will be disappointed. You may even blame your partner for being unhappy now because you are so disappointed in him/her. That is how it is with happiness depending on external factors. In one moment a person makes us happy, and in the next moment we blame the same person for feeling unhappy.

In fact, it is not real happiness when we have found it on the outside. Instead, it is a short-term substitute emotion enabling us to feel happy for a little while. It is just a short high and can be compared with an experience under the influence of drugs. These overwhelming and uncontrollable emotions let us fall into disappointment after they have receded because the feeling of happiness is gone. We are even frustrated because we believed that we found *it* and now we realize that we were wrong. We can only *be* happy when it comes from inside of us. Then it has become a condition instead of an emotion. We can never lose this happiness because we can never lose ourselves. Happiness has much to do with contentment, and contentment is closely connected to gratitude. When we are thankful, we realize how many gifts and blessings are continually reaching us. This insight generates the feeling of contentment, which leads us to real inner happiness.

With this awareness of inner happiness, we see the world from a different, more thankful perspective. Even in difficult times we are able to have access to our inner oasis of happiness. External circumstances are subject to continual change, but it is up to us if our inner world remains harmonious and peaceful. The True Self always stays the same. Only the circumstances change. So if we are aligned with our True Selves, we do not allow the external circumstances to knock us off track anymore. Whatever happens in our external world does not have anything to do with us. We can make use of these circumstances in order to experience our talents, to make friends, and to surround ourselves with things we enjoy. We can also take advantage of our circumstances by drawing insights from our experiences. However, circumstances have nothing to do with the value of our nature. Even if we are deeply offended and insulted, it does not have anything to do with our personal being. Offenses and insults are only expressions from people who have difficulties with themselves or with their external circumstances. As long as we do not take their behavior personally but let it be a part of our external circumstances, it cannot touch our inner oasis. What happens in our world of emotions is and remains our own decision.

It is a widespread phenomenon that many people have a bad conscience when they are pacing through the world with smiles in their faces. Many think that they are only taken seriously when they are serious or put on an air of suffering or stress. Why is that? Even if some people seem to prefer dealing with persons who are playing the role of victims, why should we accept this idea when we know that it does not do us any good? As long as we make ourselves dependent on the approval of our external world, we will experience the feeling of disappointment over and over again. The external world consists of billions of subjective viewpoints, and it is simply impossible to live up to them. So when we know that we cannot meet the expectations of others anyway and when we know that their viewpoints are not necessarily in alignment with our own convictions (as perfect as they might be for them), we should better pay attention to our inner feelings. When we feel good, we emit the feeling toward our environment. So we are doing good not only for ourselves but also for our environment. The better off we are and the more happiness we allow ourselves to feel, the more authentic we become. And the more the vibrational rate of our feelings is aligned with our Source, the more self-reliant we are.

The decision of being happy is ours alone. Just as negative thoughts make us feel bad, we can feel good through positive thoughts. It just seems to be more difficult to feel good because we are not used to it. For years or even decades we habitually "had to face reality." Reality, however, was something that basically had to do with dreariness, struggle, pain, and stress. When we were children, we were still lighthearted. We did not have any sense of time. We did not worry about the future, and the past was quickly forgotten. That changed throughout the years. We had to grow up, which meant that we had to become serious, reasonable, and even hard. Who does not know the phrase, "Business before pleasure"? But why does one have to be separated from the other? Why can't work be fun at the same time, and why should it not be fun to work? It is our separated way of thinking with which we divide everything into good and bad. As children, we accepted everything the way it was. As adults, we had to learn to differentiate.

There is a fast and pretty simple way to experience real happiness, namely through conscious giving. With conscious giving, I mean giving without expecting anything in return, giving out of the pure joy of it. Chose a person or an opportunity and give something. You can simply give your attention, or you can contribute your skills or services. It really does not matter what. You can also let somebody go ahead when you are standing in line. Or even better, if somebody is jumping the line, you can simply allow him or her to go first. Or you can allow somebody to go ahead at the crossways in front of you. Maybe a person you do not feel very close to is asking you for something. It could be a perfect opportunity to let old anger or prejudices go and to consciously help that person. Simply search for an opportunity to give, no matter how small it may appear to you, and feel the happiness in you emerging from the knowledge that you have given something you really *wanted* to give and not because somebody asked you or you even felt obligated to give.

Nobody can force us into something unless we permit it. Everybody has the birthright to be happy, and through the love that always resides in us, we always have happiness inside of us. All we have to do is give ourselves permission to be happy.

WAYS TO REAL INNER HAPPINESS

View the outside world without judgment. Free yourself from the approval of others. View your reality how you want to see it. Accept that others view their reality the way they want to see it. Let go of your identifications with your body and everything else that is perishable. Regard your past as a collection of learning experiences and your present as the place of creation in which you create your future in accordance with your conscious imagination. Be thankful. Give from your heart without expecting something in return.

Happiness is the love of your True Self that is glowing within you, and it will spread in you like a bushfire. Real happiness, however, has nothing to do with emotional outbursts. Actually it is not even an emotion but rather a state of consciousness. It is the state of absolute inner contentment, contentment with yourself and with all that is without categorizing it into good and bad.

This is how it feels when we have found our true nature again.

> Happiness cannot be travelled to, owned, earned, worn
> or consumed. Happiness is the spiritual experience of
> living every minute with love, grace and gratitude.
> —Denis Waitley

HAPPINESS AND PAIN

If it is our birthright to be happy, then what about the statement that pain and suffering need to be experienced as well in order to learn? It is simple. We only experience pain and suffering if we do not learn the happy way. If we are able to recognize the beauty within us and to follow our inner light, we automatically assimilate many things we have to learn so that these lessons do not have to be brought to us through painful experiences. Often we do not even know that we have not mastered a certain issue yet and therefore have to go through a crisis. As already described in part 2 of this book, a lesson is only learned when the insight from it has really become a conscious part of ourselves. However, our learning process does not necessarily have to be painful, even if we are facing a crisis. There are two options of how to handle this.

- When we accept what is, we do not offer resistance. This alone makes it easier to deal with any situation. When we understand the reason behind our crisis, namely that it was sent to us so that we can go through our voluntarily chosen experiences, we are able to accept the challenge and view it as a chance to grow. With open hearts, we see that another point on the checklist of our life experiences can be checked off. We will remain in faith that after overcoming a challenge something wonderful will unfold which we cannot see yet.

• When we have learned to be satisfied with ourselves and with our pure existence, we automatically increase our vibrations and open up for a higher level. Therefore, all tasks that needed to be dealt with on the lower levels are automatically resolved. Opening up for the real light means learning many lessons the soft way. Thus, many challenges are easier to handle and can be accomplished faster because we bring the necessary openness with us.

The purpose of all that we experience here on earth is to integrate our time into part of our being. Through our way of approaching and handling our experiences, we ourselves determine how the integration happens. The more conscious we are, the easier and faster we get our insights and learn. Joy in the heart, accepting and letting go, true inner happiness, love for ourselves, and the love we share with others form the basis for less painful experiences and lives in pleasant circumstances.

GRATITUDE

or a long time I was not sure in which chapter the section "Gratitude" would fit in best. As gratitude is of major if not essential importance, I finally decided to devote a separate chapter to it.

On the one hand, gratitude is the natural consequence of the realization of what we are and what has been given to us. At the same time gratitude is the basis through which we are able to realize our connection with an unbelievable force—a force that guides us through our whole existence and that loves us in a manner that cannot be set into words. Gratitude is the key to many insights and the consequence of insights at the same time. Through honest, deeply felt gratitude and appreciation, we connect ourselves with the Source. We become aware of the True Self, of our own value, and of our connection with the Source. We recognize its everlasting presence and feel deep, real love without wanting to define it, without even being able to define it. In this state of consciousness we cannot but act out of our inner light. Gratitude leads us to ourselves.

We can be thankful for so many things—the beginning of a new day in which we can experience new adventures, our warm beds in which we slept last night, the roof above our heads, the ability to simply walk into the kitchen in order to prepare a nice breakfast, our families, all the people who help us in all kinds of situations, our friends who are always there for us and who will laugh and cry with us, the new chances we get every day, a moment of relaxation in which we enjoy a cup of coffee, a beautiful sunny day, the green traffic lights on our route, a simple smile, electricity, the tree providing shade, the flowers blooming in our gardens, the gift of being able to recognize this life as a gift, and much more. When we start to think about all the things we can be thankful for, we can easily get carried away because we discover the tiniest details and recognize them as real treasures that surround us.

Now what does real gratitude feel like? Real gratitude manifests itself in a feeling of deep contentment. A warm, pleasant feeling of contentment spreads in our chests. We feel awe, and at the same time we realize that we somehow must be special because we are blessed with so many gifts. A clear sign of feeling real gratitude is when we catch ourselves lifting our heads and looking upward … or when we close our eyes and deeply breathe in and out with a smile on our faces. Through deeply felt gratitude, we perceive the world around us in a totally different light. We are able to feel love arising from our hearts. This love feels like something long forgotten yet very familiar. We feel an enormous power living in our bodies. When we feel this power, we feel ourselves and at the same time feel the connection with the one who created us. As we are part of what created us, we feel God, and God is pure love. This love is a power emitting vibrations of an unknown energy. Therefore, we are sending signals to our Source, which in turn supplies us with even more that we can be thankful for. When we are consciously thankful for what we have, we focus our energy on the positive and comfortable outlooks of life, enhance the vibrations we emit, and draw more positive energies and situations into our lives. Or we intensify what we already have. The more we receive, the more grateful we are and then the more we receive. It is a positive spiral.

However, if we worry a great deal and if a crisis threatens to drown us, it is particularly difficult to maintain the feelings of gratitude and happiness. At these times it becomes evident how deeply rooted our achieved insights and the belief in us are. If we do not apply what we have read, heard, experienced, and practiced particularly in times of crisis, then when? We experience easy times in order to get prepared for times of hardship. Hard times give us the opportunity to apply what we have learned. In difficult times gratitude helps us to recognize that there is still much light beside the darkness. Even if we think that we have reason to feel sad, angry, or depressed, there are so many other things we can be happy about and grateful for.

Be grateful for what you already have and do not focus your attention with melancholy and anxiety on things or circumstances that are lacking. Gratefulness for what we are and for what we have immediately removes energy from things that burden, frighten, or worry us. Hence, we only concentrate on what we really want and therefore produce positive thoughts. Through positive thinking we create positive vibrations, and consequently we receive the corresponding positive results. Positive results in turn create joy, positive feelings, positive thoughts, and gratitude again. Deeply perceived gratitude makes it easy for us to feel happiness in the heart. When we see the positive in everything or when we at least are able to trust that the positive is definitely there even if we are not aware of it at this moment, we do something good not only for ourselves but also for our environment. With our positive vibrations we also have a positive effect on others, which makes it is easier for them to improve their own frequency and promotes their spiritual growth.

Probably every mother and every father already experienced the feeling that they wanted to give their children special treats, but instead of happiness and bright eyes, they harvested bad moods, tears, and rejection. Of course, it is quite understandable that the children's reactions caused a feeling of disappointment in the parents. If we ourselves do not want to be ungrateful and defiant beings facing our Creator only with criticism and complaints, we should eventually begin to understand that it's our own creations that are continually being fulfilled in perfection. We wanted it, and we are getting it. Living a happy life generates gratitude.

By consciously being grateful and feeling the loving energy spread within you, you can attract and become even more thankful. Be grateful for all the dreams that live within you, and be consciously pleased about the possibility that they can become true because of your gratitude and your understanding that you can attract everything you want. When you perceive real gratitude, doors will open that otherwise would have remained closed for you. With real gratitude, we become much more alert. We see many more things as gifts and become more open. This attitude in turn lets our gratitude grow again. Where there is gratitude, there is no bitterness. Where there is gratitude, there is love at the same time. Where there is love, there is no room for fear. Be grateful at all times and be happy with your whole heart for feeling this. You are continually given gifts. All you have to do is open your eyes and see them. When we are grateful, we also know how the love feels from which we are created. When we perceive gratitude, we are close to God.

Gratitude

I'm thankful for my feelings from happiness to pain.
I'm thankful that none of it I experience is in vain.

I'm thankful for nature, for the ocean's amazingly wide range.
I'm thankful for each person who gives my view a change.

I'm thankful for my body the way it simply is.
I'm thankful for its boundaries to keep my self-made promises.

I'm thankful for the joy that life brings every day.
I'm thankful for each soul that comes across my way.

I'm thankful for my friends. They never let me fall.
I'm thankful for the fact that I'm there when they call.

I'm thankful for the knowing that love is all around.
I'm thankful for the love inside of me that I've found.

I'm thankful for each chance to make somebody smile.
I'm thankful that we're treasures and everyone's worthwhile.

I'm thankful for my calling that keeps me on my path.
I'm thankful for believing and having a deep faith.

I'm thankful for the chance to create this life I've found.
I'm thankful for the connection to my Source, to whom I'm always bound.

I'm thankful for the chance that I've come here to thrive.
I'm thankful for the insight that I'm born to be alive.

I'm thankful that I know that I always have a choice.
I'm thankful that I listen to my unique inner voice.

I'm thankful that each challenge is a chance for me to grow.
I'm thankful that it leads me my inner self to know.

I'm thankful for the one I am, that I'm divine creation.
I'm thankful that this knowing always is the greatest salvation.

PART 4
REALIGNMENT

I rearrange my life and prepare myself for a new beginning.
—Source unknown

THE CHOICE IS OURS
A SPIRITUAL FAIRY-TALE

I took a walk through the forest. It was a beautiful early summer day. The sunlight found its way through the tiniest spaces between the already leafy treetops, and nature seemed to reach out its arms to me, full of energy. I perceived the humid, spicy scent of the forest air, which gave me a feeling of connection with this place. Although birds were chirping exuberantly and something was rustling in the undergrowth now and then, the atmosphere was so peaceful and harmonious that I almost had the feeling of being in a different world.

After a while I reached a large clearing with a big pond in the middle. In the center of the pond I saw a big flat rock. What really caught my attention was the woman who stood on that rock in an upright position. She looked into the pond and observed with happiness and satisfaction the excited fish underneath her. A long, light blue, flowing robe surrounded her in an almost playful, yet majestic manner. When I arrived on the bank, the woman lifted her head and looked in my direction. Now I saw that her entire shape was surrounded by a glow. That glow seemed to emanate from her body. No, it was not a glow. It was a light. And although she stood in the full sunlight, I was able to see her rays of light glowing. A loving energy radiated from the woman.

She indicated that I should come closer. So I looked for a path leading across the pond to the rock. I walked around the entire waters until I returned to the starting point without having found a way to get there. Inquiringly I looked up to the woman. She smiled compassionately but with awareness for my problem. One more time she indicated that I should come to her. This time I realized that I should simply take the direct way and not make a detour. In my mind I asked myself how I could manage to cross the pond without getting wet. Then I heard words in my head. "Why do you doubt? You are a child of God. The path to the goal is simpler than your mind can imagine. All that you need to reach safe ground is the belief in you and in the goal itself. With faith in your heart, you have confidence in the ways that open up for you." I looked up to the woman and had a premonition of what was to be revealed to me here. She looked at me, and I understood what she was trying to get me to do. Her soft and encouraging gaze eventually led me to put a foot on the water. Although a part of me wondered about what was happening, another part of me seemed to recall how natural it was to walk on water. I remembered that there had already existed someone who accomplished that. While I kept my view on the glowing figure of light, I walked over the water. Dry and without any difficulty, I climbed onto the rock.

Only now I asked myself what I was actually here for. No word came out of the woman's mouth, but while she lifted her arm and pointed to the surroundings in order to bring them closer to me, I heard the following words: "All this had been created by you. This and many more wonderful places are your creations. Enjoy them! That is what you are here for—to experience yourself and to create the world you want to live in. You shall create the world you need in order to live the kind of life you truly desire."

"But," I said with astonishment and a little confused, "then why do we also create places of perdition, of fear, of darkness, and of cruelty? Why do we create battlefields, and why do we level jewels like this place to the ground?"

"My child, not *you* as a community of all creatures in the world are doing that. It is a community of individuals who want to experience this for at least a while … or who have created these experiences for themselves with their own conviction and therefore must go through this. Just as there are oases of peace like this one, there are places that tear you apart from alignment and harmony. They are creations as well. It is up to every individual to decide in what kind of world he or she wants to live in. Only because there is a desolate, cold side, it does not automatically mean that you have to experience it. It is your decision on which side of life you want to live. You only dwell in the dark world if you unconsciously turn to it or if you believe in those who try to convince you that the dark world is the only true world. You create the kind of world that arises from your thoughts and emotions. That's the world you live in. If you change your thoughts and convictions, your feelings change as well … and then your world will soon be different.

"It is at all times possible to recreate the world you live in. Nobody is cursed to remain in a world once created. You are eternal creators of your circumstances. Your thoughts are your tools to see what you want to see. If you turn to the painful side, you see and experience pain, limitations, and grief. If you turn to the peaceful, happy side, you live your life in harmony, fulfillment, and abundance. The choice is yours.

"It is important for you to understand that at any moment you can switch to a desired world, even if you are currently feeling that you are trapped in an unwanted world. All you have to do is choose the kind of thoughts that make you aware of what you want and avoid what you do not want. You are children of God, and you have the right to live the life you dream of.

"Always remember, there are no detours needed on the path to your desired world. The world you want to live in is only one thought away."

When I woke up that morning, I was still aware of the gentle yet very present voice in my head. Was that really a dream? It felt so unbelievably real as if I had really visited that place. I still had the peaceful feeling within me, a feeling that I could achieve anything if

I only decided to. That day I enrolled at the university and began to study archaeology. I always wanted to do this, but I was prevented by my parents and my surroundings. One reason was that my parents were of a humble background, and for them it was obvious that after school one immediately had to enter a respectable profession to earn money. Additionally the financial resources to pay for my studies were simply not available. So I buried the dream, and after school I took up an apprenticeship in a joinery workshop. It was a good job, and I was able to put some money aside. My dream of studying archaeology was already forgotten. Now, however, something seemed to be different. I remembered my dream, and through this memory fuel was added to the little flame within me. I felt that if I ever really wanted to realize this dream, it had to be done now. With the help of my financial buffer, I was indeed able to get it accomplished. I had the money, and I was willing to study. I was fifty-four years old at that time.

Today fifteen years later I hold a doctorate and a chair at the university, and I am an internationally renowned author of specialist books. I own a house with a big garden and a swimming pool and a holiday home on the Riviera. However, it was not my possessions that brought me fulfillment but the fact that I had only been able to get my goal accomplished by not allowing myself to get confused or distracted any longer. I was convinced of my goal, and I pursued it confidently and without detours. I am completely happy with what I made out of my life. Every day I am filled with satisfaction and gratitude about what I do. I have never forgotten this sentence: The world you want to live in is only one thought away.

DELETE AND RESTART

You can't solve a problem with the same mind that created it.
—Dr. Wayne W. Dyer

Deep inside we all have our wishes and longings. We deny many of these wishes, or we push them aside with excuses. "I have no time." "I cannot afford it." "It is going to be too difficult." Why are so many people doing that? This can be regarding the beginning of an apprenticeship or a study. It can be about changing your job or moving. It can also be about expressing one's creativity or to one's talent as a painter, singer, poet, or author. Of course, we are never guaranteed that the result will exactly correspond to our ideal vision, but we are not guaranteed that it will not work out either. There is a chance that it will go wrong, and there is a chance that we will succeed. Now I would like you to ask a question. If there is no guarantee in either one direction or the other, why should we decide against it just for safety reasons? Only because we do not want to experience a disappointment? Or because we do not want others to make fun of us? Yes, we can listen to outside voices and refrain from doing what we really would love to do. We can give in to reason and oppress the voice of our fate, which we clearly perceive within us, just to agree with other people who have no clue about our life plan. Yes, we can be against our own being and deny our right to be ourselves, to create our own world, to be happy, and to enjoy doing what we want to do. We can deny ourselves the reason for being here, namely to be conscious creators and to experience our world by means of our own creative powers. We have the choice, and we have our free will. However, if we submit to fear or negative thought patterns, we will never find out that we can free ourselves through changing our way of thinking.

In his book *Excuse BeGone*, Dr. Wayne W. Dyer puts it in a nutshell. He recommends that we ask this question any time we use an excuse to justify not doing something: "Is it true?" Is it really true that I am too weak to change my life? Is it really true that I am too old to find a new job? Is it really true that I am too young to give a speech in front of a crowd? Is it really true that it is too risky to build a house? Whatever it may be, is it really true? If we cannot categorically say, "Yes, that's how it is," we should ask another question. "Can I afford it anyway? Am I really too young? Do I possibly have enough power for that? Will we be able to keep peace in the family nevertheless?" The answer to these questions may not be a clear yes either. Dyer concludes logically that if there is neither an obvious yes that something will work nor a no indicating that it will not work, why should we decide in favor of the alternative that will definitely never lead us to our goal?

Perhaps we cannot be 100 percent sure that it will work, but we cannot be 100 percent sure that it will not work either. If we continually tell ourselves, "I can't. It is too expensive. I am not intelligent enough," our conviction will certainly deliver us the matching result through our connection with the same energy of the expected outcome. So we should do ourselves a favor and begin to rethink our positions. Substitute every negative thought that could jeopardize your project for a positive thought. Let's assume that you have the wish to begin studies that you could not realize at the age of twenty. Now at the age of fifty, you can find many reasons for not putting this idea into action. "I am too old. It is too expensive. I am not receptive enough anymore. It will take too long." Yes, studies take time, and our age cannot be changed. So what? You must accept what you cannot change. It does not matter. Let us say instead, "Hey, I am happy about my decision to begin these studies. I am still able to make it. At the right time I will always have all necessary financial means. No matter how the studies develop, I will have a lot of experiences and gain new impressions. I take the time that I need, and in every moment I am happy to be living my dream."

When?

The right time to do anything is now.
The right place to do anything is here.
So if you want to do anything, do it now ... here.
Don't wait
till it's too late!

—*Erika Kind*

We are only able to know if something is really for us when we have tried it out. And only when we are doing it with enthusiasm, conviction, and passion—when we are doing it from our hearts—is it going to be fulfilling and successful. It will even be a fulfilling experience if it does not develop the way we would have expected, for we can finally say, "Yes, I had the courage, and I dared to do it!"

REPROGRAMMING OF THOUGHT PATTERNS

All that we think and believe is our reality. As we get what we are and what we believe in, it is inevitable that we must first change our inner world (the thoughts) before we can move something outside of ourselves. Real changes can only be made from the inside out. By changing our thoughts and beliefs, we are able to see things, occurrences, and persons in a different light. Therefore, we act and behave differently, and as a consequence, our circumstances and our environment change according to our new perspectives and the different way we encounter life and everything and everyone in it.

A conscious shift in our way of thinking is mostly triggered by a wish, a vision, or an unexpected occurrence. The stronger our wish is, the easier and more intensive we are able to believe in our desired reality. In order to let it become true, we must passionately identify with the manifested wish. We must *be* it. Ways that had been hidden until now will become evident since we haven't looked in their direction yet. Out of a conviction, we take steps that make waves. New doors open, which bring us closer to our desired goal.

An unmotivated trial to think differently, however, only remains in the head and does not generate enough power to produce the emotions and energetic vibrations necessary for any kind of manifestation.

The whole secret of manifesting our dreams is the absolute focus on the final result. We must leave the way to get there open because otherwise we get lost in details and cannot see the true path anymore. When we mentally and emotionally focus on the result, we will not allow disturbing and distracting thoughts to enter our minds that could delay or prevent the manifestation. Any kind of thoughts or doubts, whether our project makes sense or not, will lead to failure. The stronger, more intense, and longer we let our thoughts and passion flow into the manifestation of our wish, the more we connect ourselves with it. The more we are connected with it, the more we become what we want. When we have reached that point, the manifestation is bound to happen because we do not give our attention to doubts or negative influences anymore. With this inner attitude and alignment, our dreams will come true.

Deep Inside

There are so many gifts surrounding us.
We only have to open our eyes and see.

There is so much beauty surrounding us.
We only have to open our minds and feel.

There are so many tools surrounding us.
We only have to open our hands and take.
There is so much joy surrounding us.
We only have to open our hearts and awake.

There is everything surrounding us
that could make our dreams come true.
But first of all every dream
has to be born inside of you.

—Erika Kind

RELEASE FROM SELF-MADE BONDS

Each of us wants to be happy and to feel good. Feeling good is a basic need. It is even a birthright. When we feel good, we are happy and do everything with joy. When we do something with joy, it is successful, and success leads to more happiness. Hence, we are encouraged to do more things that make us happy. Positive thoughts cause positive feelings, and the resulting inner happiness emits to the outside. Therefore, we are able to have an influence on our environment because it reacts according to the frequency of our charisma. As I said, everyone wants to feel good. When someone observes a truly happy person living a happy life, he or she will try to follow suit.

Dr. Wayne W. Dyer has said, "If you get pushed around, you've been sending push me around signals."

It's no use to lament how bad things are because as long as we are swirled around in the same counterproductive whirl of thoughts, nothing will change. Changing only one single thought can be the beginning of a new life. One single thought can help us to see things from a different perspective, and therefore, changes in the old thought patterns occur. It is a chain reaction. Through different thoughts and the connected change in our emotions, we emit different vibrations that attract appropriately adapted circumstances and people into our lives. The experiences we make through our altered circumstances and new acquaintances lead to a realignment of our thoughts and to a confirmation of our new alignment. It is hard to believe, but if we manage with only one single thought to break out of our habitual way of thinking, a huge wall that has tremendously blocked our view begins to crack.

It is not necessary to always analyze everything. All we have to know is how to get rid of problems and bad feelings that prevent us from pursuing our path. If we continually lose ourselves in the questions of *why* and *for what* or excuse ourselves with a *but*, we cannot become free of the problem. Our thoughts continually circle around it, and we cannot avert our gaze from it. If we, however, readjust our thoughts and focus on what we really want, namely to be happy and free and to do what provides us with pleasure, we withdraw our energy from the negative focus. Through removing our energy from what burdens us, we relieve ourselves and let our energy flow in the direction we really want it to flow. Directing our energy toward our goal gives us a good feeling and increases the positive energy.

As already mentioned, having fear does not make sense. Fear arises from a lack of confidence and a feeling of separation caused by negative thought patterns. When we are connected with the True Self, we recognize that we are guided, that everything happens for a reason, and that all has its time and its place. Through our oneness with our Source, there are no doubts and no negative and hindering thoughts anymore. For anything new to be created, something must come to an end first. We cannot pour fresh water into a glass as long as it is full of stale water.

Fear is like a rope tied inside of us and behind us. As long as we do not detach ourselves from the rope, we will not be able to move one step forward. It is up to each of us individually to detach ourselves from it in order to proceed on our path. We acquired this rope ourselves. We have tied ourselves up by absorbing the convictions of others and by influencing ourselves through negative suggestions. Before we are able to untie ourselves, we must understand that we cannot successfully do so by using the same thought patterns with which we tied us up in the first place. So we must approach the problem from the other side.

These fear-inducing thoughts and influences have developed in the past and do no longer correspond to our current state of development. We are still carrying them around with us because we are used to them and because we believe that they are a part of us. Actually that is what they have become because of our belief in them, but in fact, they are not part of the True Self but of the ego self. Today, however, we have reached a new level of knowledge. This knowledge contradicts our former thoughts and suggestions. The mere decision to read a book about letting go of fears and blockages proves that your basic concept has already changed a little.

So let us little by little delete our old thought patterns and replace them with new ones. By shifting negative thoughts to positive ones, we consciously learn to control our thoughts. Positive thoughts create positive feelings. When positive feelings dominate, faith develops. Where there is faith, there is no fear. In the beginning, though, it seems to be very hard to delete our old reflexive thoughts, but it is only a matter of practice and routine. It is about spontaneous thoughts like *I cannot do that*. Stop! Immediately delete this thought and replace it with a new, positive, and goal-oriented one like *I am glad that I am given this chance, and I will see where it leads me. I can only win*. Whenever you notice a counterproductive, negative thought arising, replace it with a positive one.

After a while it not only gets easier but even becomes fun. It is a great feeling to know that we are really able to influence our lives the way we want and that we have the power to decide what kind of thoughts and external influences we allow to enter our minds. In one of his books Wayne Dyer quoted the story of an enlightened master. One of his devotees asked why he could be so kind and peaceful in the face of disparaging invective he just experienced. The master responded, "If someone offers you a gift and you do not accept that gift, to whom does the gift belong?" At any time it is your personal decision what gift you accept and which one you refuse. Through the goal-oriented control of your thoughts, you will find out that it lies in your own hands whether you feel good or not, even if the outer circumstances do not seem to be very pleasant. But above all, you will become aware of something incredible. Imagine how it feels if there is no "I cannot" anymore. When you are no longer subject to a self-suggested border, you can feel all obstacles dissolve. Feel that you can achieve anything you ever wanted. Imagine that there is just an "I will make it" and that your wish can easily and effortlessly manifest. Feel it. Try to describe this feeling. How does it feel? Doesn't it simply feel great, but is it hard to put into words? The moment we are able to detach from self-hindering patterns of thought and behavior, we are free— free from chains that we have tied around us and that we can untie at any time. Each person can follow his or her own heart and fulfill his or her own wishes. The only thing required is the decision that he or she wants it.

Through the realignment of our thoughts, a new perspective that enables us to find a solution easier opens up. At the same time our charisma changes. We emanate a different energy. Hence, people treat us differently, and new people who match our altered energy field come into our lives.

Once you allow this new orientation and begin to accept yourself as a Vibrational Being who attracts all the things that come into your experience, then you will begin the delicious journey into Deliberate Creation. Once you begin to understand the correlation between what you are thinking, what you are

feeling, and what you are receiving, now you have it. Now
you hold all the keys that are necessary to get from wherever
you are to wherever you want to be, on all subjects.
    – Abraham – Esther and Jerry Hicks

WE RECEIVE WHAT WE SEND OUT

Whether you think you can or think you can't, either way you are right.
    – Henry Ford

In terms of interpersonal relationships, we often experience
situations in which we feel excluded, criticized, humiliated, and
treated in a disrespectful way. Actually this can really be the
case. But why is it so? If we, for example, have a colleague who is
continually picking on us and criticizing us, who considers us to be
too slow, too inaccurate, or whatever, although we are convinced
we are doing our work properly, what is going on? There is a saying,
"As one calls into the canyon, so it echoes back." This very old saying
is absolutely justified. We receive what matches the vibrations
we send out. We receive what we are identified with. Supposing
we really made a mistake on our first working day or we really
were too slow and the said colleague made a comment (perhaps
it was only a joke) on that, then it could be that we identified with
these thoughts right away since that joke rubbed us up the wrong
way. From that moment on we have developed a negative attitude
toward that person. Now every time that we think of our work,
we automatically see the picture of that colleague before our inner
eye. In our minds we are already getting upset about anything he
or she might say to us the next day. We encounter our colleague
with this resentment within us, and accordingly we receive more
reprehensions and criticizing comments.

   Yet all of us have certainly experienced the opposite of this. No
matter how bad-tempered we are, when somebody smiles at us, we
reflexively smile back. This is how it also works in connection with

the previously mentioned example. As long as we project negativity on the other person, we will harvest negativity. We expect to be attacked and criticized again, so this is the kind of vibration we transmit. It is only logical that we receive exactly what we send out. The law of attraction always works, whether we are aware of it or not. So if we want our environment to respect us, we must respect our environment as well. If we do not want to be criticized for no reason, we should not criticize the respective persons as well, not even in thoughts. When we transmit criticism, we harvest criticism. When we transmit tolerance and understanding, we harvest tolerance and understanding. You get what you are. You are what you feel. You feel what you had thought about. Our thoughts are the first step to the manifestation of an idea.

Now if our thoughts have such a great power and influence on our emotions and our emotions in turn affect our vibrations, then it would be clever to use them *on behalf of* us and not against us.

"A mind at peace, a mind focused on not harming others, is stronger than any physical force in the universe," Dr. Wayne W. Dyer once said.

Our decision to give a new direction to our thoughts and consequently to our lives, to review old thought and belief patterns, and to either leave them behind us or replace them with new constructive ones is a really powerful new start into a new period of life. From this moment on we consequently work on a shift in our behavioral patterns. Our new period of life is going to be very eventful. We will encounter new people, and people we already know will treat us differently. Any little change we make has an effect on something in our lives. This can be very strenuous, for we draw situations and circumstances into our lives that we have not known before. We will have to go through heavy emotional struggles within ourselves because our heads are not always realigned yet but often irritated by the new developments. From the highest mountain peaks we will fall into the deepest valleys and then ascend again. We will move from hope to despair to renewed hope. During the period of realignment we will go through a continuous up-and-down process. We will feel ourselves deep down into our innermost being and say good-bye to all shadows from the past. We will hate it, and we will love it. Of course, our environment will perceive that there is something going on. People may make comments on our changed behavior, which can increase the pressure or even motivate our new state of mind to keep going. These comments can vary between admiration and total rejection. Therefore, it is shown again how subjective each individual's perspective is. As we know that we cannot make everybody happy and that we above all are not responsible for another person's happiness anyway, we should recognize these reactions as evidence that we are really in the process of changing our alignment. But no matter what kind of new situations or people we encounter and no matter what kind of changes happen, whenever there is something moving, we can be sure about being on the right track. It is apparent that we ourselves are the cause for what happens to us and for what is in our lives. We will unmask and resolve all those patterns of belief and behavior that have been obstacles on our path. The more we dispose of that which we carry from the past, the calmer the pendulum movements become. They become weaker and softer until one day we rest in our center.

A realignment is the beginning of the search for ourselves. It is a process that may take a while, possibly many years for something that has our whole life to dig up inside of us cannot be dug up within a few days. However, with every item that we are able to tick off, negative energy is set free, and hence, we are coming closer to the vibration of our true nature. The released energy gives us the strength we need to deal with the next item on our lists or the next boxes in our backpacks. This gives us a better motivation to resolve this subject as well, which in turn sets free more energy and provides us with the strength to face the next challenge. Therefore, a positive spiral has been put into action, one that we do not want to turn around anymore, no matter how heavy our processes may be. Every discovery we make leads us to more discoveries, and every time it goes faster and is more intensive than before. The more we discover, the more connections become clear and the more confirmations of our realignment we receive. It becomes increasingly evident for us what we really want and what we do not want, and it becomes increasingly natural for us to act accordingly. We feel that we are gradually bringing our vibrations into harmony with our true nature and that we are therefore coming ever closer to it.

A deep peace spreads within us even when the biggest tornado rages around us. We become aware of the incredible power that enables us to cope with all the challenges facing us and to put our dreams into action. With our conscious decision to live according to our inner voice, a time of awakening begins.

Act from a place of love. Send out what you can give away since you can only give away what you have, and you will get back what you have given. Let it be love!

Face Your Fears!

Turn your face to the sun, and your shadow will fall behind you.
—Chinese wisdom

Fears are there to be overcome. In every fear there is something hidden that needs to be cleared. Fears are pointers for tasks to be done and obstacles to be overcome. If it was different, we would not perceive these fears. Therefore, the best time to face our fears is when we feel them most intensely.

For almost thirty-nine years of my life I ran away and hid from ghosts that did not exist. Out of fear I would rather back off in humiliation instead of take hold of my interests, so I used to be the last in the queue and often felt disappointed and frustrated. But since I began to face my fears, a huge tornado has been sweeping across my whole life. I began to tackle all those things I had turned away from until then. With every breath I took, I have been freeing myself from all the things preventing me, from experiencing the incredible potential of my True Self, from pursuing my path, and from finding my fate. It is not easy to put into words how it feels to throw away these burdens and to realize that they never were a part of my True Self. It was always only in my head.

I made a list of all the things I was afraid of, but this obviously prevented me from reaching my goals. It felt as if there was a big gap between me and the goals. As I considered my fears as parts of myself, my goals seemed to be inaccessible. So I sat down at my computer and listed everything I was afraid of in red letters. I made it a sport to work myself through this list. Whenever I managed to overcome a fear, I changed the color from red to green. In fact, when I tackled a fear without having managed it yet, I changed the color to yellow. It began to really be fun! My list turned from a list of fears into a list of motivations. Within a short period of time, there were hardly any red notes left, but there were many green and yellow ones.

At the top of the list there was this entry: "Being on my own."

I had always been afraid of doing something on my own from the beginning to the end. Actually I was afraid of taking on responsibility for my decisions and actions, accepting their consequences, and handling upcoming challenges myself. Then a dear friend of mine drew my attention to upcoming seminars in Los Angeles and San Diego. He was living in that area. Of course, I buried the thought of attending these seminars immediately. After all, I had never traveled alone by air until then, especially not so far. However, this time I was hooked because I loved America, California above all. I said to myself, "Hey, girl, this is your chance. Grab it now, for you don't know when you'll get the next one." And I did it. I booked everything myself, including a rental car. It was about a one-hour drive from the airport to the South. And ... it was no problem at all. From the moment I made my decision, I stood behind it, did not question it anymore, and simply went with it. It was almost unbelievable what had happened. From that moment on I defiantly faced my fear and decided to say, "I'll do it." The fear simply faded away. It dissolved like a drop of water falling on a hot plate. There was not one single moment I felt insecure or had doubts during the preparation for the trip, the flight, or the stay. I had already grown on the implementation of this plan against all odds, for there had been enough adversities and reluctant voices. As I felt this deep wish to make this journey, I would not let myself be distracted by fears or external comments because I simply knew that I did the right thing. While I was traveling, I realized how right it was and enjoyed amazing coincidences that went along with this trip. Out of these experiences, for example, came the idea for this book.

Another fear I was able to get rid of was the fear of flying. Perhaps some of you agree with this one, nodding. Weeks before a planned flight I used to panic when I would just think about it, and the days prior to departure were occupied by persistent thoughts of flying. The first things I did when I finally sat in the airplane were to check if the life vest was in its proper place and locate the closest exits. When the plane began to roll, I became a nervous wreck. It was especially unpleasant when the plane increased its speed on the runway. Panicking, I dug my fingers into the armrest (if I had had long fingernails, I would have worn them out badly), stared at the seat in front of me with eyes wide open, and braced my feet into the ground. With rising panic, I awaited the moment when the plane took off, almost mockingly showing me that on earth the force of gravity ruled which began to push my stomach against the spine. Only after we had reached the cruising altitude and the plane flew relatively calmly could I slowly relax. As long as no air pockets or turbulences occurred, I was pretty calm. When this was the case, however, my armrests were in demand again. But the tension started to flare up at the latest again as soon as the descent was initiated. On landing I felt the touchdown of the plane long before it actually touched the ground. Stressed, I waited for the moment of the real touchdown. When the plane was finally on the runway, I "helped it to slow down" with all my strength just as if I sat in my car and slammed on the brakes.

Today when I am sitting in an airplane, I am happy about a few hours of forced rest when I can read, listen to music, write, relax (yes, really!), and let my thoughts wander. How did this change? It happened exactly the same year I decided to tackle my fears and to tick off one by one. Actually the end of my fear of flying was even the beginning of my adventure because it was the first fear—actually phobia—I was able to face down. Through letting go of this deep-rooted fear, I realized that I could let go of any fear.

So I dared to travel alone to California. It had been about half a year since my husband and I had been there for the first time to visit my best friend. My friend and I were in contact by e-mail, and we had not seen each other since that visit. I was looking forward to this first reunion after so long. Above all, I was also happy about being able to finally have a real conversation with him. I was looking forward to seeing him so much that I only thought of the impending time in California but not the route to get there. The priorities had shifted completely. I was sure that we would meet again, and thus, nothing could happen. I had no fearful thought about the flight prior to it. On the contrary, my heart was full of anticipation. When my husband and I sat in the plane, we had the opportunity to experience both the start and the landing on a screen by means of a camera on the nose of the aircraft. My husband was amazed that I watched, fascinated by all these happenings. Even before the departure I was aware that I was no longer afraid of flying. In that year I approached five destinations altogether, four of them being twelve-hour flights.

Actually it is no secret. It is about withdrawing energy from the fear and directing it into something positive—your goal. Instead of focusing my attention on the flight, my entire focus was on the destination itself. I had the belief that nothing could go wrong because I was so positive anyway. Indeed, I didn't have the slightest doubt, and thus, I sent out waves of confidence. The longer I felt no fear, the more certain I became. Through the experience of overcoming it, the fear did not return. Actually it never was a reality. It was only made up by me. It was an idea, an imagination, an illusion, but never reality. With every fear, we are devoting our lives and the quality of our lives to an idea. Isn't that ironic?

The biggest problem is the fear of fear. The fear of looking at it is bigger than the reason for the fear itself. Why is that so? The answer is as simple as it is complicated. We don't know what is behind it. Since we are conditioned to basically assume the worst, we do not even bear to look. We ask our ego, and it urges us to simply turn our heads away, for it will surely be terrible. If we realized that there is nothing and that it is only an invention of the mind (like the ego itself), the ego would be weakened.

But in the moment when you decide to not let others let you down anymore and when you do not shy away from facing the fear any longer, you will notice that it is not real. It is only in your head. So when you have changed your alignment, your priorities, and your thoughts, fearful thoughts will not arise any more. One cannot be anxious and confident at the same time just as one cannot be happy and sad at the same time. Basically you do not have to think at all. You can resolve every negative emotions (including fear) by simply watching it. Look at it without judging it. Just look at it. As you stop to think, it simply dissolves after a while. So you have proven to yourself that negative emotions arise from negative thoughts. Yes, it is primarily a matter of finding the right thoughts. Once we have positive thoughts that give us a good feeling, that strengthen us, and that fill us with joy, a feeling of security spreads within us.

The longer I dealt with the subject of overcoming fears, the clearer a particular thought formed within my mind. This thought gave me the last kick to face my fears. It was the idea of looking back someday in the future and having to say to myself, "It is too late!" and the thought of admitting to myself that I had not done certain things out of fear that really scared.

Dr. Wayne W. Dyer has said, "Don't die with your music still in you."

There are various reasons why we postpone things out of fear. We can hide behind excuses like these: "I am too old or too young. I cannot afford it. What would the neighbors say?" But what is life all about? Is it about living a fulfilled life? If you, as I have already mentioned, want to study, then do it, no matter how old you are. It is possible, and that is all that counts. If you want to emigrate, do it, no matter what your environment thinks and says. You have to live with and feel comfortable with it. Your neighbors don't matter. If you think that you do not have enough money for a specific purchase, then consider ways to get it. If you feel it inside of you, then it is meant to be. With the divine power, you can become and achieve everything. The burning flame inside of you is the seed that waits to be watered with your attention and that expands with the light of your passion.

Absolutely nothing is impossible.

NEW CHALLENGES

We often ignore challenges because we do not dare to try something new. That is the fear of risk, the unpredictable factor! Perhaps we cannot estimate how it will turn out. Or we just do not trust ourselves because we have never done it before. I think this is basically one of the biggest fears. However, as already mentioned, we are not really in control of what happens around us. But we have full control at all times of what we make out of what happens around us. Just because we do not know how things develop, it does not mean that the result must be a disadvantage for us.

Do not be afraid to try something new only because you do not know how it will end or because you could possibly fail. There is no failure because everything we do brings us an experience. Experiences are of the greatest benefit for us when we make them ourselves. Words can never be as insightful as lived experiences. No one can make a decision for you because only you are you. Only when *you* decide can you evaluate whether something is right for you or not. Furthermore, you can never blame yourself for not having tried it. No matter how it turns out, you will draw your experiences from it in any case—even if it is only the promise to yourself that you will never do it again. As I already said, it is much worse to look back someday and to say, "I wanted it, but I never tried it. And now it's too late."

THE FEAR OF ONESELF

We ourselves are the cause for our biggest fears. We have buried our true, bright identities deep within us and forgotten that these exist. But identity is there, and it continually makes itself felt by ideas, wishes, and feelings. Our inner light cannot be annihilated. It is an eternal flame. But since we cannot remember it, we are frightened of the feeling it sends out. Eventually we are trained to use our minds in order to be responsible. As the mind is unable to classify the impulses of the soul, they declare them unidentifiable and push them aside. As a result, these impulses get more and more diffuse in the course of our lives, and we are afraid of these uncontrollable emotions. Fear prevents us from engaging in soul-searching. We are afraid of tapping into our innermost where our fears may be confirmed, made worse, or where dormant demons may be reawakened.

What a fatal mistake. Precisely because we have buried the True Self so deep within us, we must enter our innermost. We will discover that the deeper we dig, the calmer and more peaceful it becomes. The deeper we penetrate into ourselves, the closer we come to the love, the warmth, and the light peacefully sleeping inside of us, patiently waiting for discovery so that we can finally become aware of our grace and preciousness. You have to dig down deeply. It is like the ocean. On the surface you feel the power of the rough sea, which can become dangerous and scary. But the deeper you dive, the calmer the waters get and the less you are irritated by superficial activities.

For many years a person very close to me had to struggle with some serious fears. He had managed to bury his True Self so deep inside of himself that he did not even know anymore that it existed. Whenever the light of his self came to the surface, he banished it without looking at it. It had become so foreign to him that he regarded it as an enemy, an enemy living within himself. This idea made it even harder for him to cope with the calls for help from his soul. Again and again he pushed everything aside that could have caused him to look inside. He was terrified that the dark abyss would open within him, gobble him up completely, and drag him into the depths.

But as in every person's life, the moment came when he had had enough of it. Finally he wanted to get rid of these uncontrolled occurring states of anxiety and the associated emotional isolation. He had had enough of the fear that caused him to lose pleasure in life. He began to read books on self-discovery and the release of self-created chains. The more he understood and applied in his life what he had read or also heard, the more he gradually realized the many errors and delusions in his belief structure. Additionally he was able to deal better with occurring fears. Within just one year he made an inner turnaround. Of course, it was not all uphill. There have been setbacks as well. But at the same time it became clear to him that there really existed something else than just cold and darkness within him. And since he realized this, he would not be discouraged through short burglaries anymore. He picked himself up and went forward. The more he opened up, the better he could get rid of his old, self-destructive behavior and thought patterns. Again and again he felt the warmth and love within his heart. And when he felt it, he knew he was on the right track. This enormously increased and further stirred his conviction and motivation.

The setbacks became less frequent and weaker. He saw the signs, perceived the wonders and gifts of life, and developed a new way of seeing things. This new perspective also changed his charisma. The environment responded to the changed vibrations he sent out. Thus, he opened further and allowed more and more light to enter him, illuminating more and more corners within him and showing him that there was nothing threatening.

About a year after his realignment with his True Self it finally got the upper hand with a thunderclap. All the love and strength that was in him and that he had hidden for so long burst out of him, triggered by a last small incident. He felt himself so deep like never before. It was as if the walls that had been blocking his view collapsed within a second. Rather than fearing the depth, he was overwhelmed by the glory of his true nature and the love that created and encompassed him. He realized that there had never been any dark abysses in him, only misinterpreted love—the same love that now returned to him the belief in himself and in his Creator.

He also saw how he needed all the sufferings of the previous years so that he could begin to develop *the will* to get out of the swamp. Only through the dark cloud in which he felt enveloped for such a long time was he able to accept the grace of this insight. Of course, his learning process is far from complete. But now the lights are green, and whatever comes, it will never be able to throw him back in his dungeon. He understood that life is a school and that we are marching from lesson to lesson. Only when we have finished a lesson can we tackle the next one. He understood that it was not punishment when he encountered difficult situations or people in the past. He had maneuvered himself into this cloud through his destructive thoughts and beliefs about himself and his environment. But now he knew how he could get into the light and how all the past experiences had strengthened him and brought him to the point where he is now. Today he walks with open eyes and ears and with much more serenity through his life. He lets his light shine and shares his wonderful experiences in various ways.

To be allowed to accompany this transformation, which he managed all by himself by iron discipline and an unwavering will, was (and continues to be) an enriching experience for me. He made the decision and went through with it with all the consequences attached. It was often very difficult to follow the new path because it brought unknown facets with it. And just for not giving up but getting up and moving on, though he did not know where this new path would lead with all the new feelings and riddles connected, he deserves the utmost respect.

We have no dark abyss within us. The deeper we go, the brighter and more peaceful it is. If we do not follow that path, we deprive ourselves of the greatest discovery a human being can make—the discovery of ourselves and all the love and creative energy, the discovery that the human being is only the transportation system for an immortal power station called the spirit. To find oneself is nothing else but a birth into a new life. It is like an awakening from a long sleep.

Fears are like potholes in the road. When we drive around them, they are still there, and we have to dodge them every time we drive along this road. These holes need to be filled so that we can quietly drive on the road of life.

Face your fears and continually make yourself aware that you are here to learn. You are allowed to make mistakes. Do not look at them as failures but as experiences pushing you forward on your way of life. You are here to enrich the world with the gift of your talents and abilities. This is your fate. When you pursue it, everything you do will fill you with happiness and satisfaction. It cannot be otherwise because it completely corresponds to what you are, what you feel, and what you want. Your fate and all that is connected with it was designed together with you. All your talents and abilities were given to you as the means to fulfill your task in reliance upon your cooperation. Thus, it is a sign of your gratitude that you pursue your task. Be assured that at any time you receive the support you need to reach your goal. Be open to it and go with the flow of life.

When you have experienced just once how fear dissolves simply because you disregard it, you will see that it is so strengthening for you. Now you know exactly that you can achieve anything if you only make the decision. Of course, despite all awareness, anxieties may arise in certain moments, but you will recognize them and see through them. You will not turn away from them intimidated, but by coping with them, you use them as springboards to the next level.

PRACTICAL EXERCISE

Think of one of your fears and look at it thoroughly. Illuminate it from all sides and ask yourself the following: "From what does this fear hold me back? Why does it stand between me and this thing/activity/person?"

Now imagine that this fear does not exist at all. Ask yourself, "How do I feel when I look at that thing, activity or person now? What else would I do without this fear? How does it feel to be able to do all the things I would do without this fear?"

Emphasize each of these questions and write down anything and everything that comes to your mind. Now concentrate on the answers of the second question block. How does it feel to visualize your ideas without limitations? Take this liberating feeling completely into your inner self. Get emotionally involved in your vision and be fulfilled in doing it. You *are* this feeling. You *are* power. You *are* joy. You *are* enthusiasm. Now look again at the activity you would like to tackle. See yourself right in the middle of this task, see the completed project in your hands and surrounding you, and say to yourself, "I did it! I did it! I did it!"

The vibrations that you send out directly come from your True Self and from the connection with your Source. They send out exactly the energy that is required for aligning you with the vibrations of the manifestation of all your wishes and dreams. Hold this feeling and this image within you. Do this exercise whenever you feel deterred by fears.

BELIEVE IN YOU!

Believe in you!

Believe in your dreams,
believe your inner voice.
Believe that you always
will have your own choice.

Believe in your strength,
believe you're unique.
Believe that your power
is enough to succeed.

Just believe in yourself
only half as I do,
And I give you my promise—
It's all coming true!

—Erika Kind

We carry within us all the power necessary to move from vision to manifestation. The only thing needed to release this power is our belief in it. The strongest force that we can ever develop is the firm belief in the truth of our inner voice and our ability to create in accordance with this voice and our own fate. There is nothing that can stop us from calling our visualized creations into being through openness, awareness, serenity, and enthusiasm. This force is nothing less than the belief in ourselves. When we believe in ourselves, we trust the divine order. We do not have to consciously do anything to prove our confidence in the divine order. It automatically goes along with the belief in ourselves. We are a part of this divine order—a part of this entire theater play. You cannot separate one from the other. So when we believe in ourselves—in what we really are—we believe in this universal power, with which we are inseparably connected. Thus, we are open for the miracles in life. And in this way the impossible is going to be possible.

Believing in us means living in accordance with the intuition. The inner self emanates the necessary emotions showing us where our paths lead. Only we alone know these feelings and their intensity. Only we alone feel our passion and our longing. Therefore, only we can decide what is good for us and what's not, where we want to go and where not. Admitting one's own true feelings is a basic requirement to be able to hear and understand the voice of our souls. To trust someone, we must be sure that he or she is not lying to us and that he or she is honest with us. It is the same with ourselves. As long as we are forbidden from admitting our true feelings to ourselves, we lie to ourselves shamelessly. What we try to deny the most vehemently is usually the biggest truth. We can only truly believe in ourselves when we are honest with ourselves and when we look into our own eyes. As long as we repress something and turn away from our true feelings, we cannot realize the True Self. Thus, we do not know what our true nature really wants and needs and most importantly, what our true nature really is. As long as we allow our minds to convince us of who or what we are, although our feelings say something else, we believe in a mind-created being that does not exist. Since this creature does not exist, we succumb to an illusion and will never achieve what we want and ought to achieve because we act out of our minds and not from the voice of our inner light. When we accept and love ourselves with all our characteristics and feelings, we are able to make use of our perceived power in order to work on our blockages, fears, and attachments. When we accept ourselves the way we are, we are able to realize what we need to work on. When we accept ourselves with all that we carry inside of us can we recognize our true needs. Only when we accept ourselves and do not suppress our inner truth, we do not try to be people we are not. So we live our own lives and not lives based on accepted belief structures from the outside. We live our opinions, beliefs, and dreams and not those of people whose reality we have assumed without realizing their perceptions do not necessarily coincide with our own.

Just because one person cannot stand caviar, it may be a delicacy par excellence for someone else. We all have the same ultimate goal, but each of us is unique. Each is at a different point on this journey, and all individuals have their own paths and their own tasks. If all had the same path to their goals, it would be absolute chaos, and there would be no counterweight. We complement one another with our individuality. And remember one important point. Each one of us is an aspect of God himself. God wants to experience himself through our physical lives in a variety of individuality. There is not one single person on this whole planet that is almighty and unites all possible abilities, talents, qualities, and characteristics. But altogether we do. Therefore, it is important that we stand behind ourselves and behind our interests and convictions and that we allow others the same. As soon as someone is acting truly authentic, the persons in his or her surroundings are feeling some kind of permission to do the same.

Even if you feel completely alone and confused with your views and thoughts, it is still absolutely correct what you feel. Just because you are supposedly the only one, it is even more important that you believe in your intuition so that you can contribute to the world what obviously does not exist (yet). Believe in yourself. Give the world what you have got to give and what only you alone can give! And make the impossible possible.

Affirm: I dedicate my life to the realization of the visions I have brought with me.

BELIEVE IN YOUR TRUE FEELINGS

> Whatever it is you are feeling is a perfect reflection
> of what you are in the process of becoming.
> – Abraham – Jerry and Esther Hicks

As short as this sentence may be, it is still so impressive and understandable. Is it not a wonderful statement? We are called to trust our feelings. What you feel inside of you is nothing else but the Higher Self connected with the universe, giving you hints on your way forward. A burning desire in you is, therefore, a call that you should follow. These feelings send out waves that attract into your life what you have felt. Consciously feel this feeling. Imagine the desired end result and give yourself entirely to it. Identify yourself with the blissful feeling of already having it or already being it. Thus, you give the universe the key word that you are now ready to receive the fulfillment of your wish. The stronger and deeper you live this feeling, the easier and earlier it will manifest. Thus, if we get and become what we feel, we must feel what we consciously want to be and have. When we feel strength, we receive strength. When we feel doubts, we will encounter doubts whipping up our own. When we feel happiness, we will be presented with occurrences confirming our happiness. When we feel sadness, we will experience pain. When we feel love, love will be brought to us. For this reason it is so important that we feel what our hearts tell us and not what the mind tries to convince us of to impress others and call for their respect and approval. The soul speaks from the heart because it knows exactly where we should move.

The mind, however, tries it with logic and can therefore prevent us from making possible what seems to be impossible. For the True Self, nothing is impossible because we are aware of the universal laws. Therefore, we should trust our inner feelings. No matter what we feel, we attract. It also works the other way around. When you experience developments in your life or in yourself, then you have to take a deep look back on what feelings you were radiating in the first place.

As Dr. Wayne W. Dyer has said, "If you're experiencing scarcity, anguish, depression, an absence of love – or any inability to attract what you desire – seriously look at how you've been drawing these circumstances into your life."

Noble Intentions

What you feel is going to manifest through the energies you emit. In this universal law it does not matter which intentions you pursue. You simply receive what you send out. If you follow ignoble intentions, they will come back to you as well, for you then send out negative vibrations. The law always works. The universe energetically connected to you gives to you nonstop in exchange for what you send out through your feelings. Therefore, we should be aware of our feelings because unconscious feelings also draw into our lives what they emit. This is often incomprehensible for us, and so we are again and again confronted with the same occurrences or people. As soon as we start thinking and feeling only what we really want to be and receive, we will experience an immediate dramatic change.

So that we find true fulfillment in the manifestation of our desires, it is essential to attract our desired end result with noble motives and love by feeling it. Faith and trust let our hearts speak and only attract what serves us and our environment for the highest good. When we fill ourselves with love, joy, and confidence, we will get it all. When we give our inner light the space to release all the feelings that guide us on our way and make us aware of what we are to receive according to our fate, then all our dreams can come true. We just have to really believe it and make each day a step in that direction to give the necessary emphasis to our feelings and the desired manifestation.

Believe that your path is always right. "Take the first step in faith. You don't have to see the whole staircase. Just take the first step" (Martin Luther King Jr.).

When we have started to go our chosen ways, we will find out that we gradually meet people and that things happen, continually providing us with big and small motivations to take the next step. Each of these pointers is a confirmation that we are on the right track. Each confirmation strengthens the faith in our intentions and the belief in ourselves. The stronger the belief and faith in ourselves is, the more pointers and confirmations we will obtain. When we have once had this experience, we approach each project in the same way. Simultaneously a deep gratitude arises, showing us how important our own paths are not only for ourselves but particularly for the other people. When we believe in ourselves, we believe in God. When we believe in God, we know that our abilities are gifts from our Source. Then we want to share our individuality with all. There is nothing better than to make oneself a tool and to share one's talents and knowledge with others. This is what we have to bring into this world. Therefore, it is a requirement that we believe in ourselves and that we are honest with ourselves so that we can actually recognize the gifts within us. We *are not only allowed* to do so, but we absolutely *should* do so. It is the biggest gift that we can share with others, and it is the biggest fulfillment that we can find by applying our talents. When happiness, joy, and knowledge are shared, they multiply.

Do Not Be Discouraged

It happens quite often that we—despite intensive and regular visualization and feeling the desired end result—encounter things that give the appearance that our dreams will never come true. Sometimes all signs are for fulfillment, but still an occurrence may happen and give us the impression that everything was in vain. Before our inner eye, our dreams seem to burst like bubbles, and we are facing a mental shambles.

But this is not at all like that. Often the time is simply not right yet. To win a time frame, the manifestation may have to be slowed down a little because the necessary circumstances or people are not ready yet. However, it will be ensured that in the meantime we are supplied with sufficient material to perfectly prepare us so that we can receive the delivery.

Very often we believe that through the combination of a variety of circumstances a manifestation is imminent. The problem in this is that the soul does not combine. It knows without thinking why and for what something is or is not. When we begin to put together a puzzle that relates to a future event, it is a sign that the head has interfered without being noticed. The head is inexorably looking for correlations and explanations. But if we start trying to explain logically why something *must* come about, we set the path and therefore block the manifestation. However, *how* we get what we want is not subject to our control.

Now if the head thinks that a particular event has to be the next in line, it is very often true that this thought is not in accordance with the universal organization. It may very well be of this yearning desire is not in the first place of your soul's list. Perhaps you first have to take a large or small intermediate step, or you even have to let your desire rest and mature for a little while in order to become ready to receive it or wait till the right people are available. When the head is strongly involved, it will try to talk you into doubts, for it is very limited in its possibilities to see the whole picture. When you have a wish, send it out as vibrations through the right thoughts and feelings and imagine the desired as already received. It will be received because this wish emerges from your deepest inside. Then you only need to trust that everything that happens, including disappointments and alleged failures, leads you to the fulfillment.

A failure, which seems to distance us more from the fulfillment than bringing us closer to it, can be an indication that our thoughts and feelings are not in line with our desire or that our belief in the manifestation is not perfect. These alleged failures shall help us to reach maturity and experience the fulfillment of our desire. Depending on which rung of the ladder of development we stand, it may take more or less time. It will become true, but only when we believe it and work on it with joy and faith.

As long as the desire to achieve something specific prevails, it is a sign that it is meant to be. The most important thing is to not give up—no matter how the circumstances may appear. Often we will not understand the reason behind many occurrences, and we do not have to either. We also do not have to understand in what way the desired will reach us. The only requirement to get to the destination of our dreams is the belief in ourselves and in the support of the power that created us and surrounds us. For with God all things are possible. Believe in yourself, follow your inner call, and expect the unexpected! Michael Beckwith has said,

> I believe that you're great, that there's something magnificent about you. Regardless of what has happened to you in your life, regardless of how young or how old you think you might be, the moment you begin to think properly, this something that is within you, this power within you that's greater than the world, it will begin to emerge. It will take over your life. It will feed you, it will clothe you, it will guide you, protect you, direct you, sustain your very existence. If you let it! Now that is what I know, for sure.

GIVING YOURSELF PERMISSION

The biggest problems are not the limits imposed by others, but those we set ourselves.

The biggest developmental step we can accomplish is probably in giving ourselves permission—the permission to grant ourselves something out of happiness, the permission to follow our inner call, the permission to appreciate ourselves, the permission to act according to our inner conviction, the permission to accept ourselves the way we are, etc. Why is it so hard to stand up for ourselves? Why do so many people believe that they do not deserve to be successful, to be happy, to enjoy their lives, and to earn a lot of money? (Actually they do *think* they are worth it; however, they don't feel it, and therefore, they act differently.) Through our environment we have been fed from a young age with negative thought patterns—*One must be modest. One has to adapt (or even subordinate). You have to fight for your rights. Nothing is given freely to you. This is too expensive for us. That is too risky. Whoever is rich is dishonest.* Many of us have grown up with these or similar restrictive patterns of thoughts and have been shaped by them. They are stored so deeply within us that we have adopted them as part of ourselves and identify with them, so it is impossible to open up to our strength and ingenuity.

From the Bible we can learn that we were created in God's image. Every spiritual teacher will confirm this. The image of God does not mean that we look like him visually but that we are of the same kind. We are what we come from. As we are the image of God, we also carry God within us. And when we carry God within us, how can there be anything we do not deserve? How can we ever be unworthy? How can we be unworthy toward another person even though we all have the same origin? Would we ever dare to call God unworthy? Probably not! Why then do we say these things to ourselves or one of our fellow human beings though we have God within us? Can we imagine that God would ever consider himself inferior? Why then do we do this to ourselves?

We all deserve only the best. There is nothing objectionable or immoral to this. Morality was invented by man and is determined subjectively. It is our birthright to be happy. When we are happy, we realize and unfold our potential, our talents, and the gifts that have been given to us for this life. Only when we are happy are we able to bring these abilities in all their glory into life. We have received them out of love and should apply them with joy and gratitude. This is the real reason why we have received them at all. We are divine creations, and thus, we are creators ourselves.

"To achieve the possible, the impossible has to be tried again and again," Hermann Hesse once said.

Trust your feelings. Believe that your dreams show you the way. Believe that it is the divine will that your dreams come true so that you can pursue your chosen path. Believe that you get everything you wish for because it is part of your path as long as it originates from a place of love inside of you. Believe that God gives you everything you want. Believe that you are a part of God. Believe that you therefore only deserve the best. Believe that you have the power to make everything happen. Believe that you are worthwhile and profoundly loved. Believe in the powerful miracle you are.

Believe in yourself, and you believe in God.

TOOLS AND AFFIRMATIONS

TOOLS

In this chapter I list some exercises that will help to gradually dissolve fears, self-doubts, and influences from the outside and/or to connect with your Source. These exercises can be applied depending on demand or practiced daily as well. Thanking should become a reflex. Perhaps these exercises will also inspire you to develop your own ideas.

CHECKLIST

Write a list of all fears and blockages that haunt you regularly or sporadically. Write down everything you turn away from for some reason or what might prevent you from realizing yourself. Also write down those things you consider to be ridiculous. Perhaps they are the ones who have been accompanying you the longest. If they really do not seem to be so important, they may be a good introduction for processing this list. The order of the points does not matter. If you write the list on your computer, you can initially write everything in red.

Now think about the point you want to start with. Chose something that is particularly annoying or something that you think you can overcome relatively easy.

For every point that you tackle, change the font color from red to yellow. Those points that you have clearly accomplished you can write in green. Some fears and blockages can only be processed in stages. Then you can, depending on how successful you think you are, write each word or phrase in both green and yellow. If you write the list by hand, then include a red dot at the beginning of each entry. Then you can erase these during the process and accordingly replace them with the colors yellow or green.

For each variant you have an overview of what you still need to work on or what you already have accomplished. This is what motivates you to get to work on the next points. Therefore, you should also write down the small, easily surmountable fears. It just gives you a good feeling and motivation when the green starts to predominate.

BEING GRATEFUL

Every day think about what you can be thankful for and write down a list of what you are grateful for at least once a week. It is helpful if you have someone with whom you can share this list. Furthermore, you become more aware of the single points that you have experienced as blessings by writing them down.

You will notice pretty quickly a feeling of satisfaction and happiness and deep confidence. This feeling immediately connects you with your Source. You perceive all the good that has been given to you. Start with obvious things, and you will find out that through the arising feeling of happiness and enthusiasm, you will not only find more things to be grateful for but also realize that you are also going into a lot more detail. Suddenly you will experience and perceive many little things as miracles.

By writing down these things, circumstances, and persons, you not only focus on the beauty in your life but at the same time withdraw your attention from all the things you do not like without having to think about them. So you only think about all the wonderful occurrences, experiences, and encounters. By sending out these positive vibrations you attract more that you can be thankful for. So thank the universe as often as possible, at least once a day or every opportunity you are aware of.

BREATHING

Stand upright and feel the solid ground beneath you. Now close your eyes. Slowly breathe in as deeply as you can. Hold your breath for a few moments and collect all negative and stressful emotions. Now breathe out slowly but very consciously and include all these emotions in the exhaled air. Send them to God so that God transforms them into positive energy. After you have exhaled, wait a moment before you inhale again. Also wait a moment before you exhale again to collect all the power to let go of the negative with the next following breath. While you inhale, feel the energy spreading out within you, and while you exhale, feel the release of all inner loads. Always breathe slowly and deeply and always make short pauses in between. If you are feeling slightly dizzy, interrupt the exercise. It is a sign that you have breathed too fast. Do this exercise as long as you feel comfortable with it but as long as possible until you feel relief.

LOOKING FOR POSITIVE THOUGHTS

Positive thoughts cause positive feelings. Positive feelings cause a happy, stress-free, and healthy life. Whenever you feel fear or frustration arising, immediately think of something that fills you with joy. No matter what it is, be it a person who is good for you, be it a beautiful experience of your life, or be it something enjoyable that lies in front of you. Think of all the positive turns in your life that you have already experienced and think of everything that you already have accomplished. This will fill you with joy after a short time. When you feel your joyful and blissful self, confidence is created. Confidence strengthens and motivates you. Thus, you will not back away fearfully but move forward forcefully.

WHO WANTS TO KNOW IT?

Whenever we feel bad, it is an indication that our minds and thus the ego have gained the upper hand. Our souls do not know any discomfort. When you feel pressed, insulted, hurt, humiliated, disappointed, or whatever, withdraw yourself from the situation and ask yourself, "Who wants to know it? Who is the questioner?" However, stay still and do not *think* about an answer. Just listen to your inner voice. The one who wants to know it is always the ego. In asking and simply listening, you detach yourself from the ego, which cuts the cord around your neck and dissolves the iron corset around your chest.

It is also very helpful to let go of trying to find an explanation for a certain situation if it starts to burden or to suppress us. Only the mind needs explanations. But only the ego causes these emotions, not you yourself. All stressful emotions belong to the ego, not to your True Self. Whatever circumstance it was that activated the ego, it has no relevance to your True Self—that which *you* truly are. The ego is a fictional character, but *you* are real. No one can hurt or offend you, for you know that you are precious and perfect and indeed inviolable. In this moment you realize that the situation that has caused the ego to appear was sent to you as a task you simply accept and move on. However, nothing can ever harm you. The only one who can be harmed is the ego, and that is why it defends itself.

Who is the questioner? Who wants to know it? Who needs an explanation? It is only the ego.

GET OUT OF THE CIRCLE

If there are moments when you are gripped by fear and when fear takes away your breath or when oppressive and stressful feelings are arising in you, then try the following: Stand with both feet firmly on the ground and mentally draw a small circle around you. Now all your sorrows, fears, and compulsions are within this circle with you. Hence, it is very tight and suppressing for you. Now simply step out of the circle and leave all your sorrows and problems within it. Feel how light and freed you feel having these feelings stripped. Take a few deep and slow breaths. Now watch all that you left in the circle. Just observe it without judging. Just look at it without identifying with it again. After a short while you will notice that much of it becomes less important as soon as you are able to observe it from a distance. But most of all you will realize that it has never been a part of you. You can detach yourself from it.

In the beginning it may be easier for you if you only take one problem or one fear at a time into the circle with you. Hence, it is simpler to focus on this single problem when you step away. If it is easier for you, you can also draw a circle with white chalks or lay a string around you on the floor. This way it is easier to visualize.

You can repeat this exercise until you have resolved all problems. This exercise works wonders!

OBSERVING

A very good way to distance yourself from fear is observing. This method is generally very helpful when you want to get rid of negative, stressful feelings. The exercise is simple and complicated at the same time. It is about focusing your attention on the unpleasant feelings within you and really feeling them. Then you begin to observe this feeling. You only watch it without judging or commenting on it mentally. You should not think anything, not even try to fathom the reasons behind the feeling. You only look at it. You can even go so far as to take a step back and observe yourself observing. You become the observer of the observer. The observation should last until the negative feelings subside. This may take a quarter of an hour or only a few minutes, depending on the intensity of the feeling and your observation routine. But one thing is certain. The feeling will subside when you distance yourself from something that is not a part of you. Once this has happened, a pleasant relief will spread. The perspective changes, and you dissolve from the identification with the particular circumstance. Now you look at it from a distance and understand that it is currently a part of your life but not a part of yourself. Otherwise you would not be able to dissociate from it as you did in the exercise before. It simply loses importance.

The point of this exercise is to stand back and to withdraw the energetic focus from the bad feeling. When you stand back and observe a situation or circumstance from the outside, you can see more, and when you withdraw your energy from it, its influence automatically decreases. This exercise can be well combined with the question, "Who wants to know it?"

NOT REACTING/NOT JUDGING

When you come into a situation where someone confronts you with statements, accusations, or insults, reflexive feelings of anger, resistance, aggression, or fear can be triggered. These emotions are mostly characterized by a dull sensation and cramping in the stomach region. When these kinds of reactions occur in you, avoid automatically counterattacking. Become aware that the other person has a problem he or she cannot cope with and that he or she is trying to pass it on to someone else. These persons act within their own reality and conviction of doing the right thing. Currently they do not know any better. To not absorb these negative energies, try the following: *Consciously* do not respond to the attacks and do not judge what is said or done. Let it pass you by. Be always aware that it is not about you but that the other persons take their dissatisfaction and frustration to the outside world. By not reacting and not even mentally judging their behavior, you withdraw energy from the confrontation. Hence, the other person has no way to hook in a reaction from your part. By becoming aware that it is not about you and by consciously not reacting and not judging, you let the negativity pass you by rather than being absorbed by it. You do not take their behavior personally but just let them be. You will be surprised, for one day they will thank you. Through your behavior, you calmed down the situation instead of whipping it up. Always know that how other people treat you is their responsibility. But how you react is yours.

Key to Dissolve Blockages and Fears

- The beginning of a new life is the decision for it.
- Change what you can change and ask yourself, "What can I make out of that? What cannot be changed?"
- Letting go of what is not allows you to accept what is.
- Love what you do and do what you love.
- Be open to everything and attached to anything.
- First dream your life and then live your dreams.
- Heal yourself and then heal the world.
- Give to those who are in need and gratefully take when you are given what you need.
- Life is a wonderful journey with many milestones.
- The journey is the ultimate goal.
- The goal is only the guide.
- Always search for the positive in every situation and person.
- Do not condemn what you have suffered from but honor what you have learned.
- Observe negative, unpleasant, and frightening feelings without judging them until they dissolve.
- Wish for everything and expect nothing. Expect the unexpected.
- The biggest problems are not the limits imposed by others but those we set ourselves.
- True freedom comes from the inside.
- The meaning of life lies in the way that we try to achieve the fulfillment of our dreams.

- Be grateful.
- Everything you encounter are pointers and steps toward the fulfillment of your dreams.
- Where there is light, darkness cannot exist.
- Where there is love, fear cannot exist.
- Stop searching for explanations.
- One must have distance to get an overview.
- Not everything is always easy, but everything is possible.
- Thoughts are the first step to the manifestation of everything.
- Positive thoughts create positive feelings, and positive feelings create our desired reality.
- God is love, and love is God. We are a part of God. We are love.
- Believe in you, and you believe in God.

AFFIRMATIONS

Below I give you some proposals for affirmations. Of course, you are also invited to create your own affirmations. Always ensure that you formulate them in the present tense and positively. Print out one or several and spread them in places where you spend much time. Speak the selected affirmations out loud in front of a mirror at least three times a day while you look deeply into your eyes. Do this until the desired effect has arrived and then continue for a few weeks to let them become a new conviction within you.

I AM

- I am grateful for my wonderful life.
- I appreciate and love myself and share this love with everyone.
- I am a shining being of God, and I am here to bring light into the world.

- I love and accept myself the way I am.
- I am pleased to be an indispensable part of this universe.
- I am happy about every opportunity to move forward, and I purposefully go toward my goals.
- I only allow positive thoughts and feelings.
- I am a valuable being of God, and I know that I am loved.
- I gratefully take what is given to me and use it to pursue my life plan.
- Today I am taking a further step to manifest my dreams.
- My earthly life is a gift from my Creator, and I show my gratitude by facing my tasks.
- I am light and love.
- I am protected, loved, and guided to follow my own path.
- I happily take full responsibility for my thoughts, feelings, and actions.
- I am eternal life, and I am connected with all my loved ones forever.
- I have chosen this physical life to experience myself with all my senses.
- I allow myself to live my life.
- I venture to say no.
- I am a creature of God and worthy of all amenities of life.
- I am free.
- My new life begins today.
- I am love, and love surrounds me.
- I am connected to an inexhaustible Source of powerful energy.
- I think, speak, and act only positively.
- I see the gift in every person and in every situation.
- I see the chance in every change. When I take the chance, I create my life consciously.

AFFIRMATIONS OF GRATITUDE

- I am thankful that I am full of love and faith.
- I am thankful that I only concentrate on and believe in what serves me.
- I am thankful that I understand that first I have to be what I want to give or do to others.
- I am thankful that I take time for myself to open up all the wonderful aspects within me and let them bloom to finally send them out to the world.
- I am thankful that I am leading the best life ever.
- I am thankful that I intend to make this the best life ever.
- I am thankful that I decided to be empathetic, tolerant, serving, and caring ... to myself!
- I am thankful that I decided to be happy since happiness is always accompanying me as an inseparable part of me.
- I am thankful that this happiness is always available and is filling me with all the enthusiasm and energy that let my life expand in the most fulfilling way.

Print these affirmations of gratitude and pin them on your mirror in the bathroom, the cupboard in your kitchen, or the dashboard of your car. Remind yourself how much there is that you can be thankful for because of your own existence. You are a treasure, a gift to the world. And I am thankful that you intended to come into this physical world to share your divinity with us.

REALIZE YOUR TRUE POTENTIAL AND FIND YOUR PURPOSE

WHAT SHALL BE WRITTEN IN MY BIOGRAPHY?

Every human would like to leave his or her personal imprint on this planet. A man wants to call something into being that makes him unforgettable after his earthly death—an invention, the commitment to a hobby or association, success in a particular sport, expression of artistic abilities, politics, or whatever. However, for many people it is difficult to find out what their purpose is. They feel somehow uncomfortable and have the feeling of not being fulfilled with their current state. But putting into words how they want to express themselves in this world is not always easy. When we ask ourselves the previously mentioned question, "What shall be written in my biography?" we reflexively see images that could bring clarity into the foggy soup. This way we can bring the idea of what we perceive within us from our subconscious into a conscious clarity. It is an overwhelming realization to clearly know what we really want from life and what we want to get accomplished in the time provided. This realization is illuminating our existence with a thousand floodlights. Determining what we really want to move and to create is the first step. This step indicates the direction. When we have made this step, many smaller and larger steps follow, which brings the project to life. Here are some examples:

- to pursue the goal against all odds
- to plan how the project can be realized
- to only allow arising doubts and critical voices from the outside to influence us when they are in accordance with our *true* conviction
- to withstand influences
- to utilize dry spells and possible setbacks as learning factors
- to not put expectations that are too high on ourselves
- to not put ourselves under unnecessary time pressure
- to want to realize this project without wanting to prove something to somebody else
- to be grateful for every perceived success and for every expected or unexpected help
- to permanently harmonize our thoughts and our feelings with the visualized result in order to avoid blocking the way through an inner conflict
- to believe in ourselves and to follow our inner voice no matter what happens

Our Higher Selves have already settled before our incarnation everything for our new adventure on earth. The experiences we shall have are waiting for us. We are designing our lives in order to have these experiences. Our inner voice is a navigation system guiding us accordingly so that we do not get lost. On our way we find everything, we need to fulfill the purpose of our existence. All aids are available. In principle, we do not have to worry about anything. We only have to move forward, and we are automatically *provided* with the required persons and circumstances needed. The amazing thing is that we have actually done this instinctively throughout our lives. We have always received exactly what we needed to make our necessary experiences. However, if we had done it consciously, if we had trusted our inner guidance and not always thought that we must retain the control, we may possibly have accepted going through these experiences much easier and faster.

All our dreams and longings are sent to us as indications of our mission. We shall get everything we dream of because it is a part of our path. Otherwise we would not have these dreams. The wonderful thing is that our dreams are also only steps that we shall take. They are also part of the happy path. Thereafter, it continues to go on and on. After we have reached a milestone, new dreams come to show us the way forward. Every new lesson builds on the previous one. The more targeted we follow our inner voice, the faster we reach the realization of our dreams. By following our inner voice, which is guiding us in the direction of our dreams, we have all those experiences we need to prepare ourselves for the big projects. Very often we only realize in retrospect how much preparation was needed, without which we would never have connected with our purpose. This was necessary in order to prepare us for the cornerstones in our lives. The universe knows exactly when it is the right time for everything. It will not *reward* us one moment too soon, for otherwise we would miserably fail. That is why we must not quarrel but face all difficulties that arise. We will learn our lessons anyway, but we have the choice of how fast and stressful or easy the process can happen.

Most of all it is a question of how faithful we are aligned with the result. The energy vibration we send out always connects to the same frequency on the outside. That's why there will always be results that match our own vibration. So if we want to achieve or to become something, we have to match up with the vibration of the desired outcome first. In the end we will get everything with the same energy frequency we have sent out in the first place. This way you can always check if you are really in alignment with what you want.

As I already wrote in the introduction, I intensively experienced everything I have written in this book. I went through feelings of being deeply insulted and humiliated and through different kinds of fear. I experienced loss, jealousy, ignorance, rejection, and exclusion but also gratitude, happiness, respect, deep understanding, resurrection, and love. I had to experience all that to be able to write this book and to have compassion with others. I had to go through it in order to find my purpose and to follow all these experiences and realizations in public. Over the years I had to learn through many painful experiences to calmly deal with criticism. I had to be able to stand up for my own opinions and thus for myself in order to develop the opposite under my own power, which thereby is much more consolidated. I had to be humiliated to build up my self-confidence on a strong basis. Today I know why all this was necessary, and I am so happy and grateful for all these lessons. Otherwise I could not realize my true purpose.

There is really nothing to be afraid of. As long as we keep on our path, everything is settled for us. The only thing we may have forgotten is the ability to see this path. However, as soon as we are one with ourselves and with the divine universe, we have found it again. We do not have to do anything else but listen to our inside, to feel within us, and to have faith in what feels right to us. We should never be afraid to try out something new just because it is new. We originally wanted to come into this world in order to collect *new* experiences. So if we feel the urge to tackle this or that, well, then let's go ahead!

WHAT ACTUALLY IS A PURPOSE?

What actually is my purpose? Is it a particular activity that we pursue? Is it something special we must achieve? Is it a combination of it all? To put it in a nutshell, purpose is what you do. You wouldn't do it if it wasn't your purpose—right here and right now. Purpose is what you feel you want to do, want to fulfill, want to extend from your inside to your outside. Your purpose is the specific way of serving others and fulfilling your fate through living your purpose, which can change depending of your life situation, your development, your age, or your family situation. Your purpose is the knots on the red cord of your fate. Living your purpose fulfills your fate. It leads you to the experiences you have or want to have, and it gives you the opportunity to serve others with their experiences. Purpose again is what you do right now. What you do at any moment is part of your life and subsequently influences it in some way.

We are here to experience ourselves in different kinds of emotional states. Therefore, we must turn many things into their opposites. If we, for example, want to experience the feeling of freedom, then we had to be locked up before. This does not necessarily refer to physical imprisonment. It can also mean emotional dependencies or attachments. So it is important that we experience from incarnation to incarnation everything that can be experienced. Before our incarnation we determine *how* we wanted to make our experiences (also in agreement with others). We may have planned to give birth to children, to enter the careers of our choice, to find our life partners, to receive doctorates, or to overcome illness—or perhaps to not overcome sickness. It is not only our purpose to achieve all that but mainly to collect all experiences related to it.

Our purpose is an integral part of our lives, and it cannot be circumvented. We have chosen this cornerstone before our incarnation so that we can achieve the desired realizations. That's what it is really all about—the path to the goal. Our perceived purpose leads us automatically to the necessary steps and circumstances and guides us through it all. Thus, we have the opportunity to determine our path as our destiny. Our goal in mind motivates us to go through the necessary lessons with the right motivation. If we did not have certain goals, we would not follow the path leading us to the signposts that are important for us. Hence, our goals are so different because everyone has to make different experiences and go different ways. The path is the goal! The path is life, and life is our goal at the same time. It is our task to experience all facets while we are on our way. This in turn explains the meaning of life—it is life itself. This knowledge fills me with the deepest gratitude for being here.

Let us recall the Buddha quote: There is no way to Happiness, Happiness is the way.

We are the creators of our lives. The checklist tailored to us is stored within us. Now it is up to us to put into practice the individual points through purposeful thoughts, firm intention, and doubtless confidence. "Only what I gave up is lost," Ernst von Feuchtersieben said.

THE DELUSION OF THE EGO

As already mentioned, our souls know our purpose to the smallest detail. When we listen to the voice of our souls, then we also feel exactly the direction in which our purpose leads, and therefore, we will follow this voice with confidence, as it will show us the way. Everyone needs different tools to fulfill their purpose. For some it may be a family with five children. For others it could be a certain profession. For some it may be material wealth. For others a retreat from civilization may be the answer. Whatever it may be, everyone can only see for themselves where their inner voice leads them and what they need on the way to fulfill their purpose. When we listen to our inner voice and follow its call, we automatically run into everything that makes it easier for us to stay on the course. Countless confirmations in many different forms occur. Sometimes these are small interim victories. Sometimes these are persons using the appropriate words at the right moment, or they may be advertisements or reports in newspapers or songs on the radio that coincidentally match the exact topic moving around in our heads at that very moment. We always get these hints and signs, but we are only able to perceive them when we go through our lives with awareness and with open eyes and ears.

How often do we see our neighbor have one success after another while we are stuck in the same jobs? Our neighbor experiences a meteoric carrier and earns a fortune in no time while we jealously observe his or her rise. We cannot understand why everything just falls into this person's lap. We ourselves, however, struggle, visualize, have faith, and are grateful, but we still do not see any progress.

When we have arrived at such a point, then it is a sure sign that we are not really happy with our lives and ourselves. Something is missing—perhaps the meaning in our lives and what we want from life—and this can cause envy.

These are the moments when we are still under the control of the ego. Why are we disturbed by our neighbor's income, by how often he or she goes on holiday, by how many cars he or she owns? Does our envious attitude change our situation in any way for the better? Or can it not even be pleasant that we do not have neighbors who take hard drugs out of frustration? Or who constantly ask us for material favors? Instead we should be glad that they live quiet and satisfied lives, for it is in accordance with their visions and ideas. We should rather see this neighbor as an example of a successfully self-created life.

What I am trying to say here is the following: When people are successful with their ways of living, it is a clear indication that they are following their inner voice. Above all, it is an obvious sign that they do not doubt. They deeply and firmly believe in what they do because it is consistent with their nature. Their heads and hearts, thoughts and feelings, spirits and souls move in the same direction. These people should not be envied. It would be better to ask them what the secret of their success is. However, what we see in the outside does not always fully correspond to what goes on behind the façade. Maybe our neighbor is really in charge of his or her life and creates it the way he or she wants. But perhaps the person even envies us for something we have that he or she doesn't (e.g., a family).

It does not make sense at all to strive for something only because we see that somebody else has achieved it. Just because somebody is happy with his or her way of living, that does not mean we have to do the same in order to be happy too. Every way of life and associated tasks are completely different and individual. The way of our neighbor is not the way of the rest of the world. We must find our own purpose—our own individual inner call. As soon as we perceive it, we realize how familiar and safe it feels. We know in the very first moment that it is our truth. It feels absolutely good and fills us with boundless energy and enthusiasm. We thereby send out exactly those vibrations that correspond to *our* true nature. If we, however, send out vibrations for something we only want to achieve because somebody else has it, these vibrations are not in tune with ourselves. Even if signs and hints indicate that the desired goal is going to manifest, we would not perceive them. As it is a superficial wish that has not arisen from our souls, we do not have feelings for it and do not notice when it is about to manifest. The whole project is driven by the ego, which reaches out for approval or wants to show others how much better you are than they are. Better, only because for example you are able to afford an expansive car? The purchase might have burned a hole into your wallet, which could annoy you. You might have chosen a color you don't even like, and perhaps you did not consider how much more fuel it needed compared to the compact car you had before. Ego-driven desires are never fulfilling. Since they don't lead to satisfaction, the ego makes you believe that you just did not try hard enough. It makes you think you need to compete more, spend more money, look better, and so on. It's a war you can never win since it never leads to true happiness but only gives exhaustion and frustration. Following the voice of the ego, we remain on the surface, and the manifestations will remain incomplete. With vibrations, however, that are in accordance with our souls, we fulfill our purpose. Thus, we draw exactly those aids into our lives that we need to be successful. The unity and satisfaction we feel when we enter the vibration of our true nature fills us with confidence and joy, which leave no doubt about the validity of our perceived path. However, when we are searching for our purpose on the outside, we might follow the path of somebody else. It will never fulfill us because it does not belong to our own program.

So it does not matter at all why somebody achieves something with ease that we do not achieve even with the biggest effort. Then we must ask ourselves, "Do I really want that?" If we have to think about whether we really want something or not, this wish cannot correspond to our inner call. Then the actual creator is not the True Self but the ego. We start to evaluate and to doubt. Because of these circumstances, negative feelings and vibrations develop and cover the access to the voice of our souls even more. Besides, effort is an indication of blockage. If we do not achieve something despite intensive efforts, it may be that it does not belong to our lives. Then we may possibly try to force something into being that does not correspond to our inner will but to that of the ego's desire. An opening to the True Self can never be achieved through effort but only through devotion, never through screaming but through stillness. Oneness with the universe is an act of absolute freedom. Freedom can never be attained through struggle. Effort and struggle arise when we want to achieve something with our heads. But when we become quiet and listen to our inner voice, we will let go and open up. When we get our unconsciousness into consciousness by listening to our souls, we go with the flow of *our* lives, and this flow brings all to us that is sent out by our vibrations, which are in tune with our inner being.

Our contribution is important. "Things do not change; we change," as Henry David Thoreau once said.

Whenever we watch the news or listen to it on the radio, there is talk of wars, hatred against strangers, and crime. How often does it happen that we feel affected and spontaneously blame the leaders of the countries and the governments? Of course, they should aim to create a safe and peaceful environment for their inhabitants. However, as already mentioned many times, we do not have any influence on the thoughts, behavior, and actions of others. If we really want to have peace on the whole earth, we have to begin with ourselves.

As I have said before, we are all energetically connected to one another without exception. All that we do has an influence on our planetary vibration. We are all in the same boat. Now if we understand that we therefore have received a big responsibility and duty, it should be easy to comprehend that with our own behavior we do not only influence our own lives but also those of others.

If every one of us identifies with the inner light and connects with the Source, then inner peace arises, and we are filled with pure love and happiness. In such a state we would never harm anyone or plan a war. We would even have the inner strength to turn away from dark energies and to consciously face the light.

Imagine that everybody in this world leads themselves into their inner light. What would happen? There would be no jealousy, no aggression, no exclusions, no greed, and no hunger for power anymore. No one would consider another person as a rival or an enemy. On the contrary, a perspective would be created in which we would cooperate with one another rather than compete. Each individual would simply be happy with him or herself and with all that is. No one would feel the need to defend themselves because they realize that there is nothing that has to be defended against. Nobody would have to have more than anybody else because they would realize that they already have everything they need for their personal lives. Additionally everyone would only possess what they really needed or wanted for their own joy instead of accumulating possessions, positions, or achievements in order to impress others.

There is an unlimited source of power in each of us. It is sufficient if only a few of us begin to realize this power. Their environment will notice it and wants to know why they are doing so well, although there are so many difficulties in the world. As soon as they have received the information, they will want to find their own inner light as well. Eventually there will be too few incarnated souls who agree to follow a power-hungry dictator. All dictatorships would collapse. Laws would gradually become more relaxed because there would be less people breaking them.

Yes, in each one of us is the power to change the world. But we are only successful when we individually begin to live what we demand of others—love, compassion, tolerance, and acceptance. We must not only bring it to the others but first to ourselves. We do not receive respect when we do not even have it for ourselves.

Excerpt from "Man in the Mirror" by Michael Jackson

I'm starting with the man in the mirror.
I'm asking him to change his ways.
And no message could have been any clearer.
If you wanna make the world a better place,
take a look at yourself and then make a change.

Fifteen Principles for a Liberated Self

1. **I live my life according to my inner call, even if others do not understand me.**
   I am the only one who knows where my path leads. Therefore, no one knows better about what is best for me than I do. By following my true path faithfully, I give others permission to do the same.

2. **I listen to the voice of my soul and believe in it.**
   Everything is saved in my soul. I need to know how to live a life in harmony with my True Self and with the Source. By following the voice of my soul, I follow the path of my fate and create a happy destiny for myself. My dreams and aspirations are expressions of my soul showing me the direction of my fate. I follow the wisdom of my soul and therefore stay on my path to live my purpose in its most fulfilling way.

3. **I accept myself and everybody else the way we are without judging.**
   I understand that everybody has come to this physical world with different tasks and a different fate. I am tolerant and compassionate, and I am willing to serve every being; however, I do not make their problems mine.

4. **I am perfect in my imperfection and do not take attacks personally.**

   When a man criticizes me, it primarily concerns the dissatisfaction of the critic with himself. He doesn't know any better at that moment and acts out of his point of view. I live according to my inwardly felt conviction and do not allow myself to be distracted. I understand that insults and mindless comments only represent the subjective view of the other person. It has nothing to do with me, and I do not take it personally.

5. **I walk through life with open eyes and ears.**

   Through every occurrence and every encounter, I experience certain feelings and receive knowledge and gifts. I learn something through every person and every circumstance. By accepting and applying to my life what I have learned, I pass on these lessons. I am also learning by teaching and teaching by learning.

6. **Every day I am grateful for all that I have.**

   I am grateful, happy, and aware of the gift I have received in order to make experiences in this physical world and to realize myself as the creator of my reality. I am grateful that I am provided with everything I need to fulfill my purpose.

7. **I create my reality to manifest my visions.**

   By connecting to my inner light, I recognize my fate. With the vibrations I send out through the harmony between my inner being and my creative thoughts and feelings, my dreams and wishes then manifest. They are therefore one with my fate.

8. **I accept circumstances that cannot be changed.**

   By consciously accepting what I cannot change, I detach myself from a self-created prison. As a result, I have free capacities of positive energy that I can purposefully use for the manifestation of my visions. I feel free and independent to move on and unfold myself through accepting what simply is.

9. **I give for the sake of giving and not for getting anything in return.**
I am aware of the blessing of giving. By consciously practicing giving, I am filled with gratitude and joy without expecting anything in return.

10. **I love to love and not to be loved.**
I see the light in others and feel the presence of the Source that connects us and that is our origin. I honor my counterpart as a precious expression of the divine. Love is what we are, and therefore, it is all we can give.

11. **The path to my goal is the ultimate goal.**
The goals that I am striving for lead me to the path I have to follow so that I can make the experiences I need for my development. The insight from an experience on the way to a goal is more important than the result. It even inspires me, and so I can strive for new goals.

12. **I go with the flow of life.**
My entire physical life is subject to change. All changes that happen on my journey are chances. I recognize the opportunities in every challenge and accept them without resistance. I then go from there with an expanded mind to keep unfolding myself in this life.

13. **I live in the here and now.**
Whatever I think, say, or do always happens in the now. It is always now. In the here and now I plant the seeds for my future now. Just as I encounter life, it will present itself to me.

14. **I am an ambassador of God.**

I see God in me and in all that surrounds me. Every single particle is God, and all together is God. While I have experiences, God experiences himself through me. While I do my best and support others in their evolution, I serve myself, others, and all that is at the same time.

15. **I am eternal life.**

This physical existence is not my true nature. I use it to have experiences and to develop. I am the awareness that enables my body to think, to feel, and to act. For this reason, I am not bound to anything physically, and I am not dependent on the approval of others. I know that I reside in this body for the purpose of self-experience and that I will leave it again in order to return to my true home. I am divine energy, an immortal part of God.

 # CONCLUSION

The point is not that we change ourselves. The point is not that we become different or better people. We are always the same. The True Self is perfect and bright. The point is to let go of what we are not, to remove all the distorting veils and chains of illusion, and to bring our True Selves to the surface again. Therefore, we realize who we really are and consciously express our uniqueness, our light, and our creative powers for our own fulfilling and for the benefit of others.

Our fears are inventions of our own mind that keep us from seeing and feeling what we are. Indeed, if we know who we are and where we come from, fears and self-doubts cannot exist. Once we have understood this, we also recognize the tasks that we have set ourselves for this lifetime. We follow our inner voices, which remind us again and again through dreams and intuition of the reasons why we wanted to enter this physical life. When we push aside the curtain of fear, uncertainty, and self-doubt, the world is open to us, and we can create the life that we have imagined before we entered this body. This is what I have realized in a staggering way, and this is what I want to pass on. As we are all connected with one another, we also increase the vibrations of others when we act in accordance with our True Selves. This helps everybody to get to the next higher level. Therefore, each individual has not only the task but also the duty to follow their inner voice and to let their own light shine. By letting your own light shine, others feel the permission to do the same. What a wonderful world this would be!

One day I swore to not shirk away from any challenge anymore. I understood that I would otherwise slow down my own progress and even torture myself with the ongoing return of the problem. I realized that I could not run away from my lessons. If I did, I would only cheat and torture myself. After I consciously began to even look out for these challenges, they immediately lost their terror. They made me aware of misconceptions about myself, and I understood that they only helped me to learn something new, to free myself from all kinds of misconceptions, and to clarify my view of the truth. After about a year while I was writing this book, a moment came when things needed to be sorted out with my mother. Suddenly I realized certain correlations and remembered some painful details of my childhood. I picked up the phone immediately and called my mother in order to clear this matter up. We arranged to meet in the afternoon the next day. After I hung up, a flash of awareness went through my body. I realized that I wanted to clarify this matter spontaneously and that I acted intuitively. Some months before I would have shirked away from any confrontation of this kind. Now the thought didn't even occur to me if I wanted to avoid the situation. All of a sudden it was completely normal for me that I wanted to face it right away.

You'll see. Once you stand up and see how great and powerful you really are and how transparent the wall of fears and self-created limitations become, you can then see all the hindering illusions, and you can feel your inner strength rising. You feel all the power and joy that has been within you all the time. It was all just buried in you because you may have felt unworthy of it. But your powers are slumbering within you all the time, and like an inner earthquake, they repeatedly try to make their presence felt through dreams and desires. In this unique moment when you become aware of your creative powers through the powerful being that you essentially are and by realizing the meaninglessness of all the preceding fearful years, all fears are gone. It simply dissolves. What is interesting is that you do not notice it right away because you will step-by-step put things into action without thinking about them or doubting if you are capable or permitted to do them. Only later you will find out that you have done things that recently presented insurmountable challenges for you. You clearly prove to yourself that all these fears and the connected psychic and physical perceptions have never been parts of your true nature. The fears have only existed in your head and have never been anything else but illusionary ideas arising from your false self.

But now the time has come, and you can recognize your errors. Even if you have to make some effort to achieve your goal, you will do it with joy in your heart, for you know why you are doing it and this is to realize your dreams. You will open your eyes and your heart to follow all the signs that help you on your way. You only deserve the best. You are a child of God, and therefore, it is impossible that you are unworthy.

You will gain the clear insight that nothing and nobody can stop you or prevent you from reaching your goals—except for yourself. It lies, and it always has rested in your own hands to get where you want to go, to feel what you want to feel, and to live the life you want to live. Once you have made the decision to move toward your goal and feel the joy and passion within you, you have already almost reached it. Now you only have to approach it faithfully. Now if you perceive the world and what surrounds you with conscious awareness, you will be able to follow the signs that your True Self gives you through your feelings. The more you perceive, the more aware you are. And the more aware you are, the more self-secure you become. Thus, you cannot get lost anymore. Naturally you may still lose your orientation every once in a while. With every learned lesson we reach the next higher level of awareness that provides us with new and unknown challenges. But thanks to your experiences with the universal laws and the belief in yourself, you will notice the warning signals right away and become aware of your inner balance again with the help of the previously learned techniques.

We all come with individual plans for this life. These plans include all that we want to experience. However, at the same time it contains our role to help others through our decisions and actions. Our hearts tell us which tasks we want to accomplish and what our plan and fate is so that we are not misled. Our heart speaks to us through our dreams, longings, feelings, likes and dislikes, talents, and abilities. Therefore, we must listen to our inner voice and trust our intuition. If we do not do this, we miss the real purpose why we have come here and thus make our lives unnecessarily difficult because we make detours. We must find our own destination. The journey to get there is this exciting adventure we call life.

On your journey to your destination you have to pass one station after the other. In other words, you can only reach specific goals when you are properly prepared and when you have acquired the necessary knowledge. You can only do the next step when you are prepared. It is not up to us to determine the right time for something to happen. However, if the right time has come and all circumstances and your development are in the right order, you will know it, and everything will happen as it is supposed to. Isn't it a big relief to know that we do not have to determine the right time ourselves? We may safely leave it to a higher power—a power that lovingly accompanies our life paths and our advancements and that always delivers the right people, occurrences, and circumstances to us at the right time. This power never interferes with our free will, not even if we are choosing the harder paths. It is so wise that it leads us into the kind of experiences that are necessary to eventually find our way back to ourselves. It knows that an answer that you yourself find can never be forgotten anymore and is the only way to reach a higher grade of awareness. This power always supports any of our decisions because it respects our free will and the individual path. If we finally turn back to ourselves and therefore open up for the universe, the switch is turned on, and our inner light connects with the Source again. In this connection, there are no limitations that we cannot overcome. We will experience the most powerful support we can ever imagine because we let the universal creative energy flow freely again.

This also means that it is sometimes necessary to say good-bye to certain things or people. This is neither good nor bad. It is simply the way it is. As your path crosses the paths of others, you may even disrupt another's plan (depending on the consciousness of that other person) if you do not pay attention to your own plan. We meet and accompany one another for a while, and sometimes our ways separate again. Of course, this often causes pain. But even if it hurts or if it is inevitable despite the biggest compassion that we hurt others.

No matter if it hurts us or how compassionate we are, sometimes it is inevitable that we hurt other people so that we are able to open the next door in our own inner selves. Every occurrence, everything that happens to us, and every decision we make helps us to climb to the next rung of our ladder of life. The faster we understand that, the sooner we stop considering every test as a betrayal to us. Equally it will be easier to climb to the next rung. Then we will openly approach each challenge that life has to offer. These challenges are not simply thrown in front of our feet. We asked for them when we chose this life. We ourselves have planned them so that they help us through this world of contrast to experience ourselves the way we wished before we came here. It is like a contract we have made with ourselves, and as long as we do not fulfill our part, it will be shown to us again and again.

You are a precious child of God. You were created because God wanted it so, and therefore, it is good. You were created out of light, and therefore, you carry that light within you. The light is your home. There you can return after you have completed your mission here on earth. You are the light. You are an important and precious part of the universe. Without your existence, the universe would not be complete and not be in balance. Always be aware of that. Follow your feelings even if other people try to convince you of the contrary. You don't know why they are doing that. Maybe it is their task at this moment to test your conviction. Or perhaps they are currently trying to solve a problem themselves and think it is easier for them to transfer these to you. Maybe you mirror their problems, and they do not notice it. Or perhaps they simply want to be like you. Maybe they cannot accept that you have the right to have your own perceptions. However, do not look for explanations because nothing changes the fact that you are a precious and deeply loved child of God and that your purpose contributes to serve yourself as well as the whole universe.

We will never be able to fully comprehend the universe and the way it is organized with our physical consciousness. It is not necessary anyway. It doesn't play a role. We always only understand as much as our minds are able to. Too much realization at once would only overwhelm our senses. Therefore, we must take one step at a time. In its complexity and size, the universe is incomprehensible for our limited brains. At the same time it is so perfect that we intuitively know and feel everything we need to fulfill in this physical life. We do not have to know in detail how everything functions. We only have to trust that it functions.

We all carry the divine light within us, the spark that is a part of the divine Creator. Become aware of this spark, feel it and connect through it with your soul and with God himself. Feel the unity, feel the infinite security, and know that all happens for your very best so that you can perceive your path in all its completeness and glory. You are loved, and you have received the gift of this physical life to have experiences. Realize this light that shines constantly is your True Self and that it is eternal. Let this light shine so that your environment can perceive it. By sending out these divine vibrations, you give your fellow men the opportunity to perceive their own light. Let us bring the light to the world.

The aim of this book was to give you information that would

help lead you to more awareness. But just as my own experiences led to my ability to relay the awareness through my writing, reading this book alone does not give you the experiences that you must have. After you read the last page, you cannot simply say, "I got it." The good news, however, is that through the reading of this and similar books from spiritual teachers, something starts to change within you and equally around you. You start perceiving yourself and all around you with a different awareness, drawing new conclusions, and realizing the connections. Therefore, a process is set into motion, bringing those themes with your particular development more clearly to you so that you can realize what is not balanced within yourself yet. The development of your awareness happens at your own pace in your unique and particular way, and it is adapted to your life circumstances. You have the choice about how fast, how intense, how happily, and how grateful you want to experience the adventure of self-discovery.

I wish you a happy and successful progress on your journey through life on earth and on filling your treasure chest of unique knowledge. Go your way with confidence and know that you are always accompanied and guided. It is your unique path that only you know yourself.

To conclude, it is important for me to pass on a message from my spiritual guide (or guardian angel – however you may call this wise and loving companion). This message gives the groundwork and basis to decide whether we want to be for or against the gifts and blessings of life and our own power of creation.

Open your heart and your mind.
Open yourself to life.
Open yourself to love.
If you are not open to love and accept everybody and everything, you are not really open. If you refuse to love only one person, being, or thing, you are not really open. Only when you are really open can your

wishes be fulfilled. To be really open means to remove all the locks and
bolts of your self-created imprisonment and to free yourself.
You cannot be open to others by staying in chains yourself.
You cannot stay in chains and be open to others at the same time.
Open yourself and see God in everything and in all creation.
See God in everything you encounter and you open yourself.

Open yourself to yourself, and you automatically open yourself to life with love. You can live your life in happiness, well-being, and harmony. It is completely up to you. Everything else happens by itself. It is the universal law!

God bless you!

BIBLIOGRAPHY

Balsekar, Ramesh S. *Pointers from Nisargadatta Maharaj*. Durham, NC: The Acorn Press, 1990.

Demartini, Dr. John F.: *The Breakthrough Experience: A Revolutionary New Approach to Personal Transformation*. Hay House 2002

Dyer, Dr. Wayne W.: *Living the Wisdom of the Tao*. Hay House, 2008

Kind, Erika: *Wie das Leben schreibt* ... Deutsche Literaturgesellschaft, 2010

Sigdell, Jan Erik: *Reinkarnationstherapie: Emotionale Befreiung durch Rückführung*. Heyne Verlag, 2005

Tepperwein, Kurt: *Die Geistigen Gesetze: Erkennen, verstehen, integrieren*. Goldmann Verlag, 2002

Dr. Helen Schucman: *A Course in Miracles: The Text Workbook for Students, Manual for Teachers*. Michael Joseph, 1997

About the Author

Erika has a practice for aromatherapy and self-development in Liechtenstein. She is also giving lectures and holding workshops and courses to help people align with their True Selves and help them rediscover the lives that they deeply feel are theirs. In other words, she is helping them find their true purpose and fulfillment.

Erika has also worked as a singer for more than twenty years. She writes song lyrics and produces her own songs. She is a spiritual healer, and she has learned card reading. She also attends seminars and workshops from several renowned spiritual teachers every year to increase her inspirations and insights. But she says that she learns the most from consciously observing the wonder of life and implementing her discoveries.

Erika was born in Vienna, Austria, in 1970. Today she lives with her husband and their three children in the Principality of Liechtenstein in the heart of Europe.

Learn more about Erika by visiting her website, www.erikakind.com.

Printed in the United States
By Bookmasters